Pro Power BI Dashboard Creation

Building Elegant and Interactive Dashboards with Visually Arresting Analytics

Adam Aspin

Apress®

***Pro Power BI Dashboard Creation: Building Elegant and Interactive Dashboards
with Visually Arresting Analytics***

Adam Aspin
STAFFORD, UK

ISBN-13 (pbk): 978-1-4842-8226-7   ISBN-13 (electronic): 978-1-4842-8227-4
https://doi.org/10.1007/978-1-4842-8227-4

Managing Director, Apress Media LLC: Welmoed Spahr
Acquisitions Editor: Jonathan Gennick
Development Editor: Laura Berendson
Coordinating Editor: Jill Balzano

Cover designed by eStudioCalamar

Cover image designed by Freepik (www.freepik.com)

Distributed to the book trade worldwide by Springer Science+Business Media New York, 1 New York Plaza, Suite 4600, New York, NY 10004-1562, USA. Phone 1-800-SPRINGER, fax (201) 348-4505, e-mail orders-ny@ springer-sbm.com, or visit www.springeronline.com. Apress Media, LLC is a California LLC and the sole member (owner) is Springer Science + Business Media Finance Inc (SSBM Finance Inc). SSBM Finance Inc is a **Delaware** corporation.

For information on translations, please e-mail booktranslations@springernature.com; for reprint, paperback, or audio rights, please e-mail bookpermissions@springernature.com.

Apress titles may be purchased in bulk for academic, corporate, or promotional use. eBook versions and licenses are also available for most titles. For more information, reference our Print and eBook Bulk Sales web page at http://www.apress.com/bulk-sales.

Any source code or other supplementary material referenced by the author in this book is available to readers on GitHub via the book's product page, located at www.apress.com/978-1-4842-8226-7. For more detailed information, please visit http://www.apress.com/source-code.

Printed on acid-free paper

Table of Contents

About the Author

Adam Aspin is an independent business intelligence consultant based in the United Kingdom. He has worked with SQL Server for over 25 years. During this time, he has developed several dozen reporting and analytical systems based on the Microsoft data and analytics product suite.

A graduate of Oxford University, Adam began his career in publishing before moving into IT. Databases soon became a passion, and his experience in this arena ranges from dBase to Oracle, and Access to MySQL, with occasional sorties into the world of DB2. He is, however, most at home in the Microsoft universe when using the Microsoft data platform—both in Azure and on-premises.

Business intelligence has been Adam's principal focus for the last 20 years. He has applied his skills for a range of clients in finance, banking, utilities, leisure, luxury goods, and pharmaceuticals. Adam is a frequent contributor to SQLServerCentral. com and Simple-Talk. He is a regular speaker at events such as Power BI user groups, SQL Saturdays, and SQLBits. A fluent French speaker, Adam has worked in France and Switzerland for many years.

Adam is the author of *SQL Server 2012 Data Integration Recipes, Business Intelligence with SQL Server Reporting Services, High Impact Data Visualization in Excel with Power View, 3D Maps, Get & Transform and Power BI, Data Mashup with Microsoft Excel Using Power Query and M*, and *Pro Power BI Theme Creation*—all with Apress.

About the Technical Reviewer

Dan Morley is a business intelligence developer from the United Kingdom. He has 15 years of experience throughout the healthcare, pharmaceuticals, utilities, and biotechnology industries, building and maintaining SQL data warehouses and reporting solutions using SQL, SSRS, and Power BI. He obtained his bachelor's degree in computing from Sheffield Hallam University.

Acknowledgments

Writing a technical book can prove to be a daunting challenge. So I am all the more grateful for all the help and encouragement that I have received from so many friends and colleagues.

First, my heartfelt thanks go, once again, to Jonathan Gennick, the commissioning editor of this book. Throughout the publication process, Jonathan has been an exemplary mentor. He has shared his knowledge and experience selflessly and courteously and provided much valuable guidance.

My deepest gratitude goes yet again to the Apress coordinating team for managing this volume through the rocks and shoals of the publication process. Special thanks go to Nirmal Selvaraj for making a potentially stress-filled trek into a pleasant and stress-free journey.

When delving into the arcane depths of technical products, it is all too easy to lose sight of the main objectives of a book. Fortunately, my good friend and former colleague Dan Morley, the technical reviewer, has worked unstintingly to help me retain focus on the objectives of this book. He has also shared his considerable experience of Power BI Desktop in the enterprise and has helped me immensely with his comments and suggestions.

Finally, my deepest gratitude has to be reserved for the two people who have given the most to this book. They are my wife and son, who have always encouraged me to persevere while providing all the support and encouragement that anyone could want. I am very lucky to have both of them.

Introduction

Business intelligence (BI) is a concept that has been around for many years. Until recently, it has too often been a domain reserved for large corporations with teams of dedicated IT specialists. All too frequently, this has meant developing complex solutions using expensive products on timescales that did not meet business needs. All this has changed with the advent of self-service business intelligence.

Now a user with a reasonable knowledge of Microsoft Office can leverage their skills to produce their own analyses with minimal support from central IT. Then they can deliver their insights to colleagues safely and securely via the cloud. This democratization has been made possible by a superb free product from Microsoft— Power BI Desktop—that revolutionizes the way in which data is discovered, captured, structured, and shaped so that it can be sliced, diced, chopped, queried, and presented in an interactive and intensely visual way.

Power BI Desktop provides you with the capability to analyze and present your data and to shape and deliver your results easily and impressively. All this can be achieved in a fraction of the time that it would take to specify, develop, and test a corporate solution. To cap it all off, self-service BI with Power BI Desktop lets you produce reports at a fraction of the cost of more traditional solutions, with far less rigidity and overhead.

The aim of this short book is to introduce the reader to this brave new world of user-driven dashboard development. This will not involve a complete tour of Power BI Desktop, however. The product is simply too vast for that. Consequently, this book concentrates on the visual aspects of BI and specifically on dashboard development. If you need to learn further aspects of the Power BI Desktop ecosystem, then two companion volumes are available:

- *Pro DAX and Data Modeling in Power BI*

- *Pro Data Mashup for Power BI*

The first explains how to extend Power BI by melding disparate data sources into a unified data model that you then extend using DAX—the built-in analytics language. The second guides you through the process of ingesting, cleansing, and shaping source datasets to underpin your dashboard creation.

Although a basic knowledge of the MS Office suite will help, this book presumes that you have little or no knowledge of Power BI Desktop. This product is therefore explained from the ground up with the aim of providing the most complete coverage possible of the way in which its components work together to deliver user-driven dashboards. Hopefully, if you read the book and follow the examples given, you will arrive at a level of practical knowledge and confidence that you can subsequently apply to your own dashboard requirements. This book should prove invaluable to business intelligence developers, MS Office power users, IT managers, and finance experts—indeed anyone who wants to deliver efficient and practical business intelligence to their colleagues. Whether your aim is to develop a proof of concept or to deliver a fully-fledged BI system, this book can, hopefully, be your guide and mentor.

You can, if you wish, read this book from start to finish, as it is designed to be a progressive self-tutorial. However, as dashboard development with Power BI Desktop is the interaction of a set of interdependent BI techniques, the book is broken down into several separate areas that correspond to the various facets of the product. They are

- *Chapter 1*: This provides a high-level overview of Power BI Desktop for newcomers to the product.

- *Chapters 2 through 5*: These chapters cover tables, matrices, and other text-based visuals such as cards.

- *Chapters 6 through 8*: These chapters are an introduction to the range of chart types that are available in Power BI Desktop.

- *Chapter 9*: This chapter introduces the other visual types that are built into Power BI.

- *Chapter 10*: This chapter takes you through a tour of drill down techniques across a range of visuals.

- *Chapter 11*: This chapter helps you to discover some of the gamut of third-party visuals that you can add to Power BI Desktop to extend the variety of data display types.

- *Chapter 12*: This chapter illustrates how you can use maps to enhance your dashboards.

- *Chapters 13 and 14*: These chapters delve into filtering and slicing data in a dashboard.

- *Chapter 15 through 17*: These chapters explain how to enhance dashboards by enhancing the interface and taking the user on a data-driven journey.

This book comes with a small sample dataset that you can use to follow the examples that are provided. It may seem paradoxical to use a tiny data sample when explaining a product suite that is capable of analyzing medium and large datasets. However, I prefer to use an extremely simplistic data structure so that the reader is free to focus on the essence of what is being explained and not the data itself.

Inevitably, not every question can be answered and not every issue can be resolved in one book. I truly hope that I have answered many of the essential Power BI questions that you will face when developing dashboards. Equally, I hope that I have provided ways of solving a reasonable number of the challenges that you may encounter. I wish you good luck in using Power BI Desktop to prepare and deliver your insights. And I sincerely hope that you have as much fun with it as I had writing this book.

Dashboard Basics

If you are reading this book, it is because you have decided to embark on a journey to deliver clear, powerful, and visually compelling analytics. The time has come for you to transform data into attention-grabbing dashboards that capture the imagination of your audience. In this chapter, you will learn about the Power BI Desktop interface and how you can use it to

- Switch between dashboards, data tables, and the data model

- Create and modify visuals

- Add and remove data from visuals

- Find fields in a data model

- Activate the Formatting pane where you enhance your visuals

These are the first steps that you need to take to understand the core software that you will be using to create dashboards—Power BI Desktop. With the basics quickly mastered, you will be able to move on in the following chapters to an in-depth look at all the key visual types that you can use.

As this book focuses on dashboard development, I have to presume that you already know how to load source data into Power BI Desktop. Consequently, the techniques that you will learn in this chapter will be based on a Power BI Desktop file that is ready for you to build on to create dashboards. This file is called C:\PowerBiDesktopSamples\ PrestigeCarsDataForDashboards.pbix. It is available on the Apress website as part of the downloadable material that accompanies this book. You can find the complete details on how to access and download the source files in Appendix A.

© Adam Aspin 2022
A. Aspin, *Pro Power BI Dashboard Creation*, https://doi.org/10.1007/978-1-4842-8227-4_1

The Power BI Desktop Window

Before we go any further, I would like to explain the Power BI Desktop window. More specifically, I want to begin with Report View. This is the default starting screen that is opened when you launch Power BI Desktop.

You always use Report View to build your dashboards (or reports, if you prefer). It is here that you add and configure visuals that use the data that you have already loaded, cleansed, structured, and enhanced in the data model.

Since it is something that you will use a lot in this book from this point onward, let's take a look at the main components of this window. The Power BI Desktop Report View window contains the elements that are outlined in Figure 1-1.

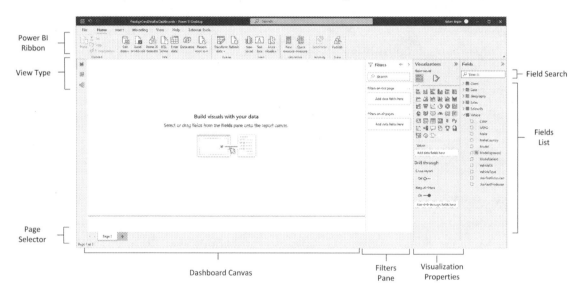

Figure 1-1. *The Power BI Desktop*

As you can see, the Power BI Desktop screen is simple and uncluttered. The various elements that it contains are explained in Table 1-1.

Table 1-1. *Power BI Desktop Options*

Option	Description
Power BI ribbon	This contains the principal options that are available to you when developing dashboards with Power BI Desktop.
View type	These three icons let you flip between Report View (where you create dashboards and reports), Data View (where you can add calculations), and Model View (where you join data from different sources).
Dashboard canvas	This is the main area, where you add visualizations and design your dashboards.
Visualizations pane	This area of the application is specific to each type of visualization and lets you set the specific attributes of each element on a dashboard. It also allows you to filter dashboards, pages, and individual visualizations. You can also format visualizations using this pane.
Fields list	Here, you can see all the available fields from the source data that you can use to build your visualizations.
Filters pane	Any filters that you have applied to the report, current page, or selected visualization appear here.
Visualization palette	This area contains all the currently available types of visualization that you can add to a dashboard.
Page selector	These are tabs that let you switch from page to page in a report.
Other panes	There are several other panes that are available in Power BI Desktop. However, they remain hidden until you choose to display them. You will learn how to use these panes in future chapters.

Power BI Desktop—like most Microsoft applications—has several available ribbons. These are explained in the course of this book.

View Types

There are three principal views over your data in Power BI Desktop. These are outlined in Table 1-2.

Table 1-2. *View Types*

Option	Icon	Description
Report View	𝄢	This is where you create reports (dashboards) in Power BI Desktop. It will be the focus of the remaining chapters in this book.
Data View	▦	This view allows you to look at the data that you have loaded and add further calculations.
Model View	🔲	This view lets you create a coherent data model by joining tables (among other things).

We will be working virtually exclusively in Report View in this book as this view is devoted to creating dashboards and reports. The Data View and Model View are explained in the companion book *Pro DAX Data and Modeling in Power BI*.

Switching to Report View

Although Report View is the default mode when you open Power BI Desktop, you need to switch back to it if you have spent any time working on the underlying data model. To activate Report View:

- Click the Report View icon at the top left of the Power BI Desktop screen.

Creating Visuals

Power BI is all about visualizing data. So the first step once data is loaded and ready (which is the case if you have opened the sample file PrestigeCarsDataForDashboards. pbix) is to see just how easy it is to create a visual-any visual.

1. Click any empty part of the report canvas (or make sure that nothing is selected).

2. Click the icon corresponding to the visual that you want to create (I will use the very first visual at the top left of the Visualizations pane—the Stacked bar chart). A blank shape with a large gray icon will appear in the report canvas. You can see this in Figure 1-2.

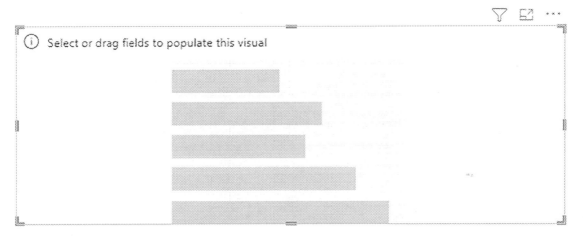

Figure 1-2. *A blank visual on the report canvas*

3. In the Fields pane, expand the Vehicle table and check the Make field.

4. In the Fields pane, expand the Sales table and check the SalePrice field.

The blank visual will become a bar chart showing the sale amounts per Make. It probably looks like Figure 1-3.

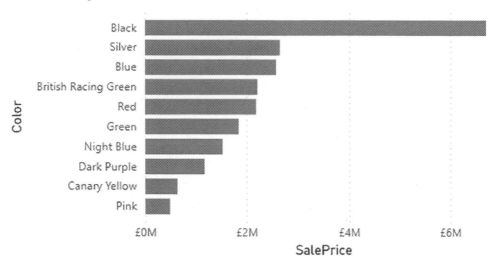

SalePrice by Color

Figure 1-3. *A first visual*

Yes, Power BI Desktop really can be that simple! The art (and science) of creating dashboards is knowing which visuals to use when and where to deliver meaningful information. This is what you are about to start discovering.

Note   The icons for visuals are described in Appendix B. The blank visual images are explained in Appendix C.

The Visualizations and Fields Panes

When you create and modify visuals in Power BI Desktop, you will spend a lot of time using the Visualizations and Fields panes at the right of the Report View. So it is worth taking a quick look at these. You can see them outlined in Figure 1-4.

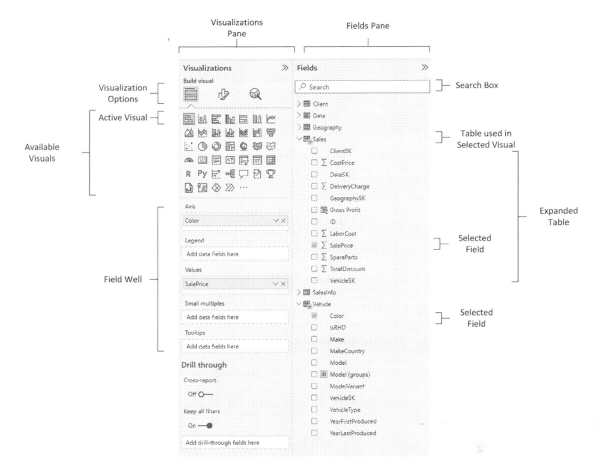

Figure 1-4. *The Fields and Visualizations panes*

In the course of the following few chapters, you will continue to learn how the Fields and Visualizations panes are used to create and edit visuals.

The Visualizations Pane

The contents of the Visualizations pane will change depending on how you are modifying a visual.

The three approaches that you can take are

- *Build*: To define the data elements that underpin a visual

- *Format*: To set and tweak the presentation of a visual

- *Analytics*: To add automated analytics to a visual

These three views are activated by clicking the icons at the top of the Visualizations pane. These are explained in Figure 1-5.

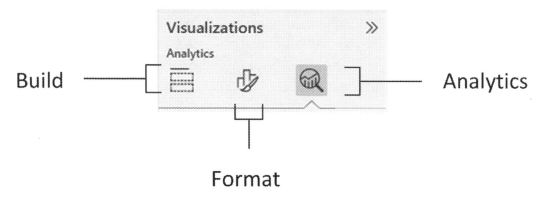

Figure 1-5. *The Visualizations pane view icons*

Ways to Add Visuals

As befits such a polished product, Power BI Desktop does not limit you to just one way of adding fields to a visual. The following are the various ways in which you can add fields to a visual:

- By dragging the field name into the field area in the Visualizations pane

- By selecting a field (which means checking the check box to the left of the field) in the Fields list—assuming that the visual is already selected

- By dragging a field onto an existing visual

You can add further fields to an existing visual at any time. The key thing to remember (if you are using any of the three techniques described) is that you must *select the visual that you want to modify first.* This is as simple as clicking inside it. After you click, you instantly see that the visual is active because tiny handles appear at the corners of the visual as well as in the middle of each side of the visual.

Note   If you do not select an existing visual before adding a field, Power BI Desktop will create a new visual using the field that you are attempting to add to a visual. If you do this by mistake, simply delete the new visual.

To create another visual, all you have to do is click outside any existing visuals in the Power BI Desktop report canvas and begin selecting fields as described earlier. A new visual is created as a result. Power BI Desktop always tries to create new visuals in an empty part of the canvas. You will see how to rearrange this default presentation shortly.

There is another way to create a visual. This is to click the report canvas to ensure that you have deselected any existing visuals, and then click the relevant visual icon in the palette of visuals in the top part of the Visualizations pane. This will create a blank visual on the report canvas.

Deleting a Visual

Suppose that you no longer need a visual in a Power BI Desktop report. Well, deleting it is simple:

1. Select the visual. You can do this by clicking anywhere on the visual. The visual borders will appear, even if you move the mouse pointer away from the visual.

2. Press the Delete key.

Another way to select a visual is to click the options button (the ellipses) that appears at the top (or bottom) right of any visual once it is selected. The options menu for the visual will appear. Clicking the Remove option will delete the visual. You can see the options (or context) menu in Figure 1-6.

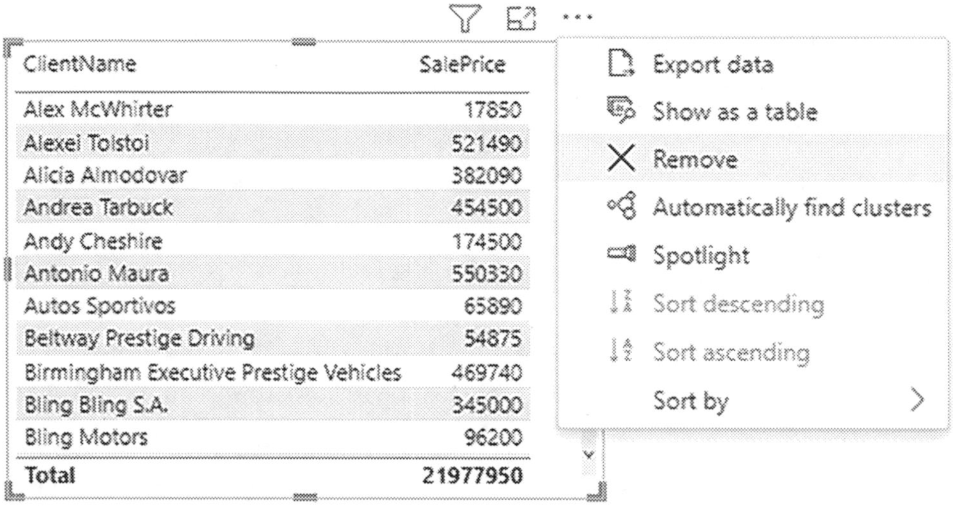

Figure 1-6. *The visual options menu*

Deleting a visual is so easy that you can do it by mistake, so remember that you can restore an accidentally deleted visual by pressing Ctrl+Z or using the Undo arrow at the top left of the Power BI Home ribbon.

Copying a Visual

You need to copy visuals on many occasions. There could be several reasons for this:

- You are creating a new visual on the Power BI Desktop report and need the table as a basis for the new element, such as a chart.

- You are copying visuals between reports.

- You want to keep an example of a Visual and try some fancy tricks on the copy, but you want to keep the old version as a fail-safe option.

In any case, all you have to do is

1. Select the Visual (as described previously).

2. In the Home ribbon, select Copy (or press Ctrl+C).

To paste a copy, click outside any visual in a current or new Power BI Desktop report, and select Paste from the Home ribbon (or press Ctrl+V).

Changing the Size and Position of a Visual

As you might expect, a visual can be resized and moved anywhere on the report canvas. Although these possibilities are fairly intuitive, I will explain them here in full for the sake of completeness.

Resizing a Visual

Resizing a Visual is mercifully easy. All you have to do is to click any of the Visual handles and drag the mouse. Lateral handles will alter the Visual width; top and bottom handles will change the Visual's height; corner handles modify both height and width by changing the size of the two sides that touch on the selected corner.

Moving a Visual

Moving a Visual is as easy as placing the pointer over the Visual so that the edges appear and, once the cursor changes to the hand shape, dragging the Visual to its new position.

You may prefer to use the keyboard when fine-tuning the position of a visual on the dashboard. The keyboard options for doing this are shown in Table 1-3.

Table 1-3. *Keyboard Shortcuts for Moving Visuals*

Option	Description
Nudge left	Left cursor key
Nudge right	Right cursor key
Nudge up	Up cursor key
Nudge down	Down cursor key

Searching for Fields

If you are building a dashboard using a new and as-yet unknown dataset, you could, potentially, waste a lot of time trawling through the available tables looking for the field that you require.

Power BI Desktop makes finding data easier using the Search field. You can see this at the top of the Fields list. Simply typing in part of a field name will instantly filter the Fields list to highlight any fields containing the text that you just entered. You can see an example of this in Figure 1-7.

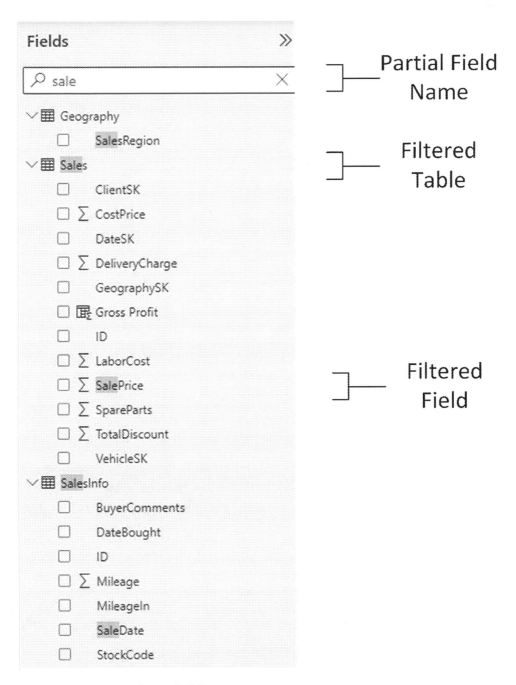

Figure 1-7. *Searching for a field*

Note   The text that you enter will be found anywhere in a field name.

To reset the field list so that it displays all the available tables and fields, simply click the cross icon at the right of the search text area (or delete the search text).

Types of Data

Not all data is created equal (or at least identical), and the data model that underlies Power BI Desktop will provide you with different types of data. The two core data types are

- Descriptive (non-numeric) attributes

- Values (or numeric measures)

Power BI Desktop indicates the precise data type by using a descriptive icon beside many of the fields, which you can see when you expand a data table in the Fields list. These data types are described in Table 1-4. The data icons are displayed for all but attribute fields.

Table 1-4. *Data Types*

Data Type	Icon	Description
Attribute	None	A descriptive element and is non-numeric. It can be counted but not summed or averaged.
Aggregates	Σ	A numeric field whose aggregation type can be changed.
Calculated column	▦	The result of a formula applied to create a new, calculated column.
Calculation	▤	A numeric field whose aggregation type cannot be changed as it is the result of a specific calculation.
Geography	⊕	This field can potentially be used in a map to provide geographical references.
Binary data		This field contains data, such as images.

Defining Aggregation

Power BI always assumes that you wish to start by aggregating data. Consequently, all numeric data will be aggregated (summed up) and all text values will be summarized to show unique values by default.

You can override this default behavior—or change the type of aggregation that is applied—by clicking the small chevron to the right of the field name in the Visualizations pane. In the context menu that appears, you can select a different type of aggregation. If you select count, you will display the *number* of elements for this attribute in the column of the table instead of the text of the element. Figure 1-8 shows you a sample pop-up field menu for a text field.

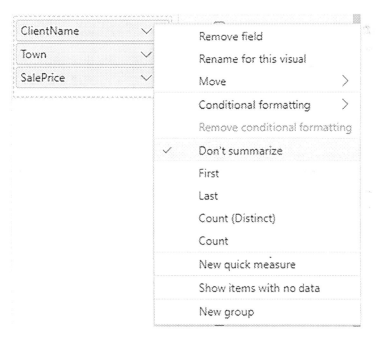

Figure 1-8. *The pop-up menu for a text field*

The available aggregation types are explained in Table 1-5.

Table 1-5. *Aggregation Types*

Aggregation Type	Applies to	Description
Sum	Numeric data	Adds up the values
Average	Numeric data	Returns the average of the values
Minimum	Numeric data	Returns the minimum of the values
Maximum	Numeric data	Returns the maximum of the values
Count	Numeric data	Returns the number of the values
Count distinct	Numeric data	Returns the number of distinct values
Standard deviation	Numeric data	Returns the standard deviation of the values
Variance	Numeric data	Returns the variance of the values
Median	Numeric data	Returns the median of the values
First	Text & dates	Shows the first element
Last	Text & dates	Shows the last element
Don't summarize	Text & dates	Displays detailed data without aggregating

The Format Pane

Although formatting options are, technically, part of the Visualizations pane, I find it easier to refer to the "formatting options of the Visualizations pane" as, simply, the Format pane.

This pane is where you add effects to your visuals in order to

- Make them visually appealing

- Display information more accurately

- Deliver actionable information to users

The detail of exactly how each visual is formatted is covered throughout this book. Clicking the Format icon in the Visualizations pane offers one final level of choice:

- *Visual*: Which offers options specific to each visual

- *General*: Which contains the standard options that you can see in
  Figure 1-9

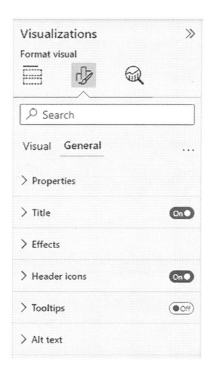

Figure 1-9. *The General format options*

It is worth noting from the start that the General formatting options are common to all visuals that you create in a dashboard. This makes learning Power BI Desktop considerably easier as you can always find these options in the same place—and you only have to learn them once. You will discover how to apply these formatting techniques in the next few chapters.

Format Pane Cards

Each of the distinct sections of the Format pane is called a *card*. You expand a card by clicking the right-facing chevron to the left of the card header. Some cards contain further cards (sublevels of formatting attributes) that you can also expand to see further options. You can see an example of this in Figure 1-10.

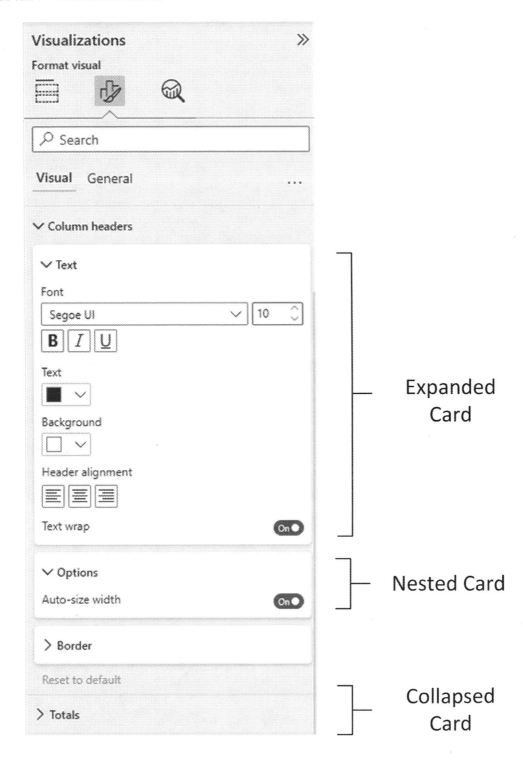

Figure 1-10. *Cards in the Formatting pane*

Conclusion

This chapter was a gentle introduction to the core elements of the tool that you will be using to create astounding dashboards—Power BI Desktop. You saw how easy it is to create simple visuals.

Then you learned all about the key interface elements that you will be using not only throughout the course of this book but also in your day-to-day work using Power BI. You discovered the Report View and the key panes that it contains—Fields and Visualizations. You then were briefed on the essentials of handling visuals in a dashboard.

There were, however, only the first simple steps. It is now time to start looking in depth at how to create text-based visuals such as tables, matrices, and cards. These will be the subject of the next four chapters, starting with table visuals in the following chapter.

CHAPTER 2

Table Visuals

This chapter and the next three take you through the process of creating text-based visualizations (or visuals if you want to call them that) in Power BI Desktop. In these three chapters, you will learn how to create and enhance

- Tables

- Matrices

- Cards

- Multirow cards

What these types of visuals all have in common is that they are designed to use *text* to convey information rather than using the more graphical display types, which you will discover in Chapters 6 through 11. Text-based visuals are essential when it comes to

- Presenting lists of detailed information

- Displaying aggregated cross-tabulations of key data

- Focusing the audience's attention on a single essential figure

- Delivering a clear overview of a few key metrics

- Drilling down into hierarchies of data

As you are on the first step of the learning curve, this chapter will focus solely on all that you can do with *tables* of data in Power BI Desktop. This will allow you to familiarize yourself with the core techniques that you can then apply to other text-based visuals—as well as many, if not all, of the vast range of graphical and geographical visualizations that Power BI Desktop lets you use to deliver your analyses.

The techniques that you will learn in this chapter use a Power BI Desktop file that has been prepared to help you learn. This file is called C:\PowerBiDesktopSamples\ PrestigeCarsDataForDashboards.pbix. It is available on the Apress website as part of the downloadable material that accompanies this book.

© Adam Aspin 2022
A. Aspin, *Pro Power BI Dashboard Creation*, https://doi.org/10.1007/978-1-4842-8227-4_2

Working with Tables

Tables are probably the simplest and most elementary way of displaying data. However, this simplicity should not detract from their usefulness. Indeed, for Power BI Desktop, the humble table is the default visualization. Moreover, the table is the default presentation style for nongeographical data.

I realize, of course, that it may seem contradictory to spend time on a subject that is generally described as intuitive. In answer to this, I can only say that, while getting up and running is easy, attaining an in-depth understanding of all of the potential of this powerful tool does require some explanation. Consequently, the approach that I am taking is to go through all the possibilities of each item as thoroughly as possible. So feel free to jump ahead (and back) if you don't need all the detail just yet—or if you want to skim over the intricacies in order to get a high-level overview of the subject.

Creating a Basic Table

The following example introduces you to tables in Power BI Desktop by creating an initial table that will display the list of clients and their total sales:

1. Open the C:\PowerBiDesktopSamples\ PrestigeCarsDataForDashboards.pbix file from the downloadable samples.

2. In the Fields list, expand the Client table.

3. Drag the ClientName field onto the dashboard canvas. A table displaying all the clients of Prestige Cars will appear.

4. Leave this new table selected and, in the Fields list, expand the Sales table.

5. Click the check box to the left of the SalePrice field. This will add the cumulative sales per client to the table. It should look like Figure 2-1.

ClientName	SalePrice
Alex McWhirter	17850
Alexei Tolstoi	521490
Alicia Almodovar	382090
Andrea Tarbuck	454500
Andy Cheshire	174500
Antonio Maura	550330
Autos Sportivos	65890
Beltway Prestige Driving	54875
Birmingham Executive Prestige Vehicles	469740
Bling Bling S.A.	345000
Bling Motors	96200
Total	**21977950**

Figure 2-1. *A basic table of sales per client*

This is a very tiny table. In the real world, you could be looking at tables that contain thousands, or tens of thousands (or even millions), of records. Power BI Desktop accelerates the display of large datasets by only loading the data that is required as you scroll down through a list, and starts with the initial few records in the data. So you might see the scrollbar advance somewhat slowly as you progress downward through a large table.

If a table contains fields that you have used in a visual, then the table name appears in yellow in the Fields list when you select the visualization. You can always see which fields have been selected for a table by expanding the table in the Fields list. The fields used are instantly displayed in both the Fields list (as selected fields) and in the field area of the Visualizations pane.

You can also add fields directly to a table by dragging them onto the table. When you do this, Power BI Desktop always adds a text field to the *right* of existing fields. However, it is always a simple matter to reorganize them by dragging the required fields up and down in the Rows and Values areas to define the correct hierarchy and the overall type of display that you want to achieve.

Changing Column Order

If you have built a Power BI Desktop table, you are eventually going to want to modify the order in which the columns appear from left to right. The following explains how to do this:

1. Activate the Fields list (unless it is already displayed).

2. In the Visualizations pane, ensure that the Fields options are displayed (by clicking the small bar chart icon under the collection of available visuals).

3. Click the name of the field that you wish to move.

4. Drag the field vertically to its new position. This can be between existing fields, at the top or at the bottom of the Fields list. A thick yellow line indicates where the field will be positioned.

Figure 2-2 shows how to drag a field from one position to another.

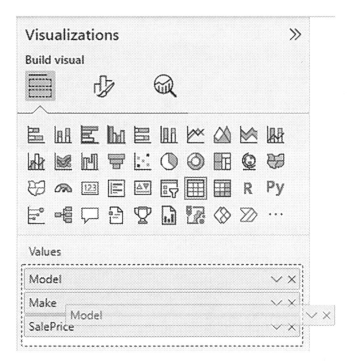

Figure 2-2. *Changing column order by moving fields in the Values box of the Visualizations pane*

Note   You cannot change the position of a column in a table by dragging it sideways inside the table itself.

Renaming Fields

You also have the ability to rename fields in visuals without having to rename the underlying column in the data table. While this can cause a certain disconnect between the data and its display, it is a technique that can be extremely useful in certain circumstances. To do this:

1. Select the visual containing the data element that you want to rename (I will use the table that you just created in this example).

2. Right-click the field to rename in the field area of the Visualizations pane (or click the down-facing chevron at the right of the field name).

3. Select Rename from the pop-up menu.

4. Edit the field name—or delete the current name and enter a new name.

5. Press Enter.

The field is now renamed. The new name will appear only in the selected visual, and the data element will keep its original name.

Note   You can also simply double-click a field name in the Visualizations pane to edit the field name.

Removing Columns from a Table

Another everyday task in Power BI Desktop is removing columns from a table when necessary. As is the case when rearranging the order of columns, this is not done directly in the table but is carried out using the Fields list. There are, in fact, several ways of removing columns from a table, so I will begin with the way that I think is the fastest and then describe the others:

1. Display the Fields list—unless it is already displayed.

2. Uncheck the field name in the Fields list.

Assuming that a visual is selected, the following are other ways to remove a field:

- In the Visualizations pane, click the cross icon at the right of the field name in the field area.

- In the Visualizations pane, either right-click the field or click the small triangle at the right of the name in the field area (remember that these are the fields used in the visualization). When the pop-up menu appears, select Remove Field.

Note   Do *not* click the pop-up menu icon (the ellipses at the right of the field name) and select Delete in the *Fields list* to remove a field from the table. Doing this deletes the field from the data model.

Table Granularity

A Power BI Desktop table will automatically aggregate data to the lowest available level of grain. Put simply, this means that it is important to select data at the lowest useful level of detail but not to add pointlessly detailed elements.

This is probably easier to understand if I use an example. Suppose you start with a high level of aggregation—the country, for instance. If you create a table with CountryName and SalePrice columns, it will give you the total sales by country. If you use the sample data given in the examples for this book (the PrestigeCarsDataForDashboards.pbix file), this table only contains half a dozen or so lines.

Then add the ClientName column after the CountryName column. When you do this, you obtain a more finely grained set of results, with the aggregate sales for *each client in each country*. If you (finally) add the InvoiceNumber, you get a very detailed level of data. Indeed, adding such a fine level of grain to your table could produce an extremely large number of records—as indicated by the appearance of a vertical scrollbar in this table. These progressive levels of granularity are shown in Figure 2-3.

CountryName	SalePrice
Belgium	£311,850.00
France	£5,882,810.00
Germany	£873,040.00
Italy	£1,170,780.00
Spain	£1,693,060.00
Switzerland	£839,415.00
United Kingdom	£9,211,375.00
United States	£1,995,620.00
Total	**£21,977,950.00**

CountryName	ClientName	SalePrice
Belgium	Diplomatic Cars	£224,000.00
Belgium	Flash Voitures	£6,950.00
Belgium	Stefan Van Helsing	£80,900.00
France	Bling Bling S.A.	£345,000.00
France	Capots Reluisants S.A.	£583,115.00
France	Casseroles Chromes	£201,050.00
France	Francois Chirac	£25,950.00
France	Jacques Mitterand	£69,500.00
France	Jean-Yves Truffaut	£1,950.00
France	Khader El Ghannam	£50,500.00
France	La Bagnole de Luxe	£497,190.00
France	Laurent Saint Yves	£1,343,950.00
France	Le Luxe en Motion	£255,950.00
France	M. Pierre Dubois	£511,675.00
France	Mme Anne Duport	£162,650.00
France	SuperSport S.A.R.L	£509,630.00
France	Vive La Vitesse	£1,269,600.00
France	Wladimir Lacroix	£55,100.00
Germany	Glitz	£589,490.00
Germany	Ralph Obermann	£11,550.00
Germany	Rodolph Legier	£99,500.00
Germany	WunderKar	£172,500.00
Italy	Bravissima!	£95,090.00
Italy	Prestissimo!	£175,540.00
Total		**£21,977,950.00**

CountryName	ClientName	Color	SalePrice
Belgium	Diplomatic Cars	Green	£125,000.00
Belgium	Diplomatic Cars	Red	£12,500.00
Belgium	Diplomatic Cars	Silver	£86,500.00
Belgium	Flash Voitures	Red	£6,950.00
Belgium	Stefan Van Helsing	Black	£79,950.00
Belgium	Stefan Van Helsing	British Racing Green	£950.00
France	Bling Bling S.A.	Red	£345,000.00
France	Capots Reluisants S.A.	Black	£43,390.00
France	Capots Reluisants S.A.	Blue	£189,500.00
France	Capots Reluisants S.A.	Dark Purple	£32,675.00
France	Capots Reluisants S.A.	Red	£7,550.00
France	Capots Reluisants S.A.	Silver	£310,000.00
France	Casseroles Chromes	Blue	£59,000.00
France	Casseroles Chromes	British Racing Green	£66,500.00
France	Casseroles Chromes	Green	£55,600.00
France	Casseroles Chromes	Red	£19,950.00
France	Francois Chirac	Black	£25,950.00
France	Jacques Mitterand	Blue	£69,500.00
France	Jean-Yves Truffaut	British Racing Green	£1,950.00
France	Khader El Ghannam	Dark Purple	£25,500.00
France	Khader El Ghannam	Green	£25,000.00
France	La Bagnole de Luxe	Black	£27,890.00
France	La Bagnole de Luxe	Night Blue	£80,100.00
France	La Bagnole de Luxe	Red	£387,950.00
France	La Bagnole de Luxe	Silver	£1,250.00
France	Laurent Saint Yves	Black	£388,050.00
France	Laurent Saint Yves	British Racing Green	£543,400.00
France	Laurent Saint Yves	Canary Yellow	£77,500.00
France	Laurent Saint Yves	Dark Purple	£269,500.00
France	Laurent Saint Yves	Green	£65,500.00
France	Le Luxe en Motion	Blue	£255,850.00
Total			**£21,977,950.00**

Figure 2-3. *Progressive table granularity*

Power BI Desktop always attempts to display the data using the information available to it in the underlying data model.

Enhancing Tables

So you have a basic table set up and it has the columns you want in the correct order. Quite naturally, the next step is to want to spice up the presentation of the table a little. So let's see what Power BI Desktop has to offer here. Specifically, we will look at

- Adding and removing totals
- Adjusting text sizes in tables
- Changing column widths
- Sorting rows by the data in a specific column

Adding and Removing Totals

Row totals are added automatically to all numeric fields. You may wish to remove the totals, however. Conversely, you could want to add totals that were removed previously. In any case, to remove all the totals from a table:

1. Create a table based on the fields ClientName (from the Client table), Town (from the Geography table), and SalePrice (from the Sales table).

2. In the Visualizations pane, click the Format icon (the small paintbrush and page icon beneath the palette of available visual types). The formatting options for the selected table will be displayed.

3. Expand the Total card by clicking the downward-facing chevron to the left of the word *Total*.

4. Drag the full circle button (to the right of Totals) to the left (or click to the left of the button or even on the button itself). It will become an empty circle and On will become Off in the formatting options. The Visualizations pane will look what is shown in Figure 2-4.

Figure 2-4. *Adding totals*

To add totals where there are none, follow the process described (with the table selected), and at step 4, click the Off button for Totals to set the totals to On.

Note   You can only add or remove totals if a table displays multiple records. If a table is displaying the highest level of aggregation for a value, then no totals can be displayed, as you are looking at the grand total already. In this case, the Totals button is grayed out.

Formatting Numbers in Reports

You cannot (as things stand) format numbers directly in tables in a Power BI Desktop report as you can in a spreadsheet. This is because all number formatting is centralized in the data model. So if you want to apply a different numeric format from the one that appears when you add a value to a table, you will have to switch to Data View and apply the formatting there. If you need to remind yourself exactly how this is done, then you can refer to the companion book *Pro DAX and Data Modeling in Power BI* for a quick refresher course on how to format numbers in Power BI Desktop.

Font Sizes in Tables

You may prefer to alter the default font size that Power BI Desktop applies when a table is first created. This is easy to do:

1. Select the table.

2. In the Visualizations pane, click the Format icon.

3. Expand the Values card by clicking the downward-facing chevron to the left of the word Values.

4. Click the up or down chevrons to the right of the current font size. The new text size in points will be displayed in the Global font size box and the actual size of the text in the table will increase or decrease.

Here are a few points regarding font sizes in tables:

- You can enter a font size in the Global font size box to specify an exact size, if you prefer.

- Altering the font size will *not* cause the table itself to grow or shrink, as Power BI Desktop will continue to display the same number of characters per column as were visible using the previous font size. So you may end up having to alter the column widths by setting Auto-size to On (this is described in the following section) or adjusting the table size (as described in the previous chapter) to make your table look exactly the way you want it.

- This formatting option only affects the size of the *records* in the table, *not* the column headings. Formatting column headers and totals are explained a little later in this chapter.

Changing Column Widths

Power BI Desktop will automatically set the width of a column so that all the data is visible when you create an initial table.

However—and as you would expect—you can also manually adjust the size of individual columns in a table. You do this more or less as you would in Excel:

1. In the column header row, place the mouse pointer over the rightmost edge of the column.

2. Drag left or right to adjust the column width.

Note   As you would probably expect from a product that aims at Excel users, you can double-click the column separator at the right of a column's header to have Power BI Desktop adjust the width of the column automatically to fit the widest data element—whether it is visible or not.

Inhibiting Automatic Adjustment of Column Width and Enabling Text Wrap

If you want to, you can prevent Power BI Desktop from resetting column widths automatically, and you can also ensure text wrap is enabled to make sure that text in a column is not truncated, but flows onto the following line. Here is how:

1. Select the table. In this example, I use the table that you saw in Figure 2-1.

2. In the Visualizations pane, click the Format icon (the second icon above the palette of available visual types). The formatting options for the selected table will be displayed.

3. Expand the Column Headers card by clicking the downward-facing chevron to the left of the word Column Headers.

4. Expand the Options card.

5. Ensure that "Auto-size width" is off. If it is not, click the On button to set it to Off.

6. Set Text wrap to On (this may already be the case). The Visualizations pane will look like Figure 2-5.

Figure 2-5. *Inhibiting automatic column resizing for tables*

You can now alter the size of the font used in the table without causing column widths to grow or shrink. Inversely, resetting the Auto-size option to On causes the column width to be readjusted automatically to display the widest element in the column.

Note   If you are formatting a table and you start to get a little confused as to which options are active and how best to start over, you can always click "Revert to default" at the bottom of each card in the Formatting pane to reapply the standard "factory settings" for tables—or for any visual.

Sorting by Column

Any column can be used as the sort criterion for a table, whatever the column data type. To sort the table, merely click the column header. The rows in the table are sorted according to the elements in the selected column. The sort order is A to Z (or lowest to highest for numeric values) the first time that you sort a column.

Once a table has been sorted, you cannot unsort it. You can use another column to resort the data, however. Alternatively, you can click the column title again to sort in the opposing order—Z to A (or highest to lowest for numeric values).

For an example of sorting a column, look at Figure 2-6 (using a table you based on ClientName, Town, and SalePrice). You can see that the data is sorted by Sale Price from highest to lowest. Moreover, you can see a small down-facing triangle below the title of the SalePrice column. This indicates that the column is sorted from the highest to the lowest value.

CountryName	ClientName	Color	SalePrice
France	Laurent Saint Yves	British Racing Green	£543,400.00
France	Vive La Vitesse	Red	£450,650.00
United Kingdom	Magic Motors	Black	£447,450.00
France	Vive La Vitesse	Black	£427,500.00
United Kingdom	Birmingham Executive Prestige Vehicles	Silver	£391,890.00

Sort Indicator

Figure 2-6. *Sorting a table by a numeric column*

Sometimes you are sorting a column on one field (as was the case in all the examples so far), but the actual sort uses another column as the basis for the sort operation. For example, you could sort by month name but see the result by the month number (so that you are not sorting months alphabetically, but numerically). Setting this option is described in the companion book *Pro DAX and Data Modeling in Power BI*.

Formatting Tables

As befits such a polished product, Power BI Desktop can enhance the presentation of even a humble table so that it stands out from the crowd, and delivers that attention-grabbing effect that your audience expects. The currently available formatting options include

- Adding automatic table styles

- Formatting titles

- Modifying the table background

- Adding and removing table borders

- Formatting rows—including alternating rows

- Adding and removing a table grid

- Formatting column headers

- Column formatting

- Formatting totals

- Conditional formatting—including color scales, font colors, data bars, and "KPI-style" icons

I confidently expect that these options will continue to be developed as Power BI Desktop matures. Consequently, you could see further presentation enhancements by the time that you read this book. However, for the moment, let's take a look at the currently available options.

Note   There are no specific options for formatting the figures in tables. You format the data by clicking the data icon on the left of the Power BI Desktop window, select the table and then the column to format, and, in the Modeling ribbon, select a number format. This format will then apply to the selected field in the same way in every visual where it is used.

Table Style

Power BI Desktop allows you to choose from nine different ways of instantly formatting a table in a few clicks. This includes the option of removing all table formatting. To format an entire table:

1. Click inside the table to format.

2. In the Visualizations pane, click the Format icon.

3. Expand the Table Style card. Select a table style from the available options.

You can see the range of available table styles in Table 2-1.

Table 2-1. *The Available Table Styles*

Matrix Style	Description
Default	Adds a gray background to alternating rows
None	Removes all formatting
Minimal	Adds a light spacing between records
Bold header	Adds a dark background to the title row
Alternating rows	Adds a gray background to alternating rows and a dark background to the title and totals rows
Contrast alternating rows	Alternates the row background between light and darker gray; adds a dark background to the title and totals rows
Flashy rows	Alternates the row background between light and darker green
Bold header flashy rows	Alternates the row background between light and darker green; adds a dark background to the title and totals rows
Sparse	Adds a dark background to the title and totals rows and removes the light line separating rows
Condensed	Adds a dark background to the title and totals rows and adds vertical and horizontal lines between rows and columns

The table styles that you can add are really nothing more than preset values. If you want to be precise in the definition of how the records in a table appear, you can apply the various options that are explained in the next few sections.

Note   To remove a table style and revert to a "plain vanilla" presentation, simply select None from the pop-up list of available table styles.

Adding and Formatting Titles

Like most visualizations in Power BI Desktop, tables can have titles. Once you have added a title, you can set its

- Font color

- Background color

- Text alignment

As simple as this is, I prefer to explain all the options for the sake of completeness.

1. Select the table. In this example, I use a table based on Town, ClientName, and SalePrice.

2. In the Visualizations pane, click the Format icon. The formatting options for the selected table will be displayed.

3. Click General to switch to the common formatting options.

4. Expand the Title card by clicking the downward-facing chevron to the left of the word Title.

5. Ensure that Title is set to On. This will activate a title for the selected table.

6. In the empty Title box, enter a title for the table. I suggest **Sales by Town**.

7. Click the pop-up menu triangle to the right of Font Color and select a color from the palette of available hues.

8. Click the pop-up menu triangle to the right of Background Color and select a color from the palette of available tones.

9. Click the middle of the Horizontal alignment icons. This will center the text relative to the width of the table.

10. Use the up- and down-facing chevrons to increase the text size of the title font.

11. Click the Bold icon.

The formatting options and the table will look like they do in Figure 2-7.

Sales by Town		
Town	ClientName	SalePrice
Newcastle	Alex McWhirter	£17,850.00
London	Alexei Tolstoi	£521,490.00
Barcelona	Alicia Almodovar	£382,090.00
Birmingham	Andrea Tarbuck	£454,500.00
Stoke	Andy Cheshire	£174,500.00
Madrid	Antonio Maura	£550,330.00
Madrid	Autos Sportivos	£65,890.00
Liverpool	Beltway Prestige Driving	£54,875.00
Birmingham	Birmingham Executive Prestige Vehicles	£469,740.00
Paris	Bling Bling S.A.	£345,000.00
Total		£21,977,950.00

Figure 2-7. *Options for titles in tables*

Note   You can, if you prefer, enter the desired font size in the Text Size field. And you can select a font and add or remove attributes such as underline and italic.

Modifying the Table Background

The table title is not the only aspect of a table that you can modify for visual effect. You can also change a couple of elements of the table itself to add pizzazz to your dashboards. The following are the two things that you can modify:

- The background color

- The table transparency

The following example illustrates both of these possibilities:

1. Select the table. In this example, I use the table that you saw in Figure 2-7.

2. In the Visualizations pane, click the Format icon.

3. Click Visual to switch to the formatting options specific to this visual (unless it is already selected).

4. Expand the Style presets card and set the Style to None.

5. Collapse the Style presets card.

6. Click General to switch to the common formatting options.

7. Expand the Effects card and then the Background card.

8. Ensure that Background is set to On.

9. Click the pop-up menu triangle to the right of Color and select a color from the palette of available colors.

10. Click the Transparency slider switch and slide it to the left to intensify the background color by reducing the percentage of transparency. The formatting options and the table will look like Figure 2-8.

Sales by Town		
Town	ClientName	SalePrice
Barcelona	Alicia Almodovar	£382,090.00
Barcelona	Prestige Imports	£456,150.00
Barcelona	YO! Speed!	£110,100.00
Berlin	Ralph Obermann	£11,550.00
Berlin	WunderKar	£172,500.00
Birmingham	Andrea Tarbuck	£454,500.00
Birmingham	Birmingham Executive Prestige Vehicles	£469,740.00
Birmingham	Boris Spry	£155,040.00
Birmingham	ImpressTheNeighbours.Com	£203,500.00
Birmingham	Magic Motors	£602,850.00
Birmingham	Peter Smith	£322,500.00
Total		£21,977,950.00

Figure 2-8. *Setting the background color for a table*

Note   You can see that, using this technique, you have only formatted the background of the table visual, not the rows and columns that make up the table itself. You will learn how to format the rows and columns in a couple of pages' time.

Table Borders

To add another flourish, you can add an outside border to any table. The following explains how to do this:

1. Select the table. In this example, I use the table that you saw in Figure 2-8.

2. In the Visualizations pane, click the Format icon and switch to the General elements.

3. Expand the Effects card.

4. Expand the Visual border card and set the border to On.

5. Select a border color from those available in the pop-up palette.

6. Drag the Rounded corners button to the right to define the rounding of the corners of the border (or use the chevrons or even enter a figure).

You can see the result in Figure 2-9.

Figure 2-9. *Setting the background color for a table*

Note   You may have to unselect the table to see the border that you added.

Shadows

You can add further pizzazz by adding a shadow to any table. Here is how to do this:

1. Select the table. In this example, I use the table that you saw in Figure 2-9.

2. In the Visualizations pane, click the Format icon and switch to the General elements and expand the Effects card.

3. Expand the Shadow card and set it to On.

4. Select a shadow color from those available in the pop-up palette.

5. Ensure the shadow offset is set to Outside.

6. Select Custom in the Position pop-up.

7. Set the Size to **5**.

8. Set the Blur to **10**.

9. Set the Angle to **55**.

10. Set the Distance to **20**.

11. Set the Transparency to **55**.

You can see the result in Figure 2-10.

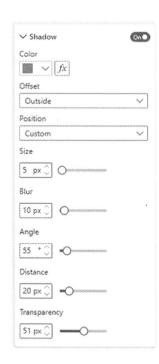

Sales byTown		
Town	ClientName	SalePrice
Marseille	Laurent Saint Yves	£1,343,950.00
Marseille	Vive La Vitesse	£1,269,600.00
Stoke	Honest Pete Motors	£947,140.00
Birmingham	Magic Motors	£602,850.00
Stuttgart	Glitz	£589,490.00
Paris	Capots Reluisants S.A.	£583,115.00
Newcastle	King Leer Cars	£581,580.00
Madrid	Antonio Maura	£550,330.00
London	Alexei Tolstoi	£521,490.00
Total		**£21,977,950.00**

Figure 2-10. *Setting the background color for a table*

In this example, you saw how to customize a shadow to the finest level of detail. If you prefer, you can select one of the shadow presets to save time.

The various shadow presets and options are explained in Table 2-2.

Table 2-2. *Shadow Options*

Option	Description
Bottom right	Adds a shadow to the bottom right of the selected visual
Bottom	Adds a shadow to the bottom of the selected visual
Bottom left	Adds a shadow to the bottom left of the selected visual
Right	Adds a shadow to the right of the selected visual
Center	Adds a shadow to the center of the selected visual
Left	Adds a shadow to the left of the selected visual
Top right	Adds a shadow to the top right of the selected visual
Top	Adds a shadow to the top of the selected visual
Top left	Adds a shadow to the top left of the selected visual
Custom	Adds a customized shadow to the selected visual
Size	Sets the size of the customized shadow
Blur	Sets the blur of the customized shadow
Angle	Sets the angle of the customized shadow to the visual
Distance	Sets the distance of the customized shadow from the visual
Transparency	Sets the transparency of the customized shadow that is applied

Row Formatting

In an earlier section, you saw how to change the font size for the row data in a table. This is only one of the available formatting options that you can apply to the data in a table. Here are some of the other possibilities:

1. Select the table that you want to enhance. In this example, I use the table that you saw in Figure 2-10.

2. In the Visualizations pane, click the Format icon and ensure that General is active.

3. Expand the Values card.

4. Select a Background Color as well as an Alternative background color.

5. Select a Text color as well as an Alternative Text color.

6. Choose a font and set a font size.

7. Select Bottom only from the available outline styles.

8. The table could look something like the one shown in Figure 2-11.

Figure 2-11. *Formatting alternate rows in a table*

Table Grid

You can extend the presentation of a table with much greater precision if you use the Table Grid card of the formatting options in the Visualizations pane.

Let's see how this works, taking the table from Figure 2-11:

1. Select the table to format, and in the Visualizations pane, click the Format icon.

2. Expand the Grid card.

3. Expand the Vertical gridlines card and switch Vertical gridlines to On.

4. Select a color from the palette of available colors for the vertical grid.

5. Enter **3** in the field for Vertical grid width (or adjust the value using the tiny chevrons).

6. Expand the Horizontal gridlines card and switch Horizontal gridlines to On (if necessary).

7. Select a color from the palette of available colors for the horizontal grid.

8. Set a different width for the horizontal grid.

9. Expand the Options card and set the Row Padding to **5**.

10. Select a color from the palette of available colors for the outline color.

11. Expand the Border card and set the width to **5**.

12. Select a border color.

13. Adjust the column widths to display all the text and numbers in the columns if this proves necessary.

You can see the results of these changes in Figure 2-12. I am in no way pretending that there is any profound aesthetic value to these enhancements—but you can, at least, see how Power BI Desktop can be used to format your data.

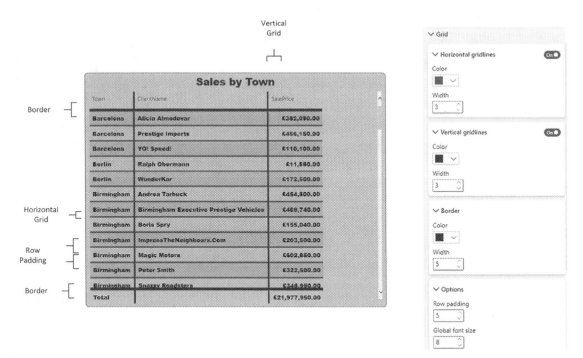

Figure 2-12. *Table grid settings*

Note   Depending on the resolution of your monitor, you might have to scroll down inside the Grid card of the Formatting pane. You do this using the gray vertical bar at the right of the Grid card.

Column Headers

Power BI Desktop also allows you to modify the formatting of column headers. You could carry out the following tweaks to see this in action:

1. Create a new table based on Town, ClientName, and SalePrice.

2. Click the Format icon in the Visualizations pane and expand the Column Headers card.

3. Set a font and background color using the appropriate palettes for each.

4. Select a different font.

5. Increase the font size for the title.

6. Switch Italic to On.

7. Click the Center alignment icon. You should see the table formatted as in Figure 2-13.

Town	ClientName	SalePrice
Barcelona	Alicia Almodovar	£382,090.00
Barcelona	Prestige Imports	£456,150.00
Barcelona	YO! Speed!	£110,100.00
Berlin	Ralph Obermann	£11,550.00
Berlin	WunderKar	£172,500.00
Birmingham	Andrea Tarbuck	£454,500.00
Birmingham	Birmingham Executive Prestige Vehicles	£469,740.00
Birmingham	Boris Spry	£155,040.00
Birmingham	ImpressTheNeighbours.Com	£203,500.00
Birmingham	Magic Motors	£602,850.00
Total		**£21,977,950.00**

Figure 2-13. *Formatting column headers*

Note   If you choose to enter a text size in the Text Size field, be aware that there are limits that you cannot exceed. For instance, if you enter a figure less than 8, Power BI Desktop will refuse to apply the requested font size and will add a red outline to the Text Size field. You will then have to enter a valid number.

Field Formatting

Each individual column can be formatted separately. You need to be aware that, in practice, overuse of this technique can easily lead to total illegibility. Nonetheless, it is worth learning how to format an individual column.

1. Select the table from Figure 2-13.

2. Click the Format icon in the Visualizations pane and expand the Specific column card.

3. Select the column header for the column that you wish to format from the pop-up list at the top of the Column Formatting card. I will choose Town in this example.

4. Set Apply to header and Apply to total to On—and ensure that Apply to values is On.

5. Expand the Values card and set a font and background color using the appropriate palettes for each.

6. You can see the output in Figure 2-14.

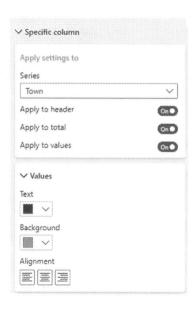

Figure 2-14. *Adding column formatting*

Formatting Totals

Power BI Desktop lets you do more to totals in tables than just switch them on and off. You can format the total to enhance the visibility (or, inversely, try and divert attention from poor figures by making them illegible), like this:

1. Re-create the table that you can see in Figure 2-14.

2. In the Visualizations pane (and, of course, leaving the table selected), activate the Format pane and expand the Totals card.

3. Expand the Values card (if it is collapsed) and ensure that it is set to On.

4. Choose a text color from those in the palette.

5. Choose a background color from those in the palette.

6. Enter an appropriate total label to override the default "Total."

7. Set a larger font size plus any font attributes that you want. You can see the result of these actions as well as the Total card of the Formatting pane in Figure 2-15.

Figure 2-15. *Formatting totals*

Conclusion

I hope that you are now comfortable with the Power BI Desktop reports interface and are relaxed about using it to present your data as tables. You learned not just how to create tables but also how to change their presentation in a myriad of subtle (and not so subtle) ways to enhance their impact. This ranges from setting font attributes to adjusting the appearance of both titles and data.

Equally, I hope that you are at ease sorting the data in your tables using the various possible techniques.

This chapter was just a taster of the many ways in which Power BI Desktop can help you analyze and display the information that you want your audience to appreciate. So, as tables are the basis for just about every other form of visual, it is well worth mastering the techniques and tricks of table creation. This way, you are well on the way to a fluent mastery of Power BI Desktop, which lays the foundations for some truly impressive presentations.

Now that you have mastered the basics, it is time to move on to the next level of dashboard creation where you will discover how to extend tables with some powerful and impressive presentation techniques. These are explained in the next chapter.

CHAPTER 3

Advanced Table Visual Techniques

In the previous chapter, you learned how to create and format tables in Power BI Desktop. Yet there are many more ways that you can enhance tables to make them into truly compelling visuals that make the information that they contain leap off the screen. These include

- Conditionally formatting the column values

- Adding data bars to visually represent the values in a column

- Adding icons (KPIs) to a column

- Adding hyperlinks

- Adding Sparklines (a kind of mini-chart inside each row of a table)

Also in this chapter, you will discover how to remove formatting—both partially and totally from any visual. Finally, you will see how to copy formatting across tables.

This chapter will continue using the sample file PrestigeCarsDataForDashboards. pbix that you can download from the Apress website.

Conditional Formatting

Tables of data may convey vast amounts of information, but they rarely enable instant understanding of the meaning of the figures. This is where conditional formatting can be applied to convert data into instantly useful information. Indeed, you may already be used to applying these kinds of enhancements to Excel spreadsheets.

In Power BI Desktop, there are two types of conditional formatting that you can apply to add meaning to your figures:

© Adam Aspin 2022
A. Aspin, *Pro Power BI Dashboard Creation*, https://doi.org/10.1007/978-1-4842-8227-4_3

- *Background color*: Add shades of color to the entire background of a table cell.

- *Text color*: Alter the color of the text as a function of a selected value.

Note   Conditional formatting can only be applied to numeric values, not to text elements.

Background Color

You can apply a background color that you apply to the cells in a column. The actual color will vary individually by row according to the value of a column that you select—which need not be the column whose background color you are modifying.

There are two ways to apply background colors:

- Using varying intensities of color to indicate a range of values. These are called *gradients*.

- Setting user-defined thresholds to apply various colors. These are called *rules*.

As an example of how gradients work, try the following:

1. Create a table using the ClientName, SalePrice, and Gross Profit fields. Make sure that you leave the table selected.

2. Click the Format icon in the Visualizations pane and expand the Cell elements card.

3. Select the name of the column to format from the pop-up list of the columns in the table (in this example, this is the Gross Profit column).

4. Set the Background Color button to On. A range of shades will be applied to the Gross Profit column.

5. Click the Fx icon for the Background color. The Background color dialog will be displayed.

6. Ensure Gradient is selected from the Format style pop-up.

7. Set the color for the minimum to a light color from the pop-up palette.

8. Click the Add a middle color check box.

9. Set the color for the center to a medium color from the pop-up palette.

10. In the pop-up for Center, select Custom.

11. Enter **100000** in the number field that is now enabled.

12. Set the color for the maximum to a dark color from the pop-up palette. The Background color dialog will look like the one shown in Figure 3-1.

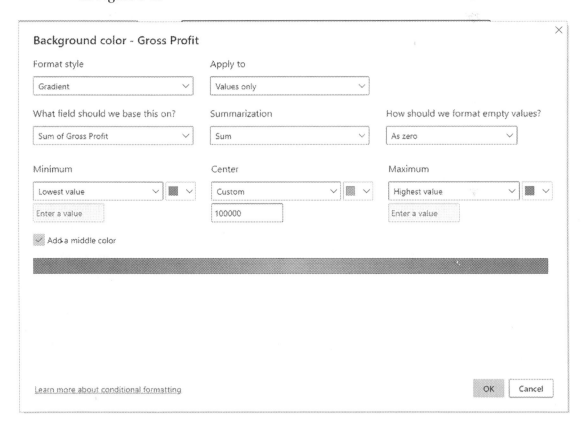

Figure 3-1. *The Color Scales dialog*

13. Click OK. The table will look like the one in Figure 3-2.

ClientName	SalePrice	Gross Profit
Alex McWhirter	£17,850.00	£3,570.00
Alexei Tolstoi	£521,490.00	£104,298.00
Alicia Almodovar	£382,090.00	£76,418.00
Andrea Tarbuck	£454,500.00	£90,900.00
Andy Cheshire	£174,500.00	£34,900.00
Antonio Maura	£550,330.00	£110,066.00
Autos Sportivos	£65,890.00	£13,178.00
Beltway Prestige Driving	£54,875.00	£10,975.00
Birmingham Executive Prestige Vehicles	£469,740.00	£93,948.00
Bling Bling S.A.	£345,000.00	£69,000.00
Bling Motors	£96,200.00	£19,240.00
Boris Spry	£155,040.00	£31,008.00
Bravissima!	£95,090.00	£19,018.00
Capots Reluisants S.A.	£583,115.00	£116,623.00
Casseroles Chromes	£201,050.00	£40,210.00
Total	**£21,977,950.00**	**£4,403,590.00**

Figure 3-2. *A table with color scales applied*

In this example, you only tweaked a few of the available options in the Background color dialog. There are many other tweaks that can be applied, so let's review the alternatives.

- You can choose any field as the basis for the background color shading—it does *not* have to be the field that actually contains the shading in the table. If you click the "What field should we base this on?" pop-up, you will see the list of all the available tables and fields in the data model, as shown in Figure 3-3.

What field should we base this on?

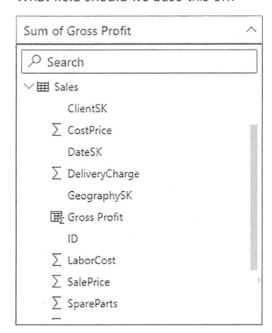

Figure 3-3. *Selecting the field to drive color formatting*

- You can either let Power BI Desktop detect the minimum, maximum, and median values when setting a background color, or you can define specific values by selecting Custom in the Minimum, Center, and Maximum pop-up lists and then enter a value in the relevant box.

- If you do not check the Add a middle color check box, you only define a range of two colors.

- The standard summarizations that you probably expect (Sum, Average, Count, etc.) are available when defining conditional formatting.

- You can define a Format style in three ways:

  - Gradient (which we did here)

  - Rules (which we will look at in the next section when defining a text color)

- Field value (which I will explain after the next section)
- You can apply the shading to
  - *Values*: So only the data (but not any totals) have a background color applied
  - *Totals*: So only the totals (but not any data) have a background color applied
  - *Values and totals*: So that both have a background color applied
- Empty values (blanks) can be treated in any of the following ways:
  - *As zero*: The color set as the minimum will be applied.
  - *Not formatted*: No color will be applied.
  - *Using a specific color*: Selecting this option displays a color palette pop-up in the dialog.

Text Color

Another conditional formatting option is to set the color of the *text* for the text of each value using conditional formatting. This is very similar to applying conditional formatting to the column background. Indeed, in this example, I will extend the previous example to apply conditional formatting to the text of the table that you just created. Only this time, we will apply rules-based formatting to the SalePrice column.

1. Select the table that you created in the previous section.

2. In the Visualizations pane, click the Format icon, and in the Visual pane, expand the Cell elements card.

3. Select the name of the column to format from the pop-up list of the columns in the table (in this example, once again, this is the SalePrice column).

4. Set Font Color to On. The Font color dialog will appear (if ever it does not, then click the *Fx* icon under Font color).

5. Select Rules from the Format style pop-up.

6. Select ID from the Sales table for the "What field should we base this on?" field.

7. Leave the Summarization as Count.

8. Set the If value to the following: Is greater than or equal to **0** (number) and Is less than **2** (number).

9. Select a color for this rule from the palette.

10. Click the + New rule button. A new rule row will appear below the rule that you just created.

11. Set the If value for this rule to the following: Is greater than or equal to **3** (number) and Is less than **10** (number).

12. Select a color for this rule from the palette. The dialog will look like the one shown in Figure 3-4.

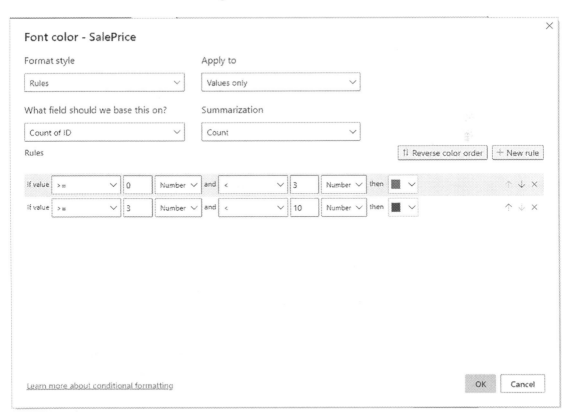

Figure 3-4. *The Background Color Scales dialog*

13.   Click OK. The table will look like it does in Figure 3-5.

ClientName	SalePrice	Gross Profit	
Alex McWhirter	£17,850.00	£3,570.00	^
Alexei Tolstoi	£521,490.00	£104,298.00	
Alicia Almodovar	£382,090.00	£76,418.00	
Andrea Tarbuck	£454,500.00	£90,900.00	
Andy Cheshire	£174,500.00	£34,900.00	
Antonio Maura	£550,330.00	£110,066.00	
Autos Sportivos	£65,890.00	£13,178.00	
Beltway Prestige Driving	£54,875.00	£10,975.00	
Birmingham Executive Prestige Vehicles	£469,740.00	£93,948.00	
Bling Bling S.A.	£345,000.00	£69,000.00	
Bling Motors	£96,200.00	£19,240.00	
Boris Spry	£155,040.00	£31,008.00	
Bravissima!	£95,090.00	£19,018.00	
Capots Reluisants S.A.	£583,115.00	£116,623.00	
Casseroles Chromes	£201,050.00	£40,210.00	v
Total	**£21,977,950.00**	**£4,403,590.00**	

Figure 3-5. *Applying conditional text color to a column*

Note   If you prefer, you can set the text and background to different colors to obtain a completely different effect from the application of conditional text.

There are a few points you may find interesting when setting the conditional formatting for a text:

- If you choose a non-numeric field as the basis for the background color shading, you can only use Count or Count distinct as the summarization.

- You can add multiple rules when defining rules-based conditional formatting.

- Rules can be deleted by clicking the cross icon at the right of each rule.

- Rules-based conditional formatting can be applied equally well to the cell background.

- If you want to alter the order in which the rules are applied, simply click the up and down arrows to the right of each rule.

- Clicking the Reverse color order button keeps the rules, but reverses the colors that are applied.

- When applying rules-based conditional formatting, be careful that you set the threshold values accurately so that you do not exclude any values.

- Applying the same rules and colors to both text and background can make the text invisible. In certain circumstances, this may even be a useful dashboarding technique.

Set a Color for the Text or Background Using a Data Field

In the two previous sections, you used rules or a gradient of colors to set the text or background color. There is, however, one other way to set the color attribute that you use for conditional formatting. This is to use a color reference that is set in a column in the source data itself.

Inevitably, this presumes that the source data contains a color setting for the rows that you wish to color. Fortunately, the sample source data contains a field—ClientFlag—that contains a color definition for some of the clients. If you switch to Data View and select the Client table, you can see the data that will be the source for the color attribution.

1. Create a table containing the fields ClientName and SalePrice.

2. In the Visualizations pane, click the Format icon, and in the Visual pane, expand the Cell elements card.

3. Select the ClientName column from the pop-up list of the columns in the table.

4. Set Font Color to On. The Font color dialog will appear.

5. Select Field value from the Format style pop-up.

6.   Select ClientFlag as the field in the "What field should we base this on?" pop-up. The dialog will look like the one in Figure 3-6.

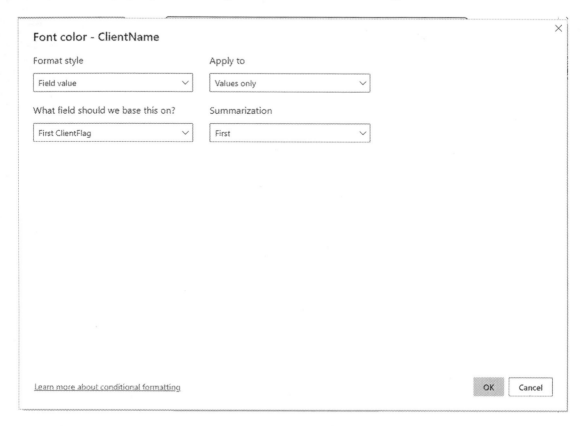

Figure 3-6. *Applying conditional text color to a column using a data field*

7.   Click OK. The table will look like the one in Figure 3-7 where Alexei Tolstoi, Antonio Maura, and Autos Sportivos are displayed in the color set in the source data.

ClientName	SalePrice
Alex McWhirter	£17,850.00
Alexei Tolstoi	£521,490.00
Alicia Almodovar	£382,090.00
Andrea Tarbuck	£454,500.00
Andy Cheshire	£174,500.00
Antonio Maura	£550,330.00
Autos Sportivos	£65,890.00
Beltway Prestige Driving	£54,875.00
Total	**£21,977,950.00**

Figure 3-7. *The result of applying conditional text color to a column using a data field*

Color References

Colors can be defined in the source data in any of the following ways:

- Color names, such as Red or Blue.

- 3-, 6-, or 8-digit hexadecimal codes that begin with the # symbol at the start of the code.

- RGB or RGBA values. These must be a comma-separated list of three or four values.

- HSL or HSLA values. These must be a comma-separated list.

Data Bars

Data bars are a visualization technique that represents the figure as a colored bar behind—or instead of—the actual value in a table cell. You can add data bars using the following steps:

1. Create a table using the Make and SalePrice fields.

2. In the Visualizations pane, click the Format icon, and in the Visual pane, expand the Cell elements card.

3. Select the name of the column to format from the pop-up list of the columns in the table (the SalePrice column).

4. Set the Data Bars button to On. Power BI Desktop applies data bars to the SalePrice column.

5. Click the Fx icon under Data bars. The Data Bars dialog will be displayed.

6. In the Minimum pop-up, select Custom.

7. Enter **250000** as the value in the number field that is now enabled.

8. Choose different colors for the positive bar and negative bar and the Axis. The dialog should look like the one in Figure 3-8.

Figure 3-8. *The Data Bars dialog*

9. Click OK. The table will look like the one in Figure 3-9.

Make	CostPrice
Alfa Romeo	£194,808.00
Aston Martin	£4,082,204.00
Austin	£51,600.00
Bentley	£1,351,392.00
BMW	£48,400.00
Bugatti	£1,524,400.00
Citroen	£80,864.00
Delahaye	£85,600.00
Delorean	£79,600.00
Ferrari	£4,432,680.00
Jaguar	£706,364.00
Lagonda	£174,400.00
Lamborghini	£1,381,720.00
McLaren	£236,000.00
Mercedes	£376,892.00
Total	**£17,574,360.00**

Figure 3-9. *Data bars applied to a table*

Once again, there are a few points you may find of note when applying data bars:

- You can choose to apply the *bars only* (and not the actual figures) by clicking the Show bar only check box.

- Data bars can only be applied to a column containing numeric values.

- Data bars can be positive or negative.

Note   You can choose to add data bars and color formatting (both text and background) to the same column at the same time. However, this may detract from the visual rather than enabling the reader to understand the meaning of the data.

Icons

Power BI Desktop also has the ability to display Key Performance Indicators as Icons. You can add these to any existing column in a table like this:

1. Select the table that you created in the previous section.

2. Click the Format icon in the Visualizations pane and expand the
    Cell elements card.

3. Select the name of the column to format from the pop-up list
    of the columns in the table (in this example, it will be the Make
    column).

4. Set the Icons button to On. The Icons dialog appears.

5. Select the SalePrice field as the "What field should we base this
    on?" field. This field is in the Sales table.

6. Select Sum as the Summarization.

7. Choose Left of Data as the Icon layout.

8. Select one of the available icon style sets from the Style pop-up.

9. Select Middle as the Icon alignment. The Icons dialog will look
    like that shown in Figure 3-10.

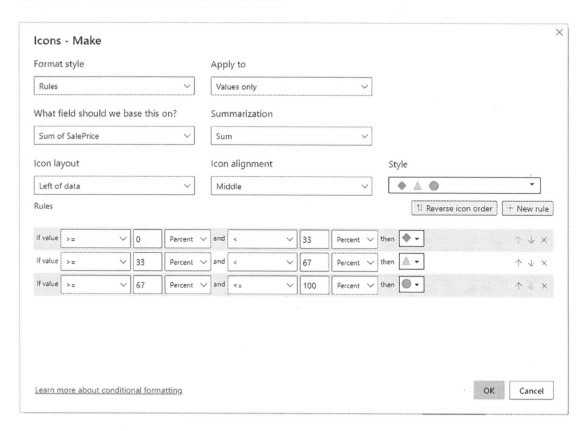

Figure 3-10. *The Icon dialog*

10.   Click OK. The table will look like that shown in Figure 3-11.

Make	CostPrice	
◆ Alfa Romeo	£194,808.00	
⬤ Aston Martin	£4,082,204.00	
◆ Austin	£51,600.00	
◆ Bentley	£1,351,392.00	
◆ BMW	£48,400.00	
▲ Bugatti	£1,524,400.00	
◆ Citroen	£80,864.00	
◆ Delahaye	£85,600.00	
◆ Delorean	£79,600.00	
⬤ Ferrari	£4,432,680.00	
◆ Jaguar	£706,364.00	
◆ Lagonda	£174,400.00	
◆ Lamborghini	£1,381,720.00	
◆ McLaren	£236,000.00	
◆ Mercedes	£376,892.00	
Total	**£17,574,360.00**	

Figure 3-11. *Icons applied to a table*

Icons are a great addition to the available data display techniques in Power BI Desktop. There are, nonetheless, a few things that you need to know:

- You can define between three and five icons for a column. The available icon sets are displayed in Figure 3-12.

Figure 3-12. *Available KPI icons*

- The number of rules that appear in the dialog will automatically map
  to the number of icons in the set that you selected.

- If you delete or add a rule, the Style switches to Custom. You can now select the type of icon that you wish for each rule.

- You can, if you wish, select a specific icon for each rule that is applied.

Sparklines

Sparklines are a recent addition to Power BI Desktop that allow you to display a high-level visual overview of trends for a row or data.

1. Select the table that you used in the previous section.

2. In the Insert ribbon menu, click the Add a sparkline button.

3. Select Gross Profit (from the Sales table) as the Y axis and leave summarization as Sum.

4. Select FullYear (from the Date table) as the X axis. The Sparklines dialog will look like the one in Figure 3-13.

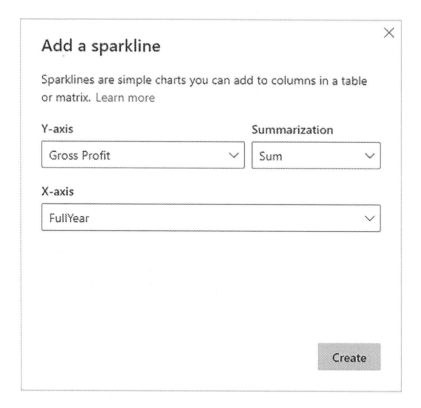

Figure 3-13. *The Sparklines dialog*

5. Click Create. A new column containing a sparkline will be added to the table.

6. Add a second sparkline with CostPrice as the Y axis, Sum as the Summarization, and DateKey (from the Date table) as the X axis.

7. Switch to the Format pane and expand the Sparklines card.

8. Select CostPrice by DateKey as the sparkline.

9. Set the Chart type to Column and choose a data color from the palette.

10. Select Gross Profit by FullYear as the sparkline.

11. Change the Data color and increase the width of the line.

12. Expand the Marker card.

13.   Uncheck all the marker check boxes. The table will look like the one in Figure 3-14.

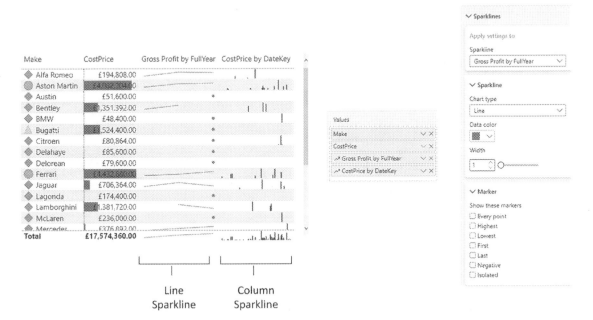

Figure 3-14. *Sparklines*

Once you have added a sparkline to a table, you will notice that the field that you added in the Values area of the Visualizations pane has a sparkline icon to its left.

Should you need to edit a sparkline, all you have to do is to open the pop-up menu for the sparkline field in the Values area of the Visualizations pane. This will display the Sparklines dialog.

Once you have created a sparkline, a new card (Sparklines) will appear at the bottom of the Visual panel of the Visualizations pane. When formatting a sparkline, be sure to select the appropriate sparkline (if your table contains more than one of them) in the Apply settings to pop-up.

Note   You can also add sparklines by clicking Add a sparkline in the context menu for any numeric field in the Values area of the Visualizations tab.

Markers in Sparklines

Sparklines can be enhanced by adding markers to the line at various points. Markers are described in Table 3-1.

Table 3-1. *Markers*

Marker	Description	Example
Every point	Adds a marker to every data point in the sparkline	
Highest	Adds a marker at the highest data point in the sparkline	
Lowest	Adds a marker at the lowest data point in the sparkline	
First	Adds a marker at the first data point in the sparkline	
Last	Adds a marker at the last data point in the sparkline	
Negative	Adds a marker to any negative data points in the sparkline	
Isolated	Adds a marker to any disconnected data points in the sparkline	

You can combine the marker options to display multiple markers if you so choose. These options do not apply to column sparklines.

Display Images

Tables can also display images. For this, the source data needs to contain the link to the image that you wish to display. The image *must* be stored as a URL on the Web.

Note   Before an image can be used in a table, it must be set as an image URL data category. This is described in the companion book *Pro DAX and Data Modeling in Power BI.*

---

1. Create a table using two columns from the Client table: ClientName and ImageLink.

The ImageLink column will display the source image. You can see this in Figure 3-15 (you will need to scroll down the table as not all clients have images).

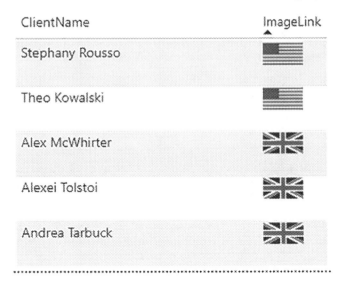

Figure 3-15. *Images*

There are, nonetheless, a couple of things to note about displaying images in tables:

- The image needs to be in one of these file formats: .bmp, .jpg, .jpeg, .gif, .png, or .svg.

- The URL needs to be anonymously accessible, not on a site that requires logging on.

Image Sizes

Once you have added images to a table, you may well want to adjust the size of the image. This is as simple as

1. Select the table that you created containing an image in the previous section.

2. In the Visualizations pane, display the Formatting pane, and in the Visual card, expand the Image height card.

3. Set an appropriate image height—either by entering a value or using the slider. You can see this in Figure 3-16.

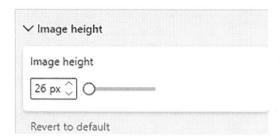

Figure 3-16. *Adjusting the image height in a table*

Display URL Links

Power BI dashboards are designed to be shared over the Web. Inevitably, they can contain URLs to link to other websites. If your source data contains URLs in a source table, there are three ways that these can be used in a table:

-   As the URL itself

-   As a link icon

-   Through setting another column as the hyperlink—and visually indicating the hyperlink status

---

Note   Before a URL can be used in a table, it must be set as a URL data category. This is described in the companion book *Pro DAX and Data Modeling in Power BI*.

Displaying URLs

To display a column as a URL, simply add the column to a table. You can see this in Figure 3-17. This is a table using two columns from the Client table: ClientName and ClientWebsite.

ClientName	ClientWebsite
Alex McWhirter	Http://www.calidra.co.uk
Alexei Tolstoi	Http://www.calidra.co.uk
Alicia Almodovar	Http://www.calidra.co.uk
Andrea Tarbuck	Http://www.calidra.co.uk

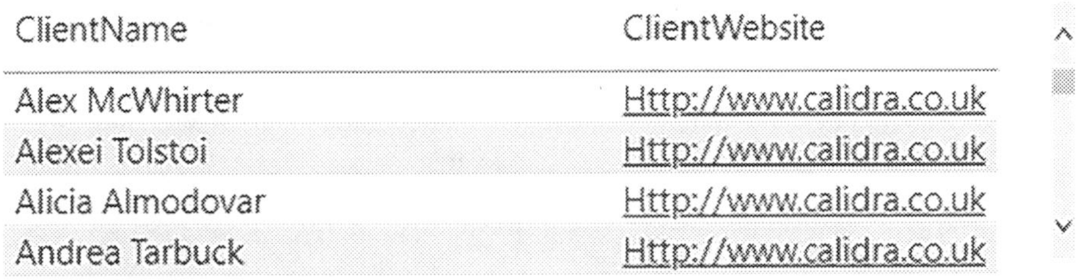

Figure 3-17. *Displaying a URL*

Displaying Link Icons

As URLs can take up a large amount of space in a dashboard column, you may prefer to display them as a link icon.

1. Create a table using two columns from the Client table: ClientName and ClientWebsite.

2. In the Visualizations pane, display the Format pane.

3. Expand URL icon and switch the URL icon to On.

You can see the result in Figure 3-18.

ClientName	ClientWebsite
Alex McWhirter	🔗
Alexei Tolstoi	🔗
Alicia Almodovar	🔗
Andrea Tarbuck	🔗

Figure 3-18. *Displaying a URL icon*

Setting Another Column As the Hyperlink

If you prefer to avoid URLs or icons to represent URLs, you can set another column as a hyperlink in a table.

1. Create a table using only the columns ClientName and CountryName from the Client table.

2. Display the Format pane.

3. In the Visual option, expand Cell elements.

4. Select the field ClientName from the Series pop-up.

5. Set Web URL to On. The Web URL dialog will appear.

6. Set the "What field should we base this on?" pop-up to ClientWebsite. The dialog will look like Figure 3-19.

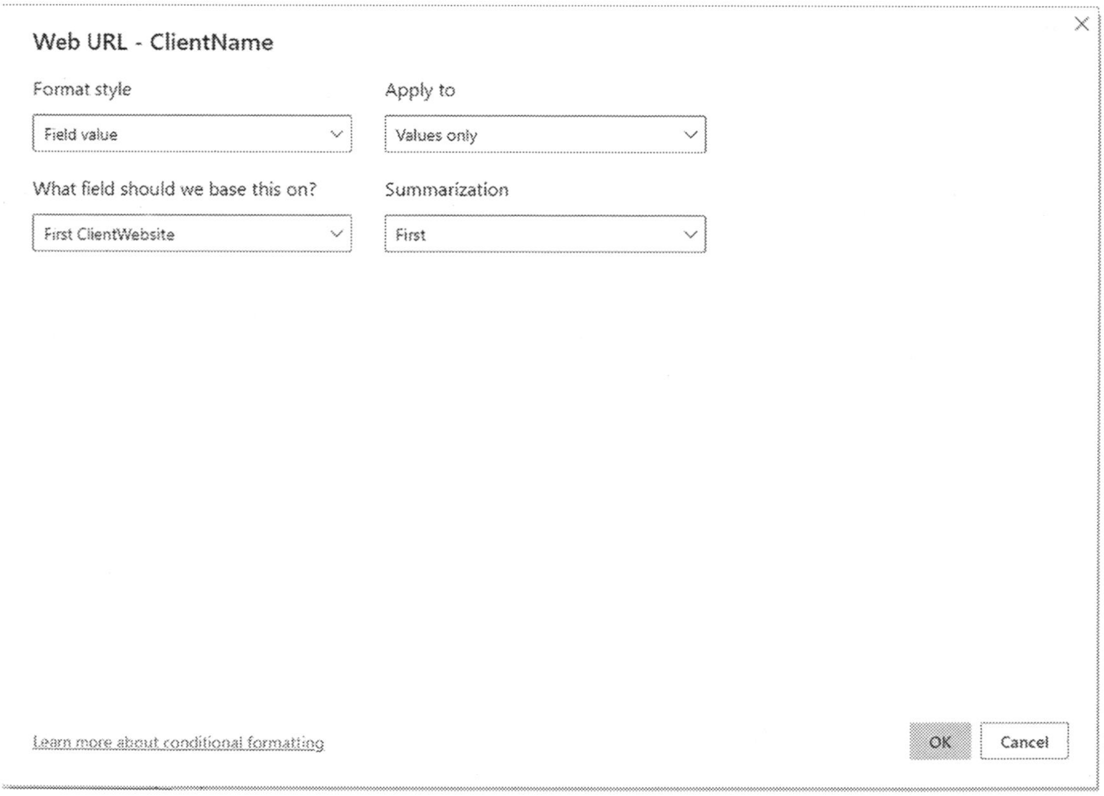

Web URL - ClientName

Format style   Apply to

| Field value ∨ | | Values only ∨ |

What field should we base this on?   Summarization

| First ClientWebsite ∨ | | First ∨ |

Learn more about conditional formatting   OK   Cancel

Figure 3-19. *The Web URL dialog*

7. Click OK.

The ClientName field will be underlined to indicate that it is now a hyperlink. You can see this in Figure 3-20.

Figure 3-20. *Displaying a field as a hyperlink*

Note   You may also want to format the values in this column (in blue, for instance) so that they are more clearly recognizable as hyperlinks.

Reset Visual Formatting

You may well spend quite a bit of time formatting visuals (including tables) in Power BI Desktop. Yet there may also be times when you want to remove the formatting for either all or part of a visual. Resetting the formatting of a table does not necessarily apply "plain vanilla" formatting. However, it will reapply the underlying standard formatting that applies throughout the current dashboard.

Reset a Card of the Formatting

If all you need to do is to reset part of the formatting, you can do this card by card in the Formatting pane.

1. Select the visual where you want to reset part of the formatting.

2. Switch to the Format pane.

3. In either the Visual or General panels (depending on where the particular card that you want to reset is found).

4. Expand the card that you want to reset.

5. Click Revert to default.

The formatting for the chosen card will revert to the initial formatting definition. This will happen without any warning—but if you have done this in error, you can just click the Undo icon (or press Ctrl+Z) to reapply the format as it was previously.

Reset All the Formatting for a Table

Should you wish to undo all the formatting that you have applied to a visual (rather than having to revert each and every card in the Formatting pane), you can

1. Select the visual whose formatting you want to reset.

2. Switch to the Formatting pane and activate the General settings.

3. Click the ellipses (…) on the right of "General."

4. Select Revert all settings to default. You can see this option in Figure 3-21.

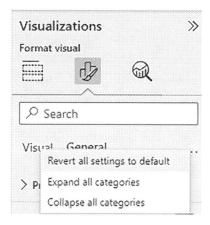

Figure 3-21. *Reset all formatting*

All formatting will be removed from the visual.

Here, again, if you have done this in error, you can just click the Undo icon (or press Ctrl+Z) to reapply the previous formatting to the entire table.

Copying Formatting

Formatting visuals is a large part of dashboard development. So you will probably need to apply the formatting that you have lovingly applied to one table to other tables. This can be done using the Format Painter—a technique that you have probably encountered in other software packages.

1. Select the table whose formatting you want to copy (the source of the formatting).

2. In the Home ribbon, click the Format Painter icon. The pointer becomes a paintbrush.

3. Click the destination table that you wish to format.

Note   This is an "all or nothing" operation. That is, you cannot copy part of a table's formatting to another table. Nor, unfortunately, can you double-click the Format Painter and then apply the format to several tables, one after the other.

If you need to format aspects of several tables on the same page at once (or indeed any set of the same visual types together), you can Ctrl-click the multiple tables to format and then apply the required formatting. All the selected tables will be formatted simultaneously. This will only work, however, for visuals of the same type.

Exporting Data from a Visualization

Finally, it is worth noting that you can export the data that underlies a visualization. This applies to any visual, from tables to charts. The amount of data that can be exported is currently limited to 150,000 rows. All you have to do is

1. Click the menu for the visual—the ellipses at the top right of the chart, table, or map. Then select Export Data from the pop-up menu.

2. Select a destination directory and file name.

3. Click OK and the relevant data will be exported. The only current export format is a CSV file.

Note   Any existing filters are applied when the data is exported. This means that, potentially, only a subset of the data will be exported to the CSV file.

Conclusion

In this chapter, you saw how to take basic tables and develop them into powerful visuals capable of delivering key insight. You saw how figures can be enhanced and draw in the user's focus by clever use of color where you define rules that accentuate thresholds in the data.

You also learned how to add sparklines and data bars to table rows to represent data more visually and tellingly. Then you saw how to add Key Performance Indicator icons to indicate trends or provide alerts based on the underlying data. Finally, you discovered how you can add hyperlinks to records in tables.

This chapter concludes the introduction to table visuals. However, there is another kind of table that is also available in Power BI Desktop. This is the matrix visual—and it is the subject of the next chapter.

CHAPTER 4

Matrix Visuals

This chapter takes you through the process of creating further text-based visualizations in Power BI Desktop. More specifically, you will learn how to create and enhance matrices. Also known as crosstabs or pivot tables, these build on the table creation techniques that you learned in the previous two chapters. They allow you to create advanced table structures containing complex hierarchies of data.

The techniques that you will learn in this chapter use a Power BI Desktop file that results from the application of much of what you saw in the last four chapters. This file is called C:\PowerBiDesktopSamples\PrestigeCarsDataForDashboards.pbix. It is available on the Apress website as part of the downloadable material that accompanies this book.

What Is a Matrix?

In the previous chapter, you saw how tables can be used to display the information as full columns of lists. Lists do not, however, always give an intuitive feeling for how data should be grouped at various levels. Presenting information in a neat hierarchy with multiple grouped levels is the task of a matrix visual.

Creating a Row Matrix

When creating a matrix, I find that it helps to think in terms of a hierarchy of information and to visualize this information flowing from left to right. For instance, suppose that we want to create a matrix with the *country name* as the highest level in the hierarchy (and consequently the leftmost item). Then we want the *make* of car to be the second level, and the next element in from the left. Finally, we want the *color* of car sold, followed by all the numeric fields that interest us. You can see this progression illustrated in Figure 4-1.

© Adam Aspin 2022
A. Aspin, *Pro Power BI Dashboard Creation*, https://doi.org/10.1007/978-1-4842-8227-4_4

Figure 4-1. *An information hierarchy*

When creating a matrix, it is important to have the Visualizations pane reflect the hierarchy. Put another way, you must ensure that the order of the fields that you select for the matrix and that you place in the field area follows the display hierarchy that you want. Consequently, to create a matrix like the one just described, you need to do the following:

1. Use the C:\PowerBiDesktopSamples\ PrestigeCarsDataForDashboards.pbix file as your source of data.

2. In the Build tab of the Visualizations pane, click the Matrix icon in the Visualizations pane. This will add a blank matrix to the dashboard canvas.

3. Drag the fields CountryName (from the Geography table), Make, and Model (from the Vehicle table) in this order to the Rows area in the Visualizations pane. Then add the fields SalePrice and SpareParts (from the Sales table) to the Values area. The data will be displayed initially as a table.

4. Click the expand icon (the small plus sign) to the left of France, then again for Bentley.

5. The matrix should look something like Figure 4-2.

Top level

Second level

Third level

Matrix icon

Figure 4-2. *A three-level matrix*

As you can see, a matrix display not only makes data easier to digest, but it automatically groups records by each element in the hierarchy and adds totals for each level as well. What is more, each level in the hierarchy is sorted in ascending order. You can expand all the levels that are available in the data that you added to the matrix definition. This final level will display all available detail at that level.

When creating matrices, my personal preference is to drag the fields that constitute the hierarchy of non-numeric values into the Rows area, which means I am placing them accurately above, below, or between any existing elements. This ensures that your matrix looks right the first time, which can help you avoid some very disconcerting double takes! Also, as Power BI Desktop will add additional fields to the Columns area if you drag new fields onto the matrix visual, it helps to be precise when building a matrix. This means carefully placing the fields for the row headers in the Rows area.

In a matrix, this means that any aggregate/numeric field is added to the right of existing aggregate fields (and appears in the Values area), whereas any text or date/time fields are added to the right of any existing hierarchy fields (and appear in the Rows area).

Column Matrix

Power BI Desktop does not limit you to adding row-level hierarchies; you can also create column-level hierarchies, or mix the two. Suppose that we want to get a clear idea of sales and spare parts cost by country, make model, and see the intersections with vehicle type, and how they impact one another. To achieve this, I suggest extending the matrix that you created previously by adding a VehicleType level as a column hierarchy.

Here is how you can do this:

1. Click inside the matrix that you created previously to select it and display the Build tab of the Visualizations pane. This will display the fields that are used for the selected table in the Rows and Values areas.

2. Drag the VehicleType field from the Vehicle table down into the Columns area in the Visualizations pane. This will make the current hierarchical table into a matrix. The matrix will look like Figure 4-3.

VehicleType CountryName	Coupe SalePrice	SpareParts	Saloon SalePrice	SpareParts	Total SalePrice	SpareParts
⊟ **Belgium**						
⊟ **Alfa Romeo**						
Giulia			£10,500.00	£750.00	**£10,500.00**	£750.00
Spider			£12,500.00	£750.00	**£12,500.00**	£750.00
⊟ **Aston Martin**						
Rapide			£86,500.00	£1,500.00	**£86,500.00**	£1,500.00
Vantage			£125,000.00	£2,200.00	**£125,000.00**	£2,200.00
⊟ **Noble**						
M600			£29,500.00	£750.00	**£29,500.00**	£750.00
⊟ **Peugeot**						
205	£950.00	£750.00	£3,950.00	£750.00	**£4,900.00**	£1,500.00
⊟ **Triumph**						
Roadster	£23,500.00	£500.00			**£23,500.00**	£500.00
TR4	£6,950.00	£457.00			**£6,950.00**	£457.00
TR6			£12,500.00	£750.00	**£12,500.00**	£750.00
⊟ **France**						
⊟ **Alfa Romeo**						
1750			£9,950.00	£750.00	**£9,950.00**	£750.00
Giulia			£2,550.00	£750.00	**£2,550.00**	£750.00
Spider			£11,500.00	£150.00	**£11,500.00**	£150.00

Figure 4-3. *A row and column matrix table*

As you can see, you now have the sales and gross margin by country name, make, model, and vehicle type, but it is in a matrix (or crosstab or pivot table, if you prefer), where the data is broken down by both rows and columns.

You can, if you wish, add further fields to the analysis by columns. As is the case for row elements, you can change the hierarchy by modifying the field order in the Columns area.

To conclude the section on creating matrices, there are a few things that you might like to note:

- If you add totals, then *every level* of the hierarchy has totals.

- Adding non-numeric data to the aggregated data makes Power BI Desktop display the Count aggregation.

- Matrices can get very wide, especially if you have a multilevel hierarchy. Power BI Desktop matrices reflect this in the way in which horizontal scrolling works. A matrix table freezes the non-aggregated data columns on the left and allows you to scroll to the right to display aggregated (numeric) data.

- Moving the fields up and down in the Columns and Rows areas of the Visualizations pane (using drag-and-drop, as described in for tables in Chapter 2) reorders the aggregated data columns in the table.

Viewing Records

When dealing with aggregated data, you can sometimes lose sight of valuable details. You might miss a large outlier that is skewing an average value, for instance. Or, perhaps, an excessive value for a single record is making a total higher than is normal—or healthy.

To help you follow your intuitions and weight aggregated values against detailed numbers, Power BI Desktop lets you view the underlying records "behind" a total at any time in a matrix. Here's an example:

1. Create a matrix based on the following fields:

   a. Make (Rows)

   b. Model (Rows)

   c. CountryName (Columns)

   d. LaborCost (Values)

   e. SpareParts (Values)

2. Right-click the subtotal for Aston Martin in either of the data columns for France. The context menu will appear as shown in Figure 4-4.

Figure 4-4. *The context menu for matrices*

3. Select Show data point as table from the context menu. You will see all the detail records that make up this total figure. This is shown in Figure 4-5.

Make	Model	LaborCost	SpareParts	CountryName
Aston Martin	DB4	£500.00	£500.00	France
Aston Martin	DB5	£2,000.00	£457.00	France
Aston Martin	DB6	£500.00	£750.00	France
Aston Martin	DB6	£660.00	£500.00	France
Aston Martin	DB6	£1,250.00	£750.00	France
Aston Martin	DB6	£1,785.00	£500.00	France
Aston Martin	DB9	£500.00	£750.00	France
Aston Martin	DB9	£1,490.00	£1,500.00	France
Aston Martin	Vanquish	£500.00	£750.00	France
Aston Martin	Vanquish	£500.00	£750.00	France

⟨ Back to report

Figure 4-5. *Displaying data records from a matrix*

4. Click the Back to Report button above the records that are now displayed to return to the normal Power BI Desktop Report View.

The figure you right-click in a matrix before selecting See data point as table will affect the list output.

- Clicking a top-level subtotal will show all the data for that element (all the models for a make of car in this example) including lower levels in the hierarchy.

- Clicking the lowest data point will only show the data for that element.

- Clicking the intersection of a row and column will restrict the data table to showing only data for that specific intersection of row and column data.

- Clicking a column subtotal will show all elements from the column hierarchy down to that level including lower levels in the hierarchy.

- Clicking the Row grand total will show data for the entire row hierarchy for the relevant column hierarchy.

- Clicking the Column grand total will show data for the entire column hierarchy for the relevant row hierarchy.

- You *cannot* display a table for the entire matrix by clicking the grand total for row and column.

Displaying Multiple Values As Rows

A feature that is really useful in Power BI Desktop is the possibility of creating complex matrices where the columns of data can now be displayed as rows. That is, instead of seeing possibly multiple data values side by side for a column hierarchy, you can see all the numeric data displayed as rows.

This is possibly best appreciated with the help of an example:

1. Create a matrix using the following elements:

   a. *Rows*: CountryName from the Geography table and Make from the Vehicle table (in this order)

   b. *Columns*: VehicleType (from the Vehicle table)

   c. *Values*: SpareParts and LaborCost (in this order)

85

2. Expand a couple of countries. The matrix will look like the one shown in Figure 4-6.

VehicleType CountryName	Coupe SpareParts	LaborCost	Saloon SpareParts	LaborCost	Total SpareParts	LaborCost
⊟ **Belgium**	**£1,707.00**	**£2,360.00**	**£7,450.00**	**£5,860.00**	**£9,157.00**	**£8,220.00**
Alfa Romeo			£1,500.00	£1,000.00	£1,500.00	£1,000.00
Aston Martin			£3,700.00	£2,500.00	£3,700.00	£2,500.00
Noble			£750.00	£1,360.00	£750.00	£1,360.00
Peugeot	£750.00	£500.00	£750.00	£500.00	£1,500.00	£1,000.00
Triumph	£957.00	£1,860.00	£750.00	£500.00	£1,707.00	£2,360.00
⊟ **France**	**£5,064.00**	**£8,980.00**	**£67,271.00**	**£141,820.00**	**£72,335.00**	**£150,800.00**
Alfa Romeo			£1,650.00	£1,500.00	£1,650.00	£1,500.00
Aston Martin	£1,500.00	£1,000.00	£5,707.00	£8,685.00	£7,207.00	£9,685.00
Austin			£750.00	£500.00	£750.00	£500.00
Bentley			£2,475.00	£4,165.00	£2,475.00	£4,165.00
BMW			£1,500.00	£1,000.00	£1,500.00	£1,000.00
Bugatti			£10,157.00	£24,000.00	£10,157.00	£24,000.00
Citroen			£1,207.00	£1,860.00	£1,207.00	£1,860.00
Delahaye			£750.00	£1,360.00	£750.00	£1,360.00
Ferrari			£13,850.00	£42,700.00	£13,850.00	£42,700.00
Jaguar	£1,857.00	£4,660.00	£3,900.00	£5,950.00	£5,757.00	£10,610.00
Lamborghini			£3,000.00	£9,750.00	£3,000.00	£9,750.00
McLaren			£3,150.00	£9,250.00	£3,150.00	£9,250.00
Mercedes	£957.00	£2,660.00	£1,000.00	£2,550.00	£1,957.00	£5,210.00
Peugeot			£1,500.00	£1,000.00	£1,500.00	£1,000.00
Porsche	£750.00	£660.00	£7,500.00	£10,135.00	£8,250.00	£10,795.00
Rolls Royce			£6,700.00	£15,415.00	£6,700.00	£15,415.00
Triumph			£2,475.00	£2,000.00	£2,475.00	£2,000.00
⊟ **Germany**	£750.00	£500.00	£12,150.00	£16,195.00	£12,900.00	£16,695.00
⊟ **Italy**	£6,350.00	£6,860.00	£14,339.00	£20,905.00	£20,689.00	£27,765.00
⊟ **Spain**			£28,100.00	£35,645.00	£28,100.00	£35,645.00
⊟ **Switzerland**	£975.00	£1,000.00	£14,050.00	£26,080.00	£15,025.00	£27,080.00
Total	£43,571.00	£76,160.00	£290,381.00	£472,060.00	£333,952.00	£548,220.00

Figure 4-6. *A standard matrix with values as columns*

3. In the Visualizations pane, switch to the Format pane and expand the Values card.

4. Expand the Options card and set Switch values to Rows to On. The matrix will now look like the one shown in Figure 4-7, where the multiple columns of data have become rows of data and all numeric values have been aggregated.

CountryName	Coupe	Saloon	Total
⊟ Belgium			
SpareParts	£1,707.00	£7,450.00	£9,157.00
LaborCost	£2,360.00	£5,860.00	£8,220.00
Alfa Romeo			
SpareParts		£1,500.00	£1,500.00
LaborCost		£1,000.00	£1,000.00
Aston Martin			
SpareParts		£3,700.00	£3,700.00
LaborCost		£2,500.00	£2,500.00
Noble			
SpareParts		£750.00	£750.00
LaborCost		£1,360.00	£1,360.00
Peugeot			
SpareParts	£750.00	£750.00	£1,500.00
LaborCost	£500.00	£500.00	£1,000.00
Triumph			
SpareParts	£957.00	£750.00	£1,707.00
LaborCost	£1,860.00	£500.00	£2,360.00
⊟ France			
SpareParts	£5,064.00	£67,271.00	£72,335.00
LaborCost	£8,980.00	£141,820.00	£150,800.00
Alfa Romeo			
SpareParts		£1,650.00	£1,650.00
LaborCost		£1,500.00	£1,500.00
Aston Martin			
SpareParts	£1,500.00	£5,707.00	£7,207.00
LaborCost	£1,000.00	£8,685.00	£9,685.00
Austin			
SpareParts	£43,571.00	£290,381.00	£333,952.00
LaborCost	£76,160.00	£472,060.00	£548,220.00

Figure 4-7. *A matrix with values as rows*

Simply switching Switch values to Rows to Off will revert the matrix to its initial format.

Formatting a Matrix

Fortunately, the techniques that you apply to format a matrix are largely identical to those you applied to tables. So I will not cover, again, the principles that you saw in the previous chapter to change the presentation of

- Matrix style (this is the table style, but applied to a matrix)
- Grid
- Column headers

- Row headers

- Values

- Totals

- Title

- Background

- Conditional formatting

There are, nonetheless, a few extra formatting tweaks that you can add to matrices. These are

- Stepped layout

- Subtotals

I will explain these in the following sections.

Stepped Layout

When expanding levels in a matrix hierarchy, you saw how Power BI Desktop indented the lower levels of the data. You can alter the indentation like this:

1. Create a matrix using the following elements:

   a. *Rows*: Make, Model, and Color from the Vehicle table (in this order)

   b. *Values*: SpareParts and LaborCost (in any order)

2. Expand a couple of makes.

3. In the Format pane, expand the Row Headers card and then expand the Options card.

4. Set the Stepped layout indentation to 30. You can see the result in Figure 4-8 where the indentation between the hierarchical levels of the row headers has increased.

Make	SpareParts	LaborCost
⊟ **Alfa Romeo**		
⊟ **1750**		
Black	£750.00	£500.00
Blue	£750.00	£500.00
⊟ **Giulia**		
Black	£2,550.00	£2,360.00
British Racing Green	£2,250.00	£1,500.00
Green	£225.00	£1,360.00
Red	£750.00	£400.00
⊞ **Giulietta**	**£5,300.00**	**£5,000.00**
⊞ **Spider**	**£2,025.00**	**£2,500.00**
⊟ **Aston Martin**		
⊟ **DB2**		
Black	£900.00	£1,860.00
Blue	£750.00	£970.00
British Racing Green	£750.00	£500.00
Green	£1,250.00	£1,860.00

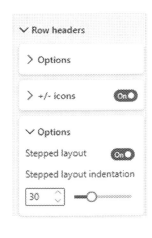

Figure 4-8. *Altering row heading indentation in a matrix*

Displaying a Row Hierarchy As Separate Columns

In Figure 4-7, you can see the multiple levels of a matrix. These are shown using levels of indentation. However, you may prefer to display each level in a separate column. Here is how you can do this:

1. Create a matrix using CountryName, and Make as the Row data, and SalePrice and SpareParts as the values.

2. Expand Belgium and Germany.

3. Switch to the Formatting pane.

4. Expand the Row Headers card and then expand the Options card.

5. Set Stepped Layout to Off.

6. Adjust the width of the matrix if necessary. The matrix will look like the one in Figure 4-9.

CountryName	Make	SalePrice	SpareParts
⊟ Belgium	Alfa Romeo	£23,000.00	£1,500.00
	Aston Martin	£211,500.00	£3,700.00
	Noble	£29,500.00	£750.00
	Peugeot	£4,900.00	£1,500.00
	Triumph	£42,950.00	£1,707.00
⊟ France	Alfa Romeo	£24,000.00	£1,650.00
	Aston Martin	£558,080.00	£7,207.00
	Austin	£6,000.00	£750.00
	Bentley	£361,500.00	£2,475.00
	BMW	£55,000.00	£1,500.00
	Bugatti	£930,500.00	£10,157.00
	Citroen	£30,500.00	£1,207.00
	Delahaye	£25,500.00	£750.00
	Ferrari	£1,750,450.00	£13,850.00
	Jaguar	£335,715.00	£5,757.00
	Lamborghini	£404,500.00	£3,000.00
	McLaren	£295,000.00	£3,150.00
	Mercedes	£134,225.00	£1,957.00
	Peugeot	£3,200.00	£1,500.00
	Porsche	£380,850.00	£8,250.00

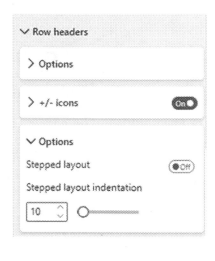

Figure 4-9. *A matrix without stepped layout*

Note   You can still expand and collapse levels of the hierarchy as you learned previously.

Formatting Drill down Icons

As a final tweak to row indentation, you can format the drill down icons themselves.

1. Use the matrix that you can see in Figure 4-8 and in the Formatting pane.

2. Expand the Row Headers card and then expand the +/- icons card.

3. Choose a different color and increase the size of the icons. You can see the +/- icons card in Figure 4-10.

Figure 4-10. *Formatting the drill down icons*

Adding or Removing Subtotals in a Matrix

By default, a new matrix will include the subtotals for every level of the data. Should you prefer to remove the subtotals from a matrix:

1. Create a matrix visual using (in this order) Make, Model, and Color as the rows and SpareParts and LaborCost as the values.

2. In the Visualizations pane, click the Format icon.

3. In the Row subtotals card, click the button to turn the row subtotals off. This will remove all the totals from the matrix and only display values for visible levels, as you can see in Figure 4-11.

Make	SpareParts	LaborCost
⊟ **Alfa Romeo**		
⊟ **1750**		
Black	£750.00	£500.00
Blue	£750.00	£500.00
⊟ **Giulia**		
Black	£2,550.00	£2,360.00
British Racing Green	£2,250.00	£1,500.00
Green	£225.00	£1,360.00
Red	£750.00	£400.00
⊞ **Giulietta**	**£5,300.00**	**£5,000.00**
⊞ **Spider**	**£2,025.00**	**£2,500.00**
⊟ **Aston Martin**		
⊟ **DB2**		
Black	£900.00	£1,860.00
Blue	£750.00	£970.00
British Racing Green	£750.00	£500.00
Green	£1,250.00	£1,860.00

Figure 4-11. *A matrix without row subtotals*

Note   Subtotals will remain visible for collapsed sections of a row hierarchy even if subtotals are set to Off.

Formatting Subtotals

Whereas a table only has a grand total (assuming that you want to display it), a matrix can—as you have seen—have subtotals for each level of data displayed. Although formatting subtotals is similar to formatting the total in a table, I prefer, for the sake of completeness, to describe the possibilities here:

1. Select the matrix visual that you used in the previous section.

2. In the Visualizations pane, click the Format icon.

3. Ensure that Row subtotals are set to On.

4. Expand the Row subtotals card.

5. In the Values card, choose a different font color from the Font Color palette and select a different font from the Font Family pop-up list.

6. Enter a number in the Text Size field (or adjust using the arrows) to set a larger font size.

7. Choose a different background color.

8. Expand the Rows card.

9. Enter a subtotal label.

10. Set Apply to Labels to On—this will ensure that the subtotal labels as well as numbers are formatted. The matrix should look like the one in Figure 4-12.

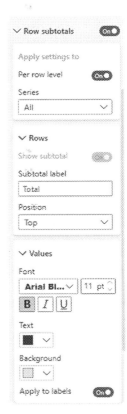

Make	SpareParts	LaborCost
⊟ **Alfa Romeo**	**£14,600.00**	**£14,120.00**
⊟ **1750**	**£1,500.00**	**£1,000.00**
Black	£750.00	£500.00
Blue	£750.00	£500.00
⊟ **Giulia**	**£5,775.00**	**£5,620.00**
Black	£2,550.00	£2,360.00
British Racing Green	£2,250.00	£1,500.00
Green	£225.00	£1,360.00
Red	£750.00	£400.00
⊞ **Giulietta**	**£5,300.00**	**£5,000.00**
⊞ **Spider**	**£2,025.00**	**£2,500.00**
⊟ **Aston Martin**	**£71,685.00**	**£96,770.00**
⊟ **DB2**	**£5,150.00**	**£7,690.00**
Black	£900.00	£1,860.00
Blue	£750.00	£970.00
British Racing Green	£750.00	£500.00
Green	£1,250.00	£1,860.00
Night Blue	£750.00	£500.00
Silver	£750.00	£2,000.00
⊞ **DB4**	**£6,650.00**	**£5,000.00**
⊞ **DB5**	**£4,107.00**	**£9,920.00**
Total	**£333,952.00**	**£548,220.00**

Figure 4-12. Formatting subtotals in a matrix

Note   As the grand total is essentially formatted in the same way as the Total for a table, I will not re-explain how to do this here. If you need to refresh your memory, then just flip back to the previous chapter.

Placing Subtotals

You can also decide whether the subtotals are placed *above* a hierarchical level, *alongside* the element header, or *under* a hierarchical level, on a separate row. Simply do the following to place subtotals:

1. Select the matrix that you used in Figure 4-12.

2. In the Visualizations pane, click the Format icon and expand the Row subtotals card and ensure that the Rows card is expanded.

3. In the pop-up for Position, select Bottom. The matrix should now look like the one in Figure 4-13.

Make	SpareParts	LaborCost
⊟ **Alfa Romeo**		
⊟ **1750**		
Black	£750.00	£500.00
Blue	£750.00	£500.00
Total	**£1,500.00**	**£1,000.00**
⊟ **Giulia**		
Black	£2,550.00	£2,360.00
British Racing Green	£2,250.00	£1,500.00
Green	£225.00	£1,360.00
Red	£750.00	£400.00
Total	**£5,775.00**	**£5,620.00**
⊞ **Giulietta**	**£5,300.00**	**£5,000.00**
⊞ **Spider**	**£2,025.00**	**£2,500.00**
Total	**£14,600.00**	**£14,120.00**
⊟ **Aston Martin**		
⊟ **DB2**		
Black	£900.00	£1,860.00
Blue	£750.00	£970.00
British Racing Green	£750.00	£500.00
Green	£1,250.00	£1,860.00
Night Blue	£750.00	£500.00
Total	**£333,952.00**	**£548,220.00**

Figure 4-13. *Placing subtotals below groups*

Custom Subtotal Settings per Level of Matrix

Power BI Desktop now lets you define whether subtotals are displayed for any level of the matrix hierarchy for both rows and columns. To see this in action for rows:

1. Select the matrix that you used in Figure 4-12.

2. In the Visualizations pane, click the Format icon and expand the Row subtotals card and ensure that the Rows card is expanded.

3. Ensure that Per Row Level is set to On.

4. Select Color from the Series pop-up.

5. In the Rows card, set the Show subtotal button to Off. As you can see in Figure 4-14, the subtotals have been removed for models (if they have been expanded).

Make	SpareParts	LaborCost
⊟ **Alfa Romeo**		
⊟ **1750**		
Black	£750.00	£500.00
Blue	£750.00	£500.00
⊟ **Giulia**		
Black	£2,550.00	£2,360.00
British Racing Green	£2,250.00	£1,500.00
Green	£225.00	£1,360.00
Red	£750.00	£400.00
⊞ **Giulietta**	**£5,300.00**	**£5,000.00**
⊞ **Spider**	**£2,025.00**	**£2,500.00**
⊟ **Aston Martin**		
⊟ **DB2**		
Black	£900.00	£1,860.00
Blue	£750.00	£970.00
British Racing Green	£750.00	£500.00
Green	£1,250.00	£1,860.00
Night Blue	£750.00	£500.00
Silver	£750.00	£2,000.00
⊞ **DB4**	**£6,650.00**	**£5,000.00**
⊞ **DB5**	**£4,107.00**	**£9,920.00**
Total	**£333,952.00**	**£548,220.00**

Figure 4-14. *Selective subtotals*

Column Subtotals

The Column subtotals in a matrix are handled in exactly the same way as row subtotals. That is, you

1. Decide which column subtotals (or all of them if you choose) you wish to format.

2. Apply the formatting in the Values card of Column subtotals.

3. Set the column subtotal text in the Subtotal label box. You can see these options in Figure 4-15.

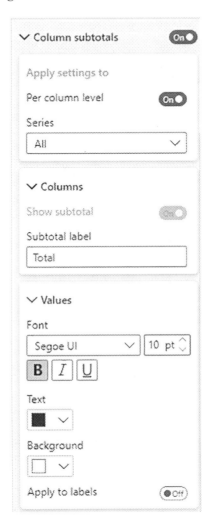

Figure 4-15. *Column subtotals formatting*

Visualize Source Data

If a formatted table or matrix becomes, paradoxically, too large or complex, you can opt to look at the underlying data without any formatting applied. This sometimes lets you see more information than you can in a carefully formatted visualization.

1. Select the table or matrix whose data you want to display without formatting.

2. In the Data/Drill ribbon, click the Visual Table button. The unformatted version of the data for the selected table or matrix will be displayed in a second window. You can see this in Figure 4-16.

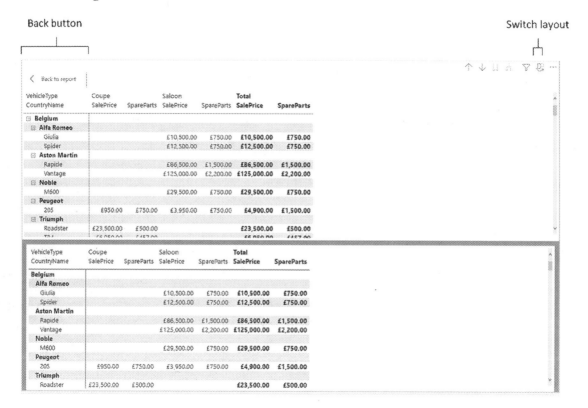

Figure 4-16.   *Visualizing source data*

3. Click the Back to Report button above the formatted table (or click again the See Data button in the Data/Drill ribbon) to return to the normal Power BI Desktop Report View.

Note   You cannot currently resize the two windows when viewing unformatted data. You can, however, scroll up and down in either window. If you prefer to see the data to the *right* of the visual (rather than underneath it), then click the Switch Layout icon at the top right of the window.

You can also switch to table view by right-clicking on a table or matrix and selecting Show as a table.

Sorting Data in Matrices

When you sort data in a matrix table, the sort order will respect the matrix hierarchy. This means that if you sort on the second element in a hierarchy (Make, in the example table we just created), then the primary element in the hierarchy (CountryName, the leftmost column) will switch back to the initial (alphabetical) sort order, as will any lower levels in the hierarchy of row elements.

If you sort by any value in a matrix, then the total for the highest level of the hierarchy is used to reorder the whole table. You can see this in Figure 4-17, where a matrix has been sorted on the total labor cost in descending order. This has made the country with the greatest labor cost move to the top of the table. Also, if you have a column matrix (as in this example), then you will end up sorting on the grand total of the columns (the two rightmost columns in this example) to make the matrix sort by numeric values, albeit in ascending order.

CountryName	Make	Color	Mileage	LaborCost
United Kingdom	Jaguar	Canary Yellow	757,220	£6,506
		Red	315,000	£5,185
		Silver	430,000	£4,500
		Dark Purple	340,500	£4,448
		British Racing Green	269,250	£4,211
		Green	337,220	£3,797
		Blue	463,250	£2,786
		Black	211,750	£2,237
		Night Blue	179,720	£736
		Total	3,303,910	£34,406
	Bentley	Canary Yellow	347,450	£8,184
		Red	445,940	£6,460
		Night Blue	267,500	£5,446
		Blue	138,050	£4,500
		Dark Purple	235,500	£2,708
		Green	57,500	£1,500
		British Racing Green	105,000	£1,473
		Black	105,000	£972
		Total	1,701,940	£31,243
	Aston Martin	Blue	289,900	£4,467
		Black	288,000	£3,807
		Silver	289,720	£3,558
		Canary Yellow	195,000	£3,349
		Dark Purple	255,000	£3,074
		Red	341,940	£2,718
		Green	105,000	£1,968
		Night Blue	284,720	£1,794
		British Racing Green	60,500	£1,533
		Total	2,109,780	£26,268
	Rolls Royce	Red	420,000	£4,923
		British Racing Green	267,500	£3,908
		Black	335,690	£3,615
		Silver	288,000	£3,178
		Green	210,000	£3,074

Figure 4-17. *Sorting a matrix on values*

Note   As was the case with tables, there are no specific options for formatting the figures in matrices. You format the data by clicking the Data View icon on the left of the Power BI Desktop window, select the column to format, and, in the Modeling ribbon, select a number format.

Conclusion

This chapter extended the knowledge that you acquired in the previous chapter to show you how to create matrices. You also learned the basic technique that you can use to drill down into any matrix to display a hierarchy of information. Then you saw the subtleties of matrix formatting—and specifically how to handle subtotals at all levels of a matrix. Finally, you learned how to display the content of a complex matrix in a more accessible form as well as how to sort data in matrices.

To conclude your tour of text-based visuals, you need to discover how to apply cards and multirow cards in Power BI Desktop. You will meet these in the next chapter.

Card Visual Types

Visuals that use text to deliver analytics are not limited to tables and matrices. In this chapter, you will build on the knowledge that you acquired in the previous two chapters to extend your range of text-based visualization techniques to cover the two final text-based visuals that are available in Power BI Desktop. These are

- Cards
- Multirow cards

This chapter uses the same Power BI Desktop file that you used in the last two chapters. This file is called C:\PowerBiDesktopSamples\ PrestigeCarsDataForDashboards.pbix. It is available on the Apress website as part of the downloadable material that accompanies this book.

Cards

On some occasions, you will want to display a single figure more prominently than others. Perhaps you need to attract the viewer's attention to your new sales record, or you would like the boss to appreciate the customer satisfaction ratings that you have achieved.

Whatever the motivation, cards are the solution. Power BI Desktop cards are a simple and powerful way to isolate and emphasize a single figure. Suppose that you want to display all vehicle sales to date in a dashboard, for instance; the following explains how you can do it:

1. Using the C:\PowerBiDesktopSamples\ PrestigeCarsDataForDashboards.pbix file as your source of data, click outside any existing visualizations.

2. In the gallery of available visuals, click the Card icon. You can see this icon in Figure 5-1. An empty card will appear on the dashboard canvas.

3. Expand the Sales table fields in the Fields list and select the SalePrice field. The total for all sales will appear in the card.

4. Resize the card so that the figure fits inside the card borders without any wasted space. The final card will look like the one shown in Figure 5-1.

Card Icon

Figure 5-1. *A card visual*

Formatting Cards

As you just saw, cards are an extremely effective way of focusing your audience's attention on key data. Yet there is a lot more that you can do to extend this emphasis, including the following:

- Change the units, number of decimals, color, and text size of the data that is displayed.

- Remove the label that is displayed automatically, as well as alter its text size.

- Add a title that you can format independently.

- Change the background color of the card.

- Modify the border style.

Let's see how to tweak the card that you just created:

1. Select the card. In this example, I use the card that you saw in Figure 5-1.

2. In the Visualizations pane, click the Format icon and then click General.

3. Expand the Effects card and then the Background card by clicking the downward-facing chevron to the left of the word Background.

4. Make sure that the switch to the right of the word Background is set to On.

5. Click the pop-up menu triangle to the right of Color and select a color from the palette of available colors.

6. Click the Transparency slider switch and slide it to the right to make the background more transparent.

7. Expand the Title card by clicking the downward-facing chevron to the left of the word Title.

8. Set the title to On by clicking immediately to the right of the On/ Off button to the right of Title.

9. Enter **Sales To Date** as the Title Text.

10. Click the pop-up menu triangle under Text and select a color for the font from the palette of available colors.

11. Click the pop-up menu triangle under Background and select a background color from the palette of available colors.

12. Click the middle icon of the Horizontal alignment icons to center the card title.

13. Choose a different font and font size if you want to.

14. Expand the Visual border card and switch the border on. Change the border color if you want to.

CHAPTER 5   CARD VISUAL TYPES

15. Adjust the Rounded corners slider to set the rounded corners of the card.

16. Switch to the Visual settings of the Format tab and expand the Category Labels card.

17. Adjust the text size either by clicking the up and/or down chevrons or entering the required font size. You can change the color and font as well if you want to.

18. Expand the Callout value card.

19. Select a color from the palette of available colors.

20. Adjust the text size—or enter the required text size.

21. Select a display unit for the figure in the card by clicking the pop-up list of Display units.

22. Select the number of decimals to be used for the card data by clicking the up and down triangles to the right of the Precision box. You can also enter the number of decimals directly, if you prefer. The card (along with the modified cards of the Format pane) will now look something like the elements that you can see in Figure 5-2.

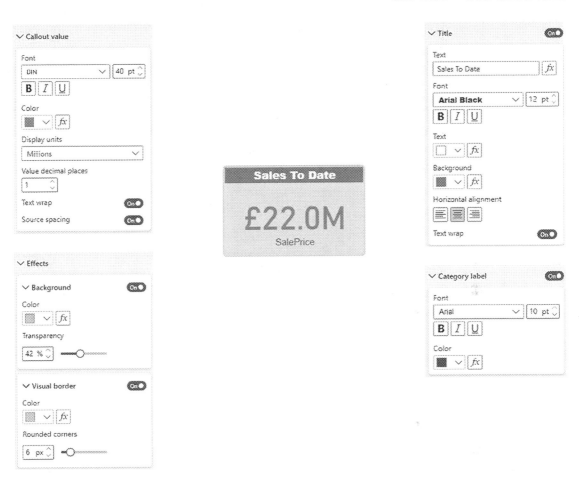

Figure 5-2. *A formatted card*

The available display units for formatting the value in a card are described in Table 5-1.

Table 5-1. *Display Units*

Display Unit	Description
Auto	Chooses an appropriate display unit from those available depending on the size of the figure
None	Displays the actual figure
Thousands	Displays the figure in thousands followed by a K
Millions	Displays the figure in millions followed by an M
Billions	Displays the figure in billions followed by a bn
Trillions	Displays the figure in trillions followed by a T

Multirow Cards

Tabular data can also be displayed in an extremely innovative way using the Power BI Desktop card style of output. As is the case with matrices, you begin by choosing the fields that you want to display as a basic table and then you convert this to another type of visual. Here is an example of how this can be done:

1. Using the C:\PowerBiDesktopSamples\ PrestigeCarsDataForDashboards.pbix file as your source of data, click outside any existing visuals.

2. In the Visualizations pane, click the Multirow card icon. An empty multirow card will appear on the dashboard canvas.

3. Add the following fields, in this order:

    a. CountryName (from the Geography table)

    b. CostPrice (from the Sales table)

    c. LaborCost (from the Sales table)

    d. SpareParts (from the Sales table)

4. Resize the multirow card to display all the countries, with all of the figures on a single row per country. The top part of the visual will look something like the one in Figure 5-3.

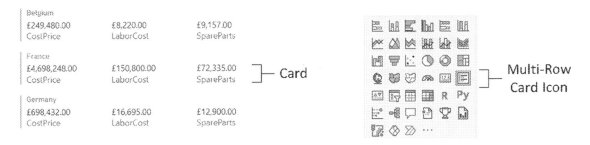

Figure 5-3. *A card visualization*

Card-type tables will display the selected fields in the order in which they appear in the field area in the Visualizations pane, and it is here that they can be reordered, as with any visual. This makes each card into a data record. The fields will flow left to right and then onto the following line in each card. What is interesting here is that adjusting the size of the table can change the appearance of the table quite radically. A very narrow table will list the fields vertically, one above the other. If you can fit all the fields onto a single row, then you will get a highly original multiple-record display.

Formatting Multirow Cards

There are several visual aspects of multirow cards that you can tweak for added effect. Let's try some of these:

1. Select the multirow card visualization. In this example, I use the card that you saw in Figure 5-3.

2. Switch to the Format pane and activate the General section.

3. Expand the Effects card and then the Background card by clicking the right-facing chevron to the left of the word Background.

4. Make sure that the switch to the right of the word Background is set to On.

5. Select a color from the palette of available tones.

6. Use the Transparency slider to set the percentage of transparency for the background.

7. Expand the Visual border card and set the border to On. Choose a border color.

8. Expand the Title card and set the title to On.

9. Enter **Key Figures By Country** as the Title Text.

10. Click the pop-up menu triangle below Text and select a color for the font from the palette of available colors.

11. Click the pop-up menu triangle below Background and select a background color from the palette of available colors.

12. Set a larger font for the title.

13. Click the icon in the center for the Alignment. This will center the title.

14. Switch to the Visual settings of the Format tab.

15. Expand the Cards card and then the Style card.

16. Click the pop-up menu triangle under Outline and select Bottom Only as the outline style.

17. Click inside the Outline Weight field and enter **4**.

18. Choose a background color from the palette of colors available for the Background.

19. Set the Padding button to **10** to reduce the padding between individual elements in the card.

20. Expand the Accent bar card and select a different bar color from the palette of available bar colors.

21. Set the Bar Thickness to **6** to increase the width of the bar.

22. Expand the Title card and increase the size of the font. Change the Font, font attributes (bold, italic, and underline), and font size if you wish.

23. Expand the Category Labels card and select the font color, font, font attributes, and font size.

24. Expand the Callout values card and select the font color, font, font attributes, and font size. The multirow card visual will now look like the one in Figure 5-4. You might have to tweak its size to get the correct effect.

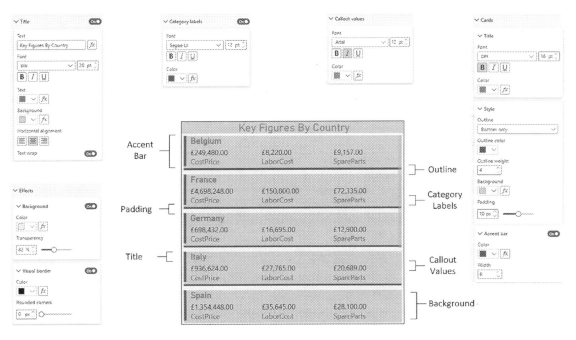

Figure 5-4. *A formatted multirow card*

Note   You can also fix the aspect ratio of a multirow card visual just as you did for the initial table at the start of this chapter. Equally, you can add a border as you saw previously for a card visual.

Sorting Multirow Cards

Like tables and matrices, multirow cards can be sorted. However, there is a specific way to apply a sort order to this kind of visual:

1. Click the ellipses at the top (or possibly bottom) right of the multirow card visual.

2. Select Sort By.

3. Select the column name to sort by from the list of columns in the pop-up menu.

The elements in the multirow card will now be ordered according to the values in the chosen column. You can see an example of the pop-up menu in Figure 5-5. This example uses the multirow card that you created previously.

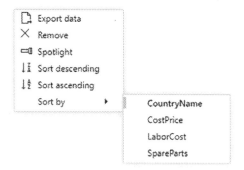

Figure 5-5. *Sorting a multirow card*

Note   Sorting on the category in a multirow card (the country in this example) will initially sort in reverse alphabetical order (as a multirow card is initially ordered in alphabetical order). Reselecting a sort on the category will reset the sort order to alphabetical. Sorting on a value will always order from highest to lowest—and re-clicking the value in the pop-up menu will remove the sort order and revert to the initial order.

Switching Between Visual Types

One of the fabulous things about Power BI Desktop is that it is designed from the ground up to let you test ideas and experiment with ways of displaying your data quickly and easily. So, quite naturally, you can switch table types easily to see which style of presentation is best suited to your ideas and the message that you want to convey. To switch table types, all you have to do is select the current text-based visualization (table, multirow card, or matrix) and select one of these options from the gallery of available visuals:

- Table

- Matrix

- Multirow card

What is even more reassuring is that Power BI Desktop remembers the attributes of the previous table type you used. So, for instance, if you set up a matrix with a carefully crafted hierarchy and then switch to a card-type table, Power BI Desktop remembers how you set up the matrix should you want to switch back to it.

To see an example of how this works in practice, take a look at Figure 5-6. This shows the same initial visual that has been copied and then switched between the text-based core types of visual. I have added the Color field to the matrix and expanded the next level to make the difference between the table and matrix clearer.

Multirow card

(Blank)		
£100,200	£1,461	£3,770
CostPrice	LaborCost	SpareParts
France		
£1,460,100	£36,471	£42,430
CostPrice	LaborCost	SpareParts
Germany		
£160,000	£1,461	£1,600
CostPrice	LaborCost	SpareParts
Spain		
£178,700	£2,272	£4,420
CostPrice	LaborCost	SpareParts
Switzerland		
£701,150	£27,207	£30,315
CostPrice	LaborCost	SpareParts
United Kingdom		
£10,193,880	£129,952	£227,250
CostPrice	LaborCost	SpareParts
USA		
£7,716,065	£113,135	£189,045
CostPrice	LaborCost	SpareParts

Table

CountryName	CostPrice	LaborCost	SpareParts
	£100,200	£1,461	£3,770
France	£1,460,100	£36,471	£42,430
Germany	£160,000	£1,461	£1,600
Spain	£176,720	£2,272	£4,420
Switzerland	£701,150	£27,207	£30,315
United Kingdom	£10,193,880	£129,952	£227,250
USA	£7,716,065	£113,135	£189,045
Total	£20,510,095	£311,959	£498,830

Matrix

CountryName	CostPrice	LaborCost	SpareParts
	£100,200	£1,461	£3,770
Blue	£42,500	£325	£400
British Racing Green	£13,500	£325	£400
Canary Yellow	£44,200	£811	£2,970
France	£1,460,100	£36,471	£42,430
Black	£97,500	£3,736	£5,590
Blue	£93,200	£4,200	£4,345
British Racing Green	£192,000	£1,056	£3,170
Canary Yellow	£422,625	£8,381	£8,440
Dark Purple	£67,000	£466	£2,570
Green	£76,125	£3,450	£2,540
Night Blue	£186,500	£4,650	£4,595
Red	£162,450	£5,620	£6,040
Silver	£162,700	£4,912	£5,040
Germany	£160,000	£1,461	£1,600
Blue	£37,500	£325	£400
Green	£42,500	£325	£400
Red	£42,500	£486	£400
Silver	£37,500	£325	£400
Spain	£178,700	£2,272	£4,420
Blue	£42,500	£325	£400
Canary Yellow	£61,200	£1,136	£3,220
Green	£37,500	£325	£400
Red	£37,500	£486	£400
Switzerland	£701,150	£27,207	£30,315
Black	£100,700	£4,236	£4,900
Blue	£97,500	£3,450	£2,585
British Racing Green	£110,700	£2,460	£7,090
Canary Yellow	£98,625	£2,582	£3,865
Dark Purple	£60,000	£2,237	£2,845
Green	£81,125	£3,450	£2,540
Red	£92,500	£4,737	£3,450
Silver	£100,000		
Total	£20,510,095	£311,959	£498,830

Figure 5-6. *Switching visuals using the same data and formatting*

The following are the main things to note here:

- The visual remains the same size when you switch types. Consequently, you will probably have to resize it.

- All formatting that can be retained is retained. This can be seen in the titles and background of all three visuals in Figure 5-6.

Conclusion

This short chapter introduced you to two more ways of using text to display metrics in Power BI dashboards. You saw how to accentuate key figures by giving them prominence as cards as well as how to isolate and accentuate groups of metrics in multirow cards.

This concludes the three chapters on text-based visuals. The next area of visualization to look at is charts. This is the subject of the following five chapters.

CHAPTER 6

Charts in Power BI Desktop

It is one thing to have a game-changing insight that can fundamentally alter the way your business works. It is quite another to be able to convince your colleagues of your vision. So what better way to show them—intuitively and instantaneously—that you are right than with a chart that irrefutably makes your point?

Power BI Desktop is predicated on the concept that a picture is worth many thousands of words. Its charting tools let you create clear and convincing visuals that tell your audience far more than a profusion of figures ever could. This chapter, therefore, will show you how simple it can be not just to make your data explain your analysis but to make it seem to leap off the screen. You will see over the next few pages how a powerful chart can persuade your peers and bosses that your ideas and insights are the ones to follow.

A little more prosaically, Power BI Desktop lets you make a suitable dataset into a whole range of chart types. To avoid swamping you with a whole plethora of chart types, we get up and running in this chapter, by looking at

- Pie charts

- Bar charts

- Column charts

- Line charts

- Area charts

- Funnel charts

- Donut charts

115

© Adam Aspin 2022
A. Aspin, *Pro Power BI Dashboard Creation*, https://doi.org/10.1007/978-1-4842-8227-4_6

In the next chapter, you will then extend some of them to create stacked bar, stacked column, and stacked area charts, 100% stacked bar and stacked column charts, as well as dual-axis charts. Once you have decided upon the most appropriate chart type, you can then enhance your visualization with a title, data labels, and legends. Consequently, in Chapter 8, you will learn how to format all of these elements to give your charts the wow factor that they deserve.

A First Chart

It is generally easier to appreciate the simplicity and power of Power BI Desktop by doing rather than talking. So I suggest leaping straight into creating a first chart. In this section, we will look only at "starter" charts that all share a common thread—they are based on a single column of data values and a single column of descriptive elements. The data will include

- A list of clients

- Car sales for a given year

So let's get charting! In this chapter, you will use the C:\PowerBiDesktopSamples\ PrestigeCarsDataForDashboards.pbix Power BI Desktop file that is available on the Apress website for download.

Creating a First Chart

Any Power BI Desktop chart begins as a dataset. So let me introduce you to the world of charts by showing you how to make a bar chart in a few clicks; the following explains how to begin:

1. Open the file C:\PowerBiDesktopSamples\ PrestigeCarsDataForDashboards.pbix from the downloadable samples.

2. Click the Stacked Bar Chart icon at the top left of the Visualizations pane. This icon is illustrated in Figure 6-1. An empty bar chart visual will appear on the dashboard canvas.

3. Leave the empty bar chart visual selected and expand the
    Geography table in the Fields list and add the CountryName field.
    This field will be added to the Axis area (although the chart will
    remain blank for the moment).

4. Leaving this new bar chart visual selected, expand the Sales table
    in the Fields list.

5. Click the check box to the left of the SalePrice field. This will place
    the data in the Values area and add the cumulative sales per
    country to the chart.

6. Resize the chart (I suggest widening it) as shown in Figure 6-1.

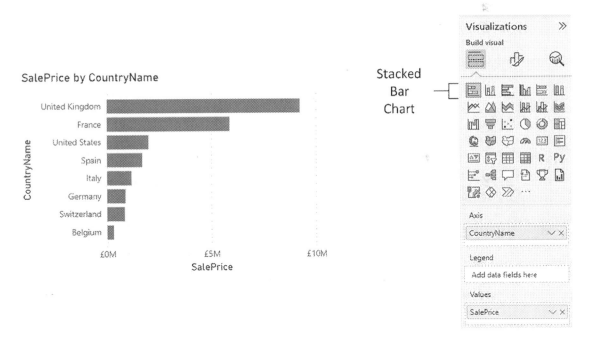

Figure 6-1. *A bar chart after resizing*

And that is all that there is to creating a simple starter chart. This process might only take a few seconds, and once it is complete, it is ready to show to your audience, or be remodeled to suit your requirements.

Nonetheless, a few comments are necessary to clarify the basics of chart creation in Power BI Desktop:

- When creating the chart, you can use any of the techniques described in Chapter 1 to add fields to visuals. So you can also drag fields into the Fields Area of the Visualizations pane or onto the visual directly if you prefer.

- When using only a single dataset, you can choose either clustered or stacked as the chart type for a bar or column chart; the result is the same in either case. As you will see as we progress, this will not be the case when the chart is based on multiple data fields.

- Power BI Desktop will add a title at the top left of the chart explaining what fields the chart is based on. You can see an example of this in Figure 6-1.

- Creating a chart is very much a first step. You can do so much more to enhance a chart and accentuate the insights that it can bring. All of this follows further on in this chapter and in the next two.

Converting a Table into a Chart

Another way to create a chart is to create a table first (by dragging the data fields onto the Power BI Desktop canvas without first clicking a chart icon, for instance). Then select the table and click a chart icon in the Visualizations pane to convert the table into a chart.

However, if you create a table first, then transform a table into a bar chart (by selecting a table and clicking the Stacked Bar Chart icon), the field area of the Visualizations pane changes to reflect the options available when creating or modifying a chart. If you select the chart that you just created, you will see that the CountryName field has been placed in the Axis box, and the SalePrice field has been placed in the Values box. Neither of these boxes exists if the visual is a table. This can be seen in Figure 6-1.

Deleting a Chart

Deleting a chart is as simple as deleting a table, a matrix, or a card. All that you have to do is

1. Click inside the chart.

2. Press the Delete key.

If you remove all the fields from the Layout section of the field area of the Visualizations pane (with the chart selected), then you will also delete the chart.

Basic Chart Modification

So you have an initial chart. Suppose, however, that you want to change the fields on which the chart is based. Well, all you have to do to change both the axis elements (the client names and the values represented) is

1. Click the bar chart that you created previously. Avoid clicking any of the bars in the chart for the moment.

2. In the field area of the Visualizations pane, click the small cross at the right of SalePrice in the Values area (or click the pop-up menu for SalePrice, and select Remove Field). The bars will disappear from the chart.

3. Drag the field LaborCost from the Sales table in the Fields list into the Values area.

4. In the field area of the Visualizations pane, click the pop-up menu for CountryName in the Axis box, and select Remove Field. The countries will disappear from the chart and a single bar will appear.

5. In the Fields list, expand the Vehicle table and drag the Color field from the Colors table into the Axis box. The list of colors will replace the list of countries on the axis, and a series of bars will replace the single bar. Look at Figure 6-2 to see the difference.

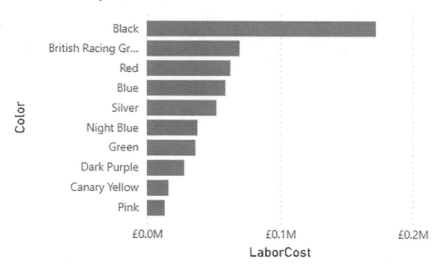

Figure 6-2. *A simple bar chart with the corresponding Layout section*

That is it. You have changed the chart completely without rebuilding it. Power BI Desktop has updated the data in the chart and the chart title to reflect your changes.

Basic Chart Types

When dealing with a single set of values, you will probably be using the following six core chart types to represent data:

- Bar chart

- Column chart

- Line chart

- Pie chart

- Donut chart

- Funnel chart

Let's see how we can try out these types of chart with the current dataset—using the Color and LaborCost fields that you applied in the previous chart you created.

Column Charts

A column chart is, to all intents and purposes, a bar chart where the bars are vertical rather than horizontal. So do the following to switch your bar chart to a column chart:

1. Select the bar chart that you previously created and modified (the one shown in Figure 6-2). Avoid clicking any of the bars in the chart to avoid cross-filtering.

2. In the Visualizations pane, click the Stacked Column Chart icon.

3. Resize the chart as required. Your chart should look like Figure 6-3.

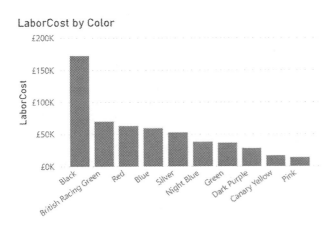

Figure 6-3. *An elementary column chart*

Line Charts

A line chart displays the data as a set of points joined by a line. Do the following to switch your column chart to a line chart:

1. Click the column chart that you created previously. Avoid clicking any of the columns in the chart for the moment.

2. In the Visualizations pane, click the Line Chart icon. Your chart should look like Figure 6-4.

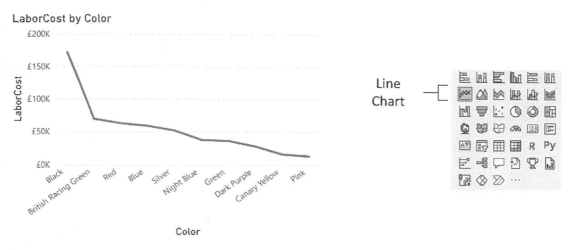

Figure 6-4. *A simple line chart*

Pie Charts

Pie charts can be used to display a limited set of data for a single series. To switch the visual to a pie chart:

1. Click the line chart that you created previously. Avoid clicking any of the lines in the chart for the moment.

2. In the Visualizations pane, click the Pie Chart icon. The line chart will become a pie chart.

3. Resize the pie chart, if necessary, to display the text for all the colors correctly. Your chart should look like Figure 6-5. You will notice that the Layout section has changed slightly for a pie chart, and the Axis box has been replaced by a Legend box.

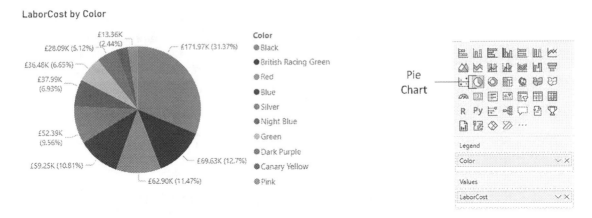

Figure 6-5. A basic pie chart

A pie chart is distorted if it includes negative values at the same time as it contains positive values. Power BI Desktop will not display the negative values. If your dataset contains a mix of positive and negative data, then Power BI Desktop displays an alert above the chart warning "Too many values. Not showing all data." What this nearly always really means is that the pie chart contains positive *and* negative values and that the negative values are not displayed. This also applies to donut charts. Negative values can make funnel charts appear a little peculiar, too.

In practice, you may prefer not to use pie or donut charts when your data contains negative values, or you may want to separate out the positive and negative values into two datasets and display two charts, using filters (filters are explained in Chapter 13).

Note   Juggling chart size and font size to fit in all the elements and axis and/or legend labels can be tricky. One useful trick is to prepare "abbreviated" data fields in the source data, as has been done in the case of the QuarterAbbr field in the Date table that contains Q1, Q2, and so on, rather than Quarter 1, Quarter 2, and so on, to save space in the chart.

Donut Charts

Donut charts are essentially a variation of a pie chart. However, they can make a welcome presentational change from their overexposed older sibling. Fortunately, they are equally easy to create. In this example, you are going to see how to visualize the parts cost incurred for each make of vehicle purchased. To vary the approach, in this example, you will first create a table and then convert it to a donut chart.

1. Continue using (or open) the file C:\PowerBiDesktopSamples\ PrestigeCarsDataForDashboards.pbix.

2. Ensure that no current visual is selected.

3. Expand the Vehicle table in the Fields list.

4. Select the box to the left of the Make field. A table containing the list of makes purchased will appear in the dashboard canvas.

5. Leave this new table selected and click the check box to the left of the SpareParts field in the Sales table. This will add the cumulative cost of spare parts per make to the table visual.

6. Click the Donut Chart icon in the Visualizations pane. This will convert the table to a donut chart.

7. Resize the chart if necessary to show the names of the makes clearly, as shown in Figure 6-6.

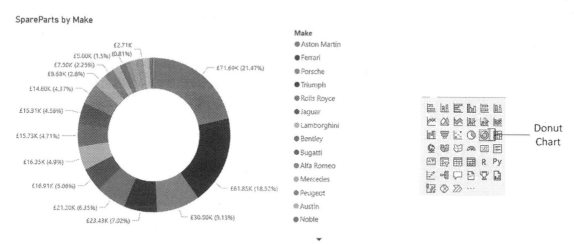

Figure 6-6. *A donut chart*

You can see in this chart that more donut sections are displayed than can be seen in the legend. So you can scroll down through the legend elements by clicking the down-facing chevron at the bottom of the legend.

Funnel Charts

Funnel charts are excellent when it comes to comparing the relative values of a single series of figures. As you are now well versed in the art of creating charts with Power BI Desktop, designing a funnel chart that displays parts cost per color should not be a problem for you.

1. Carry on using the file C:\PowerBiDesktopSamples\ PrestigeCarsDataForDashboards.pbix.

2. Expand the Vehicle table in the Fields list and drag the Color field onto an empty part of the dashboard canvas. A table containing the list of vehicle colors will appear.

3. Click the Funnel Chart icon in the Visualizations pane. This will convert the table to an empty funnel chart.

4. Leave the funnel chart selected and click the check box to the left of the SpareParts field in the Sales table. The funnel chart will display the color with the highest value for the cost of spare parts at the top of the visual.

5. Resize the chart if necessary to show the names of the colors clearly as well as making the relative weights for all the colors more clearly comprehensible, as shown in Figure 6-7.

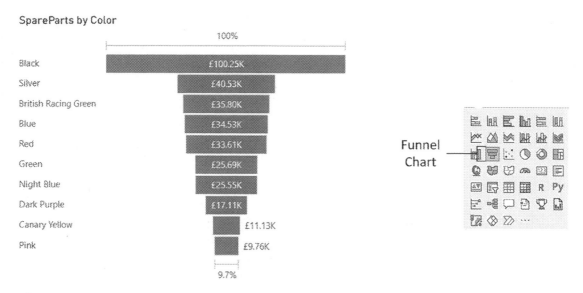

Figure 6-7. *A funnel chart*

Multiple Data Values in Charts

So far, in this chapter, we have seen simple charts that display a single series of data. Life is, unfortunately, rarely that simple, and so it is time to move on to slightly more complex, but possibly more realistic, scenarios where you need to compare and contrast multiple data elements.

For this set of examples, I will presume that we need to take an in-depth look at the following indirect cost elements of our car sales to date:

- Parts

- Labor

Consequently, to begin with a fairly simple comparison of these indirect costs, let's start with a clustered column chart:

1. Open the file C:\PowerBiDesktopSamples\ PrestigeCarsDataForDashboards.pbix from the downloadable samples.

2. Starting with a clean Power BI Desktop report, create a table that displays the following fields:

    a. ClientName (from the Client table)

    b. SpareParts (from the Sales table)

    c. LaborCost (from the Sales table)

3. Leaving the table selected, click the Clustered Column icon in the
    Visualizations pane.

4. Resize the chart to make it clear and comprehensible, as shown in
    Figure 6-8. (I have included the field areas from the Visualizations
    pane so that you can see this, too.)

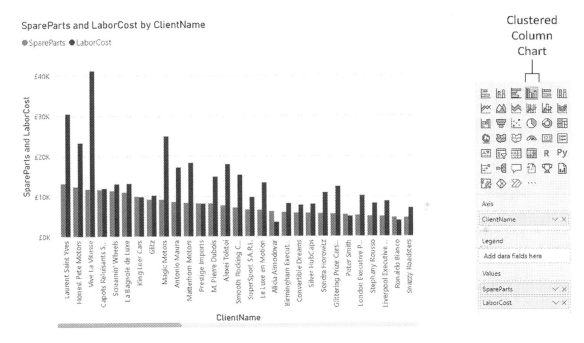

Figure 6-8. *Multiple data values in charts—a clustered column chart with the
Layout section shown*

You will notice that a chart with multiple datasets has a legend by default and that
the automatic chart title now says SpareParts and LaborCost By ClientName. Also,
you will note that the chart is automatically sorted with the highest values on the left.
Moreover, as all the clients cannot fit on the X axis, a scrollbar is added automatically to
allow the user to scroll through the clients.

The same dataset can be used as a basis for other charts that can effectively display
multiple data values:

- Clustered bar and stacked bar

- Clustered column and stacked column

- Line charts

- Area charts

- Stacked area charts

Since column charts are essentially bar charts pivoted 90 degrees, I will not show examples of bar charts. However, in Figures 6-9, 6-10, 6-11, and 6-12, you will see examples of a stacked column chart, a line chart, an area chart, and a stacked area chart—all created from the same data. You also see that when creating these types of visualization, the Layout section of the field area of the Visualizations pane remains the same for all of these charts.

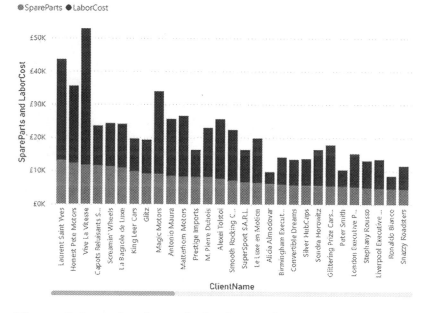
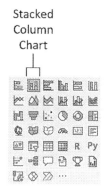

Figure 6-9. *A simple stacked column chart*

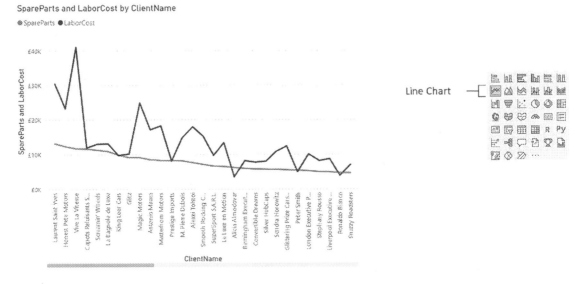

Figure 6-10. *A line chart that displays multiple values*

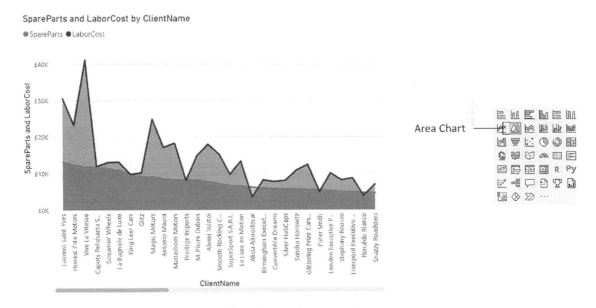

Figure 6-11. *An area chart displaying multiple values*

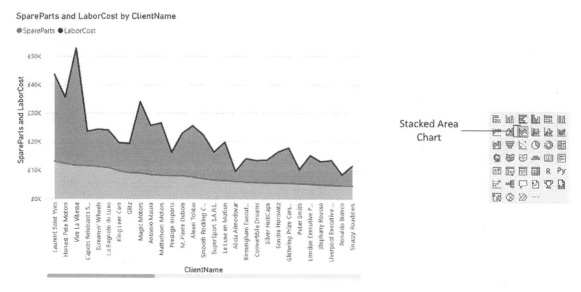

Figure 6-12. *A stacked area chart based on multiple values*

These four charts all display the same data in different ways. Knowing this, you can choose the type of chart that best conveys the information and draws your reader's attention to the point that you are trying to make.

If you are not sure which chart best conveys your message, then try them all, one after another. All it takes is a single click of the relevant icon in the visuals gallery to convert a chart to another chart type. Indeed, sometimes the differences can be extremely subtle. For instance, the essential difference between the area chart and the stacked area chart is the X (vertical) axis. In the case of Figure 6-11, this is a cumulative value. Figure 6-12, in contrast, shows two values directly compared one to the other with the higher value placed behind the lower value.

Note   Any of these chart types can be used to display a single data series if you want to. It all depends on the effect and the clarity of the insights that you are projecting using the chart.

100% Stacked Column and Bar Charts

One way to compare data from multiple datasets is to present each individual data series as a percentage of the total. Power BI Desktop includes two chart types that can do this "out of the box." They are the 100% stacked column and 100% stacked bar charts.

Since you now know how to create charts that use multiple series of data, I will not explain how to produce these two chart types in detail; all you have to do is select the correct chart icon from the Visualizations pane. So instead, I suggest that you look at Figures 6-13 and 6-14, which show an example of each of these charts using the same data that you used to create the clustered column chart shown in Figure 6-9.

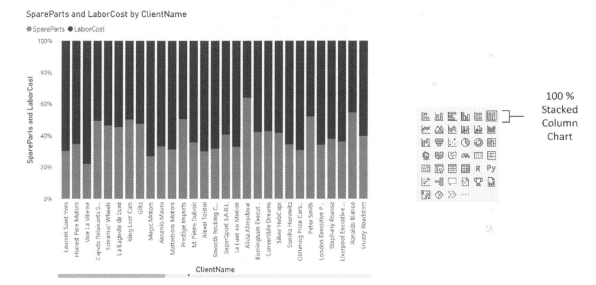

Figure 6-13. *A 100% stacked column chart*

SpareParts and LaborCost by ClientName

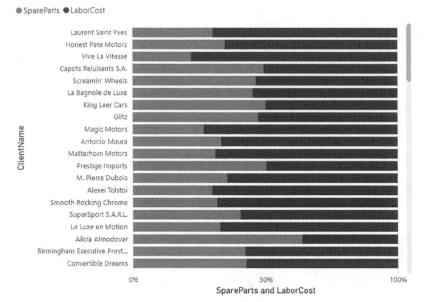
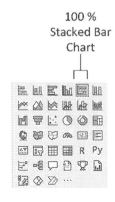

Figure 6-14. *A 100% stacked bar chart*

Essential Chart Adjustments

I hope you will agree that creating a chart in Power BI Desktop is extremely simple. Yet the process of producing a telling visualization does not stop when you take a dataset and display it as a chart. At the very least, you want to make the following tweaks to your new chart:

- Resize the chart

- Reposition the chart

- Sort the elements in the chart

None of these tasks is at all difficult. Indeed, it can take only a few seconds to transform your initial chart into a compelling visual argument—when you know the techniques to apply.

Resizing Charts

A chart is like any other visual on the Power BI Desktop dashboard canvas and can be resized to suit your requirements. The following explains how to resize a chart:

1. Click inside the chart (but not on any of the bars, columns, lines, or pie segments).

2. Place the mouse pointer over any of the eight handles that appear at the corners and in the middle of the edges of the chart that you wish to adjust. The pointer becomes a two-headed arrow.

3. Drag the mouse pointer to resize the chart.

Note   Remember that the lateral handles let you resize the chart only horizontally or vertically and that the corner handles allow you to resize both horizontally and vertically.

Resizing a chart can have a dramatic effect on the text that appears on an axis. Power BI Desktop always tries to keep the space available for the text on an axis proportionate to the size of the whole chart.

For column, line, and bar charts, this can mean that the text can be truncated, with an ellipsis (three dots) indicating that not all the text is visible. With column and line charts, the text may even be angled at 45 degrees or possibly swiveled to appear vertically.

If you reduce the height (for a bar chart) or the width (for a column or a line chart) below a certain threshold, Power BI Desktop will stop trying to show all the elements on the non-numeric axis. Instead, it only shows a few elements and adds a scrollbar to allow you to scroll through the remaining data. What is more, if axis labels cannot be displayed in their entirety, they will be truncated (and ellipses added).

All that this means is you might have to tweak the size and height-to-width ratio of your chart until you get the best result. If you are in a hurry to get this right, I advise using the handle in the bottom-right corner to resize a chart, as dragging this up, down, left, and right will quickly show you the available display options.

Repositioning Charts

You can move a chart anywhere inside the Power BI Desktop report, as follows:

1. Place the mouse pointer over the border of the chart.

2. Drag the mouse pointer.

Sorting Chart Elements

Sometimes you can really make a point about data by changing the order in which you have it appear in a chart. Up until this point, you have probably noticed that when you create a chart, the elements on the axis (and this is true for a bar chart, column chart, line chart, or pie chart) are in alphabetical order by default. If you want to confirm this, then just look at Figures 6-5 to 6-8.

Suppose now, you want to sort by the color of the vehicle in alphabetical order so as to find a color easily. The following steps explain how to do this:

1. Select the bar chart type for Color and LaborCost, as described earlier (and shown in Figure 6-2).

2. Place the mouse pointer over the chart. You will see that the chart border and options button (the ellipses at the top right) appear.

3. Click the ellipses to display the chart menu and then click the chevron to the right of Sort axis and select the appropriate field to order the data (Color in this example).

4. Click Sort Descending. This is shown in Figure 6-15, where the columns are sorted in reverse alphabetical order.

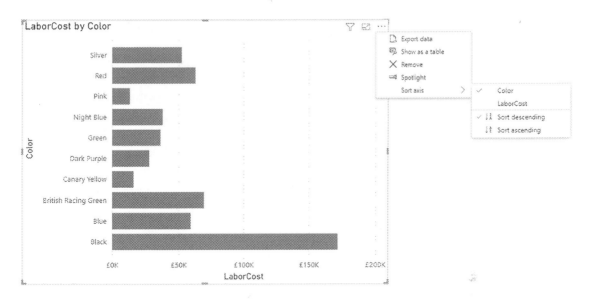

Figure 6-15. *Using the pop-up menu in a chart to sort data*

As you can see, the initial sort is in descending order when you sort by a numeric value. Let's suppose now that you want to see the sales by color in *ascending* order. All you have to do is repeat the operation that you just carried out and the chart will be resorted. Only this time, it is sorted in ascending order. Equally, the *first* time that you sort on a *text* element the chart is sorted in *ascending* order and the *second* time it is sorted in *descending* order.

I should add just a short remark about sorting pie charts. When you sort a pie chart by a numeric field, the pie chart is sorted clockwise, starting at the top of the chart. So if you are sorting colors by LaborCost in descending order, the top-selling color is at the top of the pie chart (at 12 o'clock), with the second best-selling color to its immediate right (e.g., 2 o'clock), and so on. An example of this is shown in Figure 6-16.

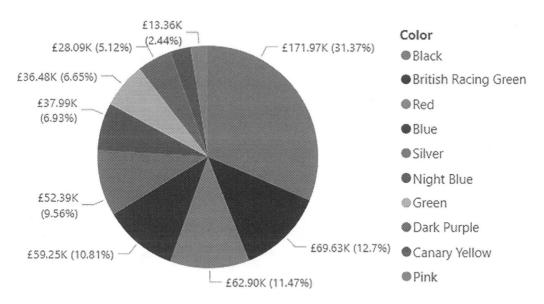

Figure 6-16. *Sorting data in a pie chart*

Data Details

To conclude our tour of chart types, I just want to make a few comments:

- You can always see exactly what the figures behind a bar, column, line, point, or pie segment are just by hovering the mouse pointer over the bar (or column, or line, or pie segment). This works whether the chart is its normal size or has been popped out to cover the Power BI Desktop report area.

- However much work you have done to a chart, you can always switch it back to a table if you want. Simply select the chart, and change it to a table in the Visualizations pane. If you do this, you see that the table attempts to mimic the design tweaks that you applied to the chart, keeping the font sizes the same as in the chart, and the size of the table identical to that of the chart. Should you subsequently

switch back to the chart, then you should find virtually all of the
design choices that you applied are still present—unless, of course,
you made any changes to the table before switching back to the chart
visualization.

- You can always juxtapose the raw data that powers a chart under
  the chart itself, as you could with text-based visuals. Simply click the
  ellipses at the top right (or occasionally the bottom left) of a chart
  and select Show as a table to display the source data. You can see an
  example of this in Figure 6-17 (where you can also see how a data
  point is displayed in line, area, and stacked area charts).

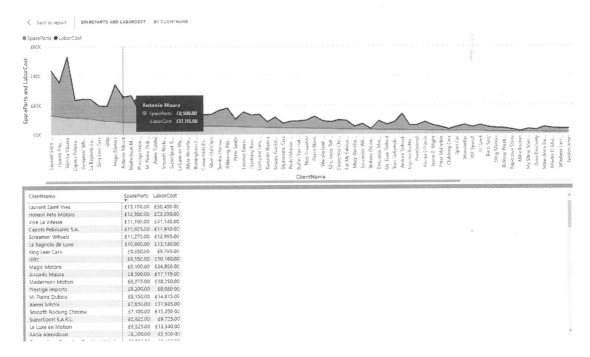

Figure 6-17. *Displaying pop-out data for a chart*

To switch back to the dashboard canvas, simply click Back to Report at the top left of
the chart.

Conclusion

This chapter took you on a tour of some of the core chart types that you can use in your Power BI Desktop reports and dashboards. These extend from the classic pie, line, column, and bar charts to the less common funnel, donut, and area charts. You saw that there are charts to suit a single data series and others that can handle multiple series of data. To add extra effect, you saw how to create mixed chart types and create 100% bar and column charts.

The charts that you met in this chapter are, it must be admitted, the simpler chart types. There are several more complex chart types that are available "out of the box." These are what you will discover in the next chapter.

CHAPTER 7

Advanced Chart Types

Now that you know the basics of how to create chart visuals, it is a perfect moment to extend the knowledge that you acquired in the previous chapter and learn some of the more advanced charting techniques that are available in Power BI Desktop. This will cover understanding how to create

- Scatter charts
- Bubble charts
- Waterfall charts
- Ribbon charts
- Dual-axis charts

Power BI Desktop can do more than create a variety of chart types. It can also extend charts with automated analytics that can make trends and exceptions stand out from the data. We will look at adding analyses to charts at the end of this chapter.

All of these charts will be based on the data in files contained in the C:\ PowerBiDesktopSamples folder. This file is available on the Apress website as is explained in Appendix A.

Scatter Charts

A scatter chart is a plot of data values against two numeric axes, and so by definition, you need two sets of numeric data to create a scatter chart. To appreciate the use of these charts, let's imagine that you want to see the sales and margin for all the makes and models of car you sold overall. Hopefully, this allows you to see where you really made money. The following explains how to do it:

© Adam Aspin 2022
A. Aspin, *Pro Power BI Dashboard Creation*, https://doi.org/10.1007/978-1-4842-8227-4_7

1. Using the file C:\PowerBiDesktopSamples\
   PrestigeCarsDataForDashboards.pbix, delete any existing
   visualizations or create a new blank page.

2. Create a Scatter chart by clicking the Scatter Chart icon in the
   Visualizations pane using the following fields:

   a. Make (from the Vehicle table) as the Details

   b. CostPrice (from the Sales table) as the X axis

   c. LaborCost (from the Sales table) as the Y axis

3. Power BI Desktop will display a scatter chart that looks like the
   one shown in Figure 7-1. Resize the chart to suit your taste.

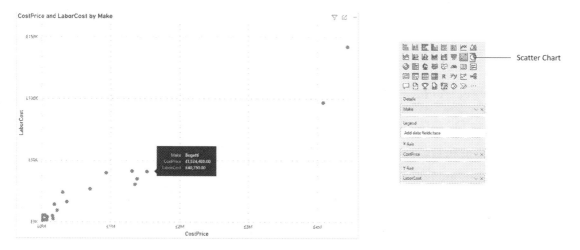

Figure 7-1. *A scatter chart*

If you hover the mouse pointer over one of the points in the scatter chart, you see the
data for the specific make of car. Figure 7-1 shows this.

Note   By definition, a scatter chart requires numeric values for both the X and Y
axes. So if you add a non-numeric value to either the X Value or Y Value boxes, then
Power BI Desktop converts the data to a count aggregation.

We made this chart by adding all the required fields to the initial table first. We also made sure that we added them in the right order so the scatter chart would display correctly the first time. In the real world of interactive data visualization, things may not be quite this coherent, so it is good to know that Power BI Desktop is very forgiving. And it lets you build a scatter chart (just like any other chart) step by step if you prefer. In practice, this means that you can start with a table containing just two of the three fields that are required at a minimum for a scatter chart, convert the table to a scatter chart, and then add the remaining data fields. Power BI Desktop always attributes numeric or time fields to the X and Y axes (in the order in which they appear in the Fields box) and places the first descriptive field into the Values box.

Once a scatter chart has been created, you can swap the fields around and replace existing fields with other fields from the tables in the data to your heart's content.

Bubble Charts

A variant of the scatter chart is the bubble chart. This is one of my favorite chart types, though of course you cannot overuse it without losing some of its power. Essentially, a bubble chart is a scatter chart with a third piece of data included. So whereas a scatter chart shows you two pieces of data (one on the X axis, one on the Y axis), a bubble chart lets you add a third piece of information, which becomes the *size* of the point. Consequently, each point becomes a bubble.

The best way to appreciate a bubble chart is to create one. So here we assume that you want to look at the following for all makes of car sold in a single chart:

- The total sales

- The net margin ratio

- The mileage

This explains how a bubble chart can do this for you:

1. Using the file C:\PowerBiDesktopSamples\
   PrestigeCarsDataForDashboards.pbix, delete any existing
   visualizations.

2. Create a scatter chart with the following fields from the SalesData table, in this order:

    a. Make (from the Vehicle table) in the Details area

    b. SalePrice (from the Sales table) in the X axis area

    c. Mileage (from the SalesInfo table) in the Y Axis area

    d. SpareParts (from the Sales table) in the Size area

3. Drag the VehicleType field from the Vehicle table into the Legend area of the Visualizations pane. Power BI Desktop will display a bubble chart that looks like that shown in Figure 7-2.

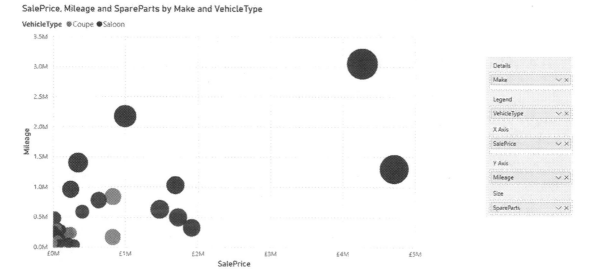

Figure 7-2. *An initial bubble chart*

4. Resize the chart if you need to.

If you look at the field area in the Visualizations pane (shown in Figure 7-2), you will see that Power BI Desktop has used the fields that you selected like this:

- *Make*: Placed in the Values box. This defines the core bubbles.

- *VehicleType*: Added to the Legend box. This creates bubbles for each combination of the detail element (make) and legend item (type of vehicle).

- *SalePrice*: Placed in the X Axis box. This is the vertical axis.

- *Mileage*: Placed in the Y Axis box. This is the horizontal axis. Each bubble is placed at the intersection of the values on the vertical and horizontal axes.

- *SpareParts*: Placed in the Size box. This defines the size of the points, which have consequently become bubbles of different sizes.

Hover the mouse pointer over one of the points in the bubble chart. You will see all the data that you placed in the Fields list Layout section for each make.

Playback over Time

So far, in this chapter, you have seen various ways of presenting data as charts and how to select and compare the data using a variety of chart types. A final trick with Power BI Desktop (one that can be extremely effective at riveting your audience) is to apply a play axis to the visualization. This animates the chart and, ideally, is suited to showing how data evolves over time. Unfortunately, it is harder to get the "wow" effect using these printed pages, so this really is a technique that you have to try yourself.

You need to know that a play axis can *only be applied to scatter or bubble charts*. Similarly, adding a play axis will not suit or enhance all types of data. However, if you have a time-dependent element that can be added to your chart as the Y axis (such as sales to date), then you can produce some powerful and revelatory effects.

The following explains how to create a bubble chart that shows the net margin ratio for colors of car sold against the sales for the year to date:

1. Select the bubble chart that you just created.

2. Add the DateKey field from the Date table to the Play Axis area. A playback bar is added to the bottom of the visual.

3. Click the play button in the visual.

The bubble chart visual will show how the data evolves over time. You can see a snapshot of this in Figure 7-3—though the printed page cannot do full justice to the wow factor delivered by a moving chart.

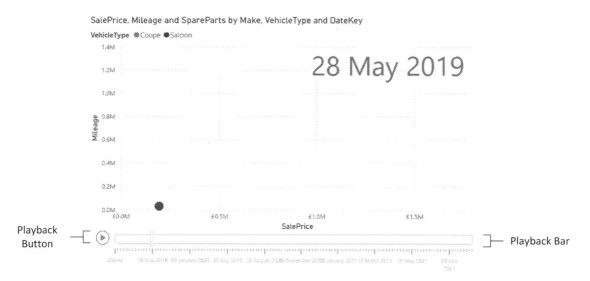

Figure 7-3. *Playing back bubble chart data over time*

There are a few points worth noting about the play axis while we are discussing it:

- You can pause the automated display by clicking the Pause icon, which the Play icon has become, while the animation is progressing. You can stop and start as often as you like.

- You can click any month (or any element) in the play axis to display the data just for that element, without playing the data before that point. This essentially means that you can use the play axis as a filter for your data.

- A play axis need not be time based. However, it can be harder to see any coherence or progression in the data if time is not used as a basis for a play axis.

- Using cumulative data (such as the YearSales figure in this example, which is the cumulative year-to-date sales) is particularly effective with a time-based play axis as it lets you appreciate the growth of sales for each data item over time.

- You can use a play axis as another interactive filter for your data, but doing this makes you miss out on a fabulous animation technique!

Waterfall Charts

What I want to look at now is one of the more original chart types that Power BI Desktop offers—the waterfall chart. This chart type is excellent at displaying the component parts of a final figure; in this example, it is used to show how the various makes sold make up the total sales figure.

1. Open the file C:\PowerBiDesktopSamples\
   CarSalesDataForReports.pbix and delete any existing
   visualizations.

2. Click the Waterfall Chart icon. You can see this in Figure 7-4. An
   empty waterfall chart will appear on the dashboard canvas.

3. Expand the Stock table and check the following fields:

   a. Make

   b. CostPrice

4. Resize the chart to suit your aesthetic requirements. It should look
   something like Figure 7-4.

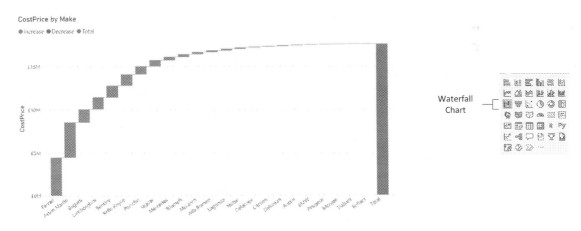

Figure 7-4. *A waterfall chart*

Waterfall charts can be extremely useful when you are analyzing the constituent elements of a whole. For instance, you could try using one to break down all the cost elements. It is worth noting that if you have any negative values in the chart, these will appear in a different color from positive values and will, inevitably, reduce the value of the total bar on the right.

145

Ribbon Charts

One addition to the range of chart options that Power BI Desktop has on offer is the ribbon chart. Ribbon charts virtually always use a time element as the X axis and are designed to show evolution over time. More specifically, they always place the highest value as the upper ribbon of the chart.

This is probably best understood with the help of an example. So I suggest that you try out the following:

1. Open the file PrestigeCarsDataForDashboards.pbix.

2. Click the Ribbon Chart icon in the Visualizations pane.

3. In the Fields list, click the following fields:

   a. MonthAbbrAndYear (in the Date table) as the Axis

   b. CountryName (in the Geography table) as the Legend

   c. SalePrice (in the Sales table) as the Values

4. Resize the chart until it looks like the one shown in Figure 7-5.

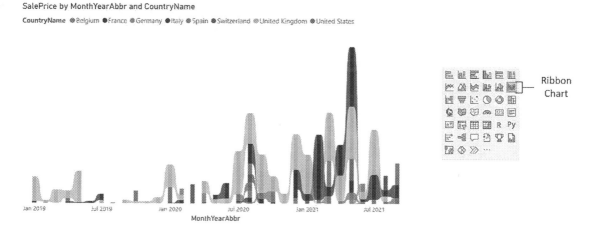

Figure 7-5. *A ribbon chart*

As you can see, the ribbon chart shows the ebb and flow of sales of different makes of vehicle over time. Indeed—and at the risk of anticipating the contents of Chapter 14—I suggest that you click one of the makes in the chart legend. This will highlight the make and show its evolution over time.

Dual-Axis Charts

To conclude our tour of chart types, let's take a look at a couple of charts that combine two of the basic chart types that you have seen previously in this chapter:

- Line and clustered column chart

- Line and stacked column chart

Let's discuss each of these in turn.

Line and Clustered Column Chart

Suppose that the upper echelons of management at Brilliant British Cars have decided to embark on an analysis of vehicle purchases. They want to isolate any interesting correlations that could influence purchases in order to maximize profits. So, determined to satisfy their request (or possibly to humor them) you have in turn decided to take a look at indirect costs and mileage to see if there are any correlations.

1. Open the file C:\PowerBiDesktopSamples\ PrestigeCarsDataForDashboards.pbix and delete any existing visual.

2. Click the Line and Clustered Column Chart icon. An empty line and clustered column chart will appear on the dashboard canvas.

3. Add the following fields:

    a. Make (this will be added to the Shared Axis box)

    b. LaborCost (this will be added to the Column Values box)

    c. SpareParts (this will be added to the Column Values box)

4. Drag the Mileage field into the Line Values box in the field area of the Visualizations pane.

5. Resize the chart to suit your aesthetic requirements. It should look something like Figure 7-6.

147

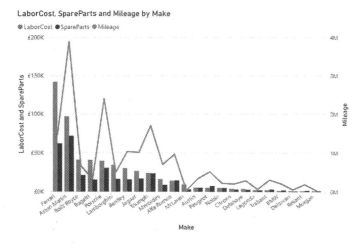

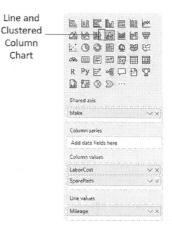

Figure 7-6. *A line and clustered column chart*

As you can see, this chart combines a clustered column chart that displays the labor and parts costs using the left axis with a line chart that displays the mileage using the right axis. Both of these charts share the X (or horizontal) axis.

Moreover, this kind of analysis makes it immediately clear that there is one make where low mileage does not necessarily mean lower repair costs. So the boss should be happy that you have isolated this unexpected correlation.

Line and Stacked Column Chart

One of the key advantages of dual-axis charts is that the two X axes can have vastly different scales. So, for instance, when you want to see how the parts and labor costs relate to the purchase cost (which is orders of magnitude higher than the other two costs), a line and stacked column chart can be really useful to get a clearer view of the data.

1. Open the file C:\PowerBiDesktopSamples\PrestigeCarsData ForDashboards.pbix and delete any existing visualizations.

2. Check the following fields to display a table on the dashboard canvas:

    a. Make

    b. LaborCost

    c. SpareParts

3. Click the Line and Stacked Column Chart icon. The table will be converted to a line and stacked column chart.

4. Also from the Sales table, drag the CostPrice field into the Line Values area of the Visualizations pane.

5. Resize the chart to suit your aesthetic requirements. It should look something like Figure 7-7.

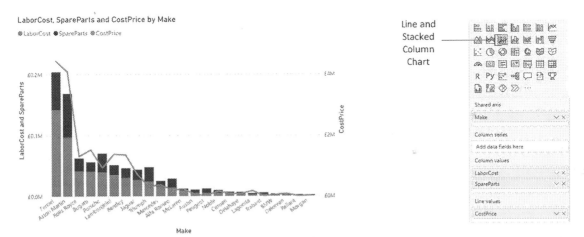

Figure 7-7. *A line and stacked column chart*

This way, you can compare values where the use of a single chart type would lead to one value (the cost price in this example) dwarfing the other values to the point of making them unreadable.

Trellis Charts

Trellis—or small multiples—charts are a way of displaying many smaller versions of a chart to allow comparison of a series of data elements. This is best appreciated using an example.

1. Open the file C:\PowerBiDesktopSamples\ PrestigeCarsDataForDashboards.pbix and delete any existing visualizations.

2. Create a stacked bar chart using the following fields:

   a. CountryName (the axis)

  b. LaborCost (values)

  c. SpareParts (values)

3. Drag the Color field into the Small multiples area of the
    Visualizations pane.

4. Resize the chart to suit your aesthetic requirements. It should
    look something like Figure 7-8 where each color is displayed as a
    separate bar chart.

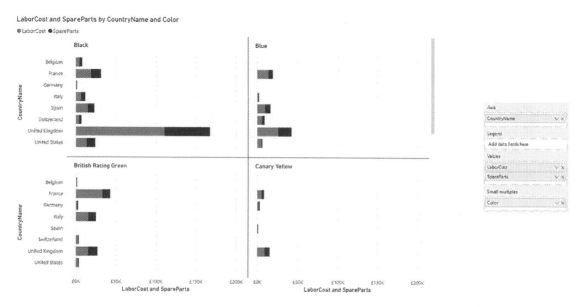

Figure 7-8. *A small multiples chart*

If a trellis chart contains a large number of small multiples elements (as is the case
here), it will automatically add a scrollbar to allow the user to scroll through the available
small multiples charts. Small multiples can use any of the following chart types:

- Column chart

- Bar chart

- Line chart

- Area chart

They cannot be used with dual-axis charts or any of the more complex chart types.

You can change the small multiples chart type to another chart type simply by selecting the small multiples chart and then clicking on a different chart type in the Visualizations pane.

Automated Chart Analytics

A fabulous way to add extra emphasis to the data in a chart is to add analytical enhancements. These are automatically calculated elements that draw the reader's attention to trends and exceptions. All these items are added as lines to a chart independently of the existing data. They include

- *Constants*: You may wish to add a specific value as an item in a chart.

- *Minimum values*: This allows you to draw attention to a lower threshold.

- *Maximum values*: This allows you to draw attention to an upper threshold.

- *Averages*: You can have Power BI Desktop calculate the average of a set of values and display this as a line.

- *Median values*: Power BI Desktop can also calculate and display a median value.

- *Percentiles*: You can specify a percentile to be displayed.

To see this a little closer, suppose that you want to add the following lines to a chart containing the selling price and mileage of all cars by make:

- The average mileage

- The maximum selling price

Here is how you can do this:

1. Click the Line Chart icon in the Visualizations pane. An empty chart visual will be created on the dashboard canvas.

2. Drag the Make field (from the Vehicle table) into the Axis area of the field area.

3. Drag the following fields into the Values area of the field area:

    a. SalePrice (from the Sales table)

    b. Mileage (from the SalesInfo table)

4. Click the Analytics icon (to the right of the Format icon in the Visualizations pane).

5. Expand the Average Line card.

6. Click Add line.

7. Double-click in the field containing the text "Average Line 1" and enter **Average Mileage**. You can, instead, click the edit icons (the small pencil) if you prefer.

8. Expand the Series card.

9. Select Mileage from the Series pop-up list.

10. Expand the Line card and choose a color from the palette of available colors.

11. Set the Style as Dotted.

12. Expand the Data label card and click the Data Label button to activate the data label.

13. Set the Style to Both (this means both name and value).

14. Set the Horizontal Position to Right.

15. Close the Average Line card.

16. Expand the Max Line card.

17. Click Add line.

18. Expand the Series card and select SalePrice from the Series pop-up list.

19. Expand the Line card and set the Style to Solid. The chart should look like the one shown in Figure 7-9.

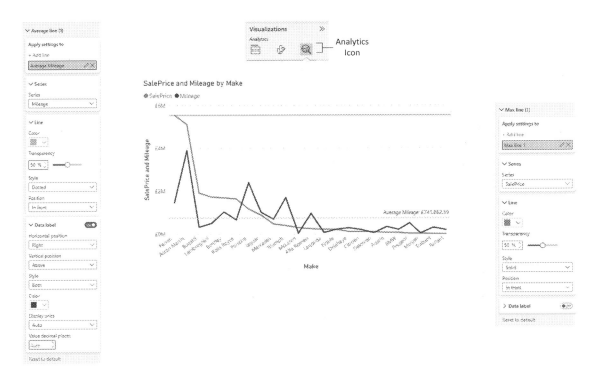

Figure 7-9. *Adding chart analytics*

It is worth noting that you can add several lines for an analytical element. That is, you can add as many averages, for instance, as there are data elements in the chart. To do this, simply click Add once more in the card where you wish to add another line and then define the settings to achieve the result that you want. This is, nonetheless, a technique that can detract from the visibility of a chart as easily as it can add to the data story that you are telling. So it is probably best used sparingly.

If you are adding a percentile line, then you have one extra element that you will probably need to alter. This is the actual percentile value of the maximum value of a data element, which you can alter using the Percentile slider.

Removing an analytical line is as simple as this:

1. Click the Analytics icon.

2. Expand the card corresponding to the line that you wish
   to remove.

3. Click the cross to the right of the line that you wish to remove.

Note   You cannot actually select an analytical line in a chart.

Scatter Chart Symmetry Shading and Ratio Line

Two features of Power BI Desktop can help you "see the wood for the trees" in scatter charts:

- Symmetry shading

- Ratio lines

They are equally simple to apply, but can really help you to see beyond a mass of data points and isolate valuable trends and salient items of data.

Symmetry Shading

This feature allows you to see which points have a higher value on the X axis compared to the Y axis (and vice versa). Like so much of Power BI Desktop, it is best understood using a practical example:

1. Open the file CarSalesDataForReports.pbix.

2. Create a scatter chart using the following elements:

   a. *Details*: Make (from the Stock table)

   b. *X Axis*: SalePrice (from the InvoiceLines table)

   c. *Y Axis*: Mileage (from the Stock table)

3. With the scatter chart selected, click the Analytics icon (the magnifying glass) in the Visualizations pane.

4. Expand the Symmetry Shading card.

5. Set Symmetry shading to On.

6. Select a color for the upper shading from the palette of available colors.

7. Select a color for the lower shading from the palette of available colors.

8. Adjust the Transparency slider to set the transparency to 50%. The chart will look like the one shown in Figure 7-10.

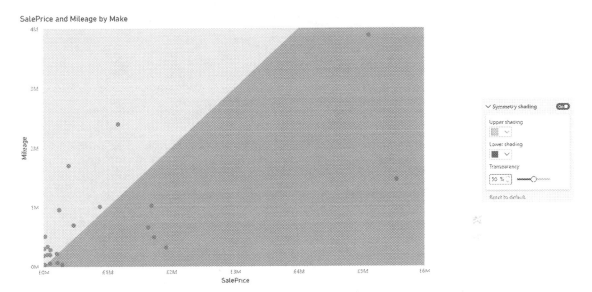

Figure 7-10. *Adding symmetry shading to a scatter chart*

You can remove symmetry shading by setting Symmetry Shading to Off in the Symmetry Shading card.

Note   Symmetry shading will only really be of use if the values on the X and Y axes are comparable in extent.

Ratio Line

One final instant analysis function that can be applied to scatter charts is the ratio line. This shows you how to apply it:

1. Follow steps 1 and 2 of the previous section to create a scatter chart.

2. Expand the Ratio Line card.

3. Set Ratio line to On.

4. Select a color for the ratio line from the palette of available colors.

155

5.   Select Solid from the pop-up list of line styles. The chart will look like the one shown in Figure 7-11.

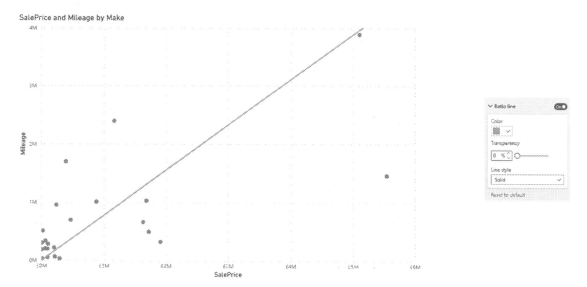

Figure 7-11. *Adding a ratio line to a scatter chart*

As was the case for symmetry shading, you can remove a ratio line by clicking the small cross at the right of the Ratio Line box in the Ratio Line card.

Conclusion

This chapter took you on a tour of the more advanced of the available chart types that you can use in your Power BI Desktop reports and dashboards. These extend the classic pie, line, column, funnel, donut, area, and bar charts to the less common scatter, bubble, ribbon, dual-axis, waterfall, and trellis charts.

Also, you saw how certain types of chart (bubble charts specifically) can even be animated so that you can add time as a descriptive factor to help your audience understand how data evolves.

Finally, you saw how to add automated trend lines and other analyses to charts. These helped you to tease out meaning from the data—with virtually no effort!

However, these charts can be presented at a higher level if you decide to add some compelling formatting. This is what you will learn to do in the next chapter.

CHAPTER 8

Formatting Charts

Now that you have mastered Power BI's core charting capabilities, it is time to move on and learn how to tweak your charts to the greatest effect. This chapter is devoted to the various techniques available in Power BI Desktop to give your charts real clarity and power. Some of these enhancements apply to all chart types, whereas others are specific to a single type of chart—or even one or two chart types.

Sometimes you change the configuration of a chart—and consequently enhance it—by altering the mapping of the data to the chart elements. However, on most occasions, you enhance a chart by modifying the various formatting options that are displayed when you select a chart and then clicking the Format icon in the Visualizations pane. I refer to this as the "Format pane" for ease of reference from now on.

In this chapter, you will use the C:\PowerBiDesktopSamples\ PrestigeCarsDataForDashboards.pbix Power BI Desktop file (that is available on the Apress website for download) as the basis for any charts that you will create.

Multiple Chart Formatting

It is worth noting from the outset that you can apply identical modifications to a set of charts on the same dashboard page by Ctrl-clicking to select multiple charts before you make any formatting changes.

However, simultaneous modification of several charts only works if *all* the selected charts are the *same type*.

If you have a chart with more than one field that provides the values on which the chart is based (or if you are creating a pie or donut chart), then you see a legend appear automatically.

© Adam Aspin 2022

A. Aspin, *Pro Power BI Dashboard Creation*, https://doi.org/10.1007/978-1-4842-8227-4_8

You can format a legend by modifying any of the following options:

- Legend display

- Position

- Legend title

Let's look at each of these in turn.

Note   A legend can only be displayed if there is more than one field added to the Values area (except in the case of pie and donut charts).

Legend Display

Power BI Desktop may automatically display legends in some cases, but you have the final decision as to whether a legend is required. To turn a legend off, do the following:

1. Select the chart whose legend you want to hide.

2. In the Visualizations pane, click the Format icon to display the Format pane.

3. In the Visual section, click the Legend button to turn off the legend.

The legend will disappear from the selected chart.

Legend Position

The default for the legend is for it to be placed at the top left of the chart. However, you can choose where to place the legend inside the chart area. Follow these steps:

1. Select the chart whose legend you want to modify.

2. In the Visualizations pane, click the Format icon.

3. In the Visual section, expand the Legend card.

4. Select one of the available legend positions from the Position pop-up.

The available options are given in Table 8-1.

Table 8-1. *Legend Position Options*

Legend Option	Description
Top	The legend is displayed above the chart on the left.
Bottom	The legend is displayed below the chart on the left.
Left	The legend is displayed at the left of the chart at the top.
Right	The legend is displayed at the right of the chart at the top.
Top Center	The legend is displayed above the chart on the left in the center.
Bottom Center	The legend is displayed below the chart on the left in the center.
Left Center	The legend is displayed at the left of the chart in the middle.
Right Center	The legend is displayed at the right of the chart in the middle.

Legends can require a little juggling until they display their contents in a readable way. This is because the text of the legend is often truncated when it is initially displayed. If this is the case, the only real option is to modify the chart size or the legend font size.

Note   You cannot add a legend to an area, column, bar, or line chart that only has a *single* data series. In these cases, the Legend card of the Visualizations pane will be grayed out.

Legend Title

You can add a title to a legend if you want.

1. Create a Clustered Column chart using the following fields (I am assuming that you are, by now, familiar enough with the source data tables to locate these fields):

    a. Make

    b. SalePrice

    c. Mileage

2. In the Visualizations pane, click the Format icon and expand the Legend card.

3. Ensure the Legend button is set to On.

4. Select a position from the pop-up list of available options.

5. Ensure the Title button is set to On.

6. Expand the Title card and enter the legend title in the Legend Name box. I suggest adding **Sales Analysis**.

7. Expand the Text card and select a color for the text in the legend from the color palette.

8. Select a font family and text size.

An example of a legend with a title is shown in Figure 8-1.

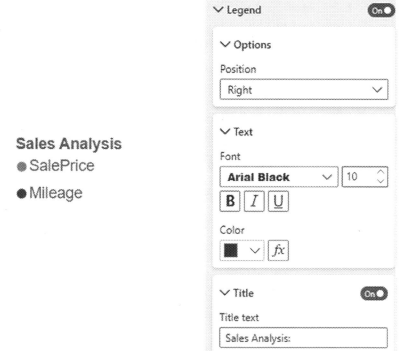

Figure 8-1. *A legend with a title*

Chart Title

Each chart is created with a title explaining what the chart is displaying; that is, the fields on which it is based. The available options are fairly simple:

- Hide or display the title

- Modify the text of the title

- Change the font color

- Change the background color for the title

- Alter the title alignment

Let's see how to apply all of these options to the title of the chart that you created earlier:

1. Select the chart that you created previously.

2. In the Visualizations pane, click the Format icon, activate the General section, and expand the Title card.

3. Ensure the Title button is set to On.

4. Replace the automatically generated title text in the Title Text box. In this example, I set it to **Profitability**.

5. Set Text wrap to On if the title needs to flow over more than one line.

6. Select a text color from the palette of available colors.

7. Select a background color from the palette of available colors.

8. Click the middle icon for Horizontal alignment. This will center the text relative to the width of the table.

9. Adjust the Text Size to set a larger font size.

10. Select any font attributes that you wish to add (bold, italic, or underline). You can see the result of these kinds of adjustments in Figure 8-2.

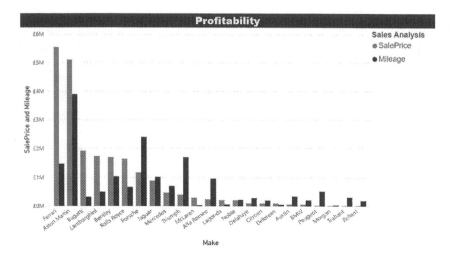

Figure 8-2. *Chart title adjustments*

You can also add further annotations to a chart using free-form text boxes. This technique is described in Chapter 15.

Data Colors

All charts allow you to specify the color of each and every data series. Of course, the amount of effort involved will depend on the number of data series that you want to alter. The way to do it is as follows:

1. Select the chart for which you wish to modify the data colors.

2. In the Visualizations pane, click the Format icon.

3. In the Visual section, expand the Columns card. The list of chart data series (or data elements for certain chart types) will be displayed.

4. Select a color for each data element or series from the pop-up palette of available colors.

Figure 8-3 shows modified data colors for the chart that you are currently working on.

Figure 8-3. *Specifying data colors*

Note   If a chart only contains a single data series (this is always the case for pie and donut charts, and can be the case for column, line, bar, and area charts), you have the option to set a color for *each data point* of a data series.

Adding Chart Data Labels

As you have seen already, you can display the exact data behind a column, bar, or point in a line chart simply by hovering the mouse pointer over the data that interests you. Yet there could be times when you want to display the values behind the chart permanently on the visualization. This is where data labels come into play.

To add data labels to a chart (in this example, I continue using the chart that you created at the start of this chapter), all you have to do is this:

1. Select the chart you created previously and switch to stacked bar chart by clicking the Stacked Bar Chart icon.

2. Remove the Make field from the Axis area and add the Color field instead.

3. In the Visualizations pane, click the Format icon and (in the Visual section) expand the Data Labels card.

4. Set the Data Labels button to On.

5. Select Mileage as the Series (this way, you will only be formatting data labels for mileage elements).

6. Expand the Options card and select Inside end as the position.

7. Expand the Values card and select Millions as the Display units for the figure in the card by clicking the pop-up list of display units.

8. Select **1** as Value decimal places.

9. Select a color for the data labels from the pop-up palette of colors.

10. Tweak the text size and attributes if you wish.

11. Expand the Background card and set the data labels background color to On—and select a color from the color palette to make the data labels appear against a specific colored background.

12. Using the slider, adjust the transparency of the data label background.

Note   When applying data labels to column, bar, and line charts, you notice that sometimes Power BI Desktop cannot physically place all the data labels exactly where the option that you have selected implies that they should appear. This is because sometimes there is simply not enough space inside a bar or column to fit the figures. In these cases, Power BI Desktop places the data outside the bar or column. On other occasions, the data cannot fit outside a line, column, or bar without being placed above the upper end of the axis. Here again, Power BI Desktop tweaks the presentation to get as close as possible to the effect that you asked for. This can mean that data labels are not displayed at all.

The various options for positioning the data labels are given in Table 8-2.

Table 8-2. *Data Label Position Options*

Data Label Position	Description
Auto	Power BI Desktop places the data label for the best effect.
Inside End	The data label is placed inside the bar at the right or inside the column at the top.
Outside End	The data label is placed outside the bar at the right or outside the column at the top.
Inside Center	The data label is placed inside the center of the bar or column.
Inside Base	The data label is placed inside the bar at the left or inside the column at the bottom.

There is one final point to note on the subject of data labels:

- Scatter charts and balloon charts do *not* display data labels.

Removing Chart Data Labels

You can, if you prefer, remove data labels from one or more selected series of data. To do this:

1. Select the chart you created previously and switch to the General section of the Formatting pane.

2. Expand the Data Labels card.

3. Select SalePrice from the Series pop-up.

4. Expand the Options card and set Show data labels to Off.

Total Labels

Stacked bar, stacked column, and stacked area charts can also display the total for the cumulative data points (the totals for all the series that make up the group). To add these:

1. Select the chart you created previously and switch to the Visual section of the Formatting pane.

2. Expand the Total labels card.

3. Set the Total labels to On.

4. Set the following attributes of the total labels:

    a. Color

    b. Display units

    c. Value decimal places

5. Expand the Background card and set the total labels background color to On—and select a color from the color palette.

6. Using the slider, adjust the transparency of the total labels background. You can see a sample of the output from this in Figure 8-4 (which also shows the formatting of the data labels that you applied previously).

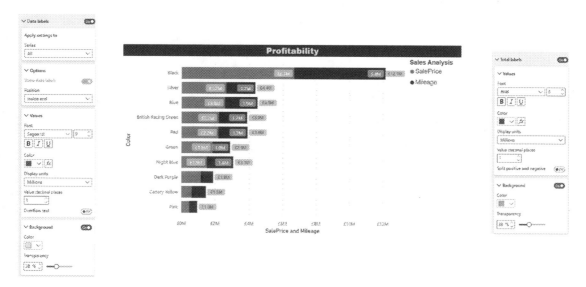

Figure 8-4. *Data labels and total labels*

Chart Background

If you need to alter the aesthetics of a chart, or should the need arise to make one chart stand out from the others in a dashboard, you can also modify the background color of the entire chart. So, continuing with the chart that you created previously, this is what you can do:

1. Select the chart whose background you wish to modify.

2. In the Visualizations pane, click the Format icon and switch to the General section.

3. Expand the Effects card.

4. Ensure that the Background On/Off switch is set to On.

5. Select a color from the palette of available colors.

6. Move the Transparency slider to the left or right to increase or decrease the transparency (and consequently the intensity) of the background color.

Plot Area

For all except pie, donut, and funnel charts, you can set an image as the background for the plot area of the selected chart. Here is an example of how to do this:

1. Select the chart that you modified in the previous section.

2. In the Visualizations pane, click the Format icon.

3. In the Visual section, expand the Plot area background card.

4. Click Browse. The standard Windows Open dialog will appear.

5. Navigate to the image file that you want to add. I will use C:\ PowerBiDesktopSamples\Images\GreenShade.png.

6. Click Open.

7. In the Image Fit pop-up, select Fit. The image will expand to fill all the plot area.

Finally, in Figure 8-5, you can see the chart with all your modifications applied. Before rolling your eyes at my (lack of) taste, please note that I am quite definitely not suggesting that you should present charts in this way (indeed, you should probably take this as an example of what *not* to do). I am merely showing the result of applying many of the available chart formatting options.

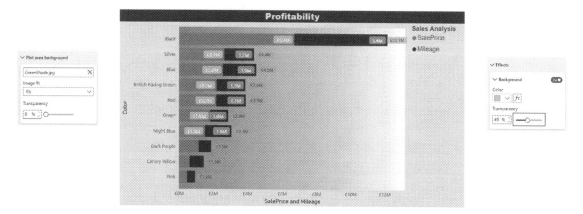

Figure 8-5. *Adding an image to a chart's plot area*

Note   To remove the image that you added, click the small cross to the right of the image file name in the Plot area background card of the Format pane.

Axis Modification

Most charts—except pie, donut, and funnel charts—allow you to tweak the axis attributes. This means modifying

- The X (horizontal) axis

- The Y (vertical) axis

We will take a look at these two separately.

Modifying the X Axis

There are several aspects of the X axis that you can alter:

- The axis display

- The axis title and presentation

- The font attributes of the axis labels

- The area height

A simple example explains how to adjust all of these aspects of the X axis:

1. Create a new stacked column chart based on Color, LaborCost, and TotalDiscount.

2. In the Visual section of the Formatting pane, expand the X-Axis card.

3. Ensure that the X Axis switch is set to On (this displays the axis and descriptive elements).

4. Select a font, font size, and color for the axis labels.

5. Set a Max area height (this defines the maximum height of the axis elements relative to the height of the plot area). You can see the Format area of the Visualizations pane for these attributes in Figure 8-6.

6. Expand the Title card and ensure the Title is set to On (this adds the axis title). Enter **Make of Vehicle** as the Title text.

7. Scroll down inside the Visualizations pane (if necessary) and select a font, font size, and color for the axis title.

Modifying the Y Axis

If your chart has a Y axis (or in the case of a dual-axis chart, two Y axes), then you can modify the following elements:

- The axis position

- The axis scale type

- The lower axis value

- The upper axis value

- The title display

- The display units

- The numeric precision

- The gridlines and gridline style

Once again, it is probably easiest to see how these various formatting options can be applied using a single example. I will continue using the chart that you saw in the previous section.

1. Select the chart to which you wish to alter the axis attributes. I will continue using the chart that we have been modifying in this chapter.

2. In the Visualizations pane, click the Format icon.

3. Expand the Y-Axis card.

4. Ensure that the Y Axis switch is set to On (this displays the axis and descriptive elements).

5. Expand the Values card, and from the Position pop-up, select Right.

6. Set (or leave) the Display units to Auto.

7. Enter the number of decimals to be displayed on the axis in the Value Decimal Places field.

8. Set the font, font size, and color for the Y-Axis elements.

9. Expand the Title card and switch Title to On to display the Y axis title.

10. Set the Style to Show Both. This way, the axis title will display both numbers and units. You can select either if you prefer.

11. Enter a title in the Axis Title field. I am adding **Massive Profit**.

12. Set the axis title font, font size, and color.

13. Expand the Range card and ensure that the Scale Type is set to Linear—or set to Log if you need a logarithmic scale.

14. Enter a Start value to set the starting figure for the axis. This can be negative, and must be a full, unformatted figure including thousands or millions. In this example, I will leave this at blank— which equates to zero.

15. Enter an End value to set the upper figure for the axis. This, too, must be a full, unformatted figure including thousands or millions. In this example, I will set it to **300000**. You can see the Format area of the Visualizations pane for the Y-Axis card in Figure 8-6.

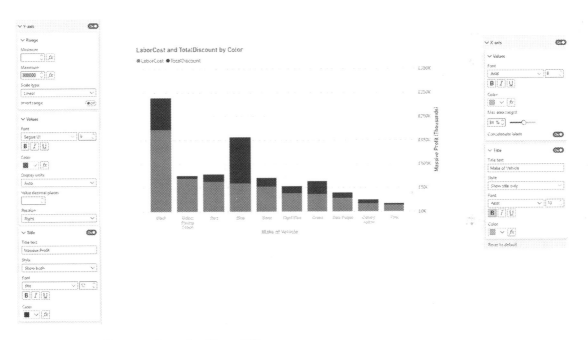

Figure 8-6. *Formatting the X and Y axes*

If you are modifying a chart that only has a single axis, you can move the axis from the left side of the chart to the right by selecting Right from the Position pop-up menu. In the case of a chart with two axes, you can swap the axes around using this setting.

If your chart contains *two* Y axes (one on the left and one on the right), then you can repeat these settings for the other axis. You may have to scroll down in the Visualizations pane to see the settings for the second axis.

Note   Remember that you can define a specific value as a measure in the data model. This can be extremely useful if you need to set reusable maximum and minimum values for the Y axis in charts.

Gridlines

Power BI Desktop also lets you modify the gridlines in a chart.

1. Select the chart whose axes you modified previously.

2. In the Visual section of the Format pane, set the Gridlines to On.

3. Choose a color for the gridlines.

4. Select a stroke width and line style. You can see the Format area of the Visualizations pane for the Y-Axis card in Figure 8-6. The final chart is shown in Figure 8-7.

Zoom Slider

Rather than setting the maximum and minimum values for a Y axis in the Formatting pane, you may refer to do this interactively using a Zoom slider. You can add one of these like this:

1. Select the chart whose gridlines you modified previously.

2. In the Visual section of the Format pane, set the Zoom slider to On.

3. Expand the Zoom slider card.

4. Set Slider labels to On.

5. Set Slider tooltips to On. The final chart is shown in Figure 8-7.

If you drag the top and bottom circles of the Zoom slider up and down, you can set the minimum and maximum thresholds for the Y axis interactively. It is worth noting that the minimum and maximum thresholds for the Y axis can only be modified within the parameters set in the Formatting pane.

Column Spacing

One potentially useful tweak can be to define the whitespace between bars, columns, or groups of bars or columns in a chart.

1. Select the chart whose Zoom slider you modified previously.

2. In the Visual section of the Format pane, expand the Columns card and then expand the Spacing card.

3. Set the Inner padding (the distance between each column or group of columns) to **30**.

The final chart is shown in Figure 8-7.

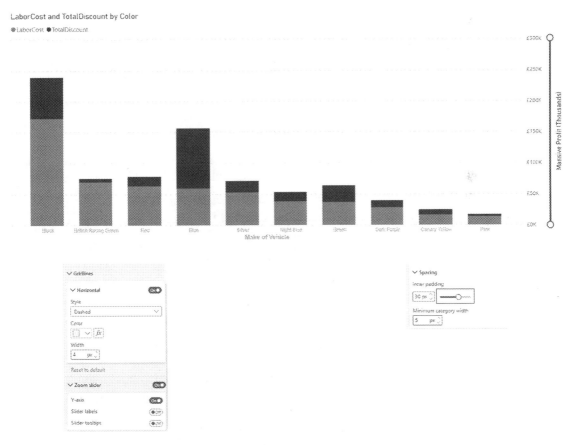

Figure 8-7. *Gridlines and Zoom slider*

Chart Borders

You can add a border to a chart just like you did to tables in the previous chapter. Simply click the Format icon and set the Border button to On. You can always choose a border color by

1. Selecting the chart

2. Clicking General in the Formatting pane

3. Expanding the Effects card

4. Setting Visual border to On

General Attributes

As was the case for the text-based visuals that you saw in the previous chapter, you can specify the exact position of a chart on the dashboard canvas in the General card of the Format area of the Visualizations pane.

Chart Aspect Ratio

As a final comment on chart formatting, it is worth remembering that you can lock the aspect ratio of a chart. This ensures that when you resize a chart, the width and height maintain their original proportions relative to each other.

To set the aspect ratio:

1. Click the chart to select it.

2. In the Visualizations pane, click the Format icon and switch to the General section.

3. Expand the Properties card and set Lock aspect ratio to On.

Now, when you resize a chart using the corner handles, it will keep its height-to-width ratio.

Specific Chart Formatting

Although most charts share many of the common formatting options that you have seen so far in this chapter, others present different formatting possibilities. This means that while bar, stacked bar, column, and stacked column charts can all be formatted using the techniques that you have recently learned, other chart types require discovering a few new tweaks.

Line, Area, and Stacked Area Charts

One group of charts that all share formatting options that are not available to bar and column charts are line charts, area charts, and stacked area charts. More specifically, they all allow you to adjust the line and point aspects of the chart. Here is an example to show you this in action:

1. Create a new line chart using the Color, SpareParts, and LaborCost fields.

2. In the Visualizations pane, click the Format icon.

3. In the Visual section, expand the Markers card.

4. Set Markers to On.

5. Set the Stroke Width to **5**.

6. Set Show Marker to On.

7. Set Customize series to On and select the series LaborCost.

8. Expand the Shape card.

9. Ensure Show marker is set to On and select a marker shape from the Marker Shape pop-up list.

10. Increase the marker size and change its color.

11. Expand the Lines card.

12. Set Customize series to On and select the series LaborCost.

13. Expand the Shape card and set the Line style to Dashed.

14. Set the Stroke Width to **2**.

15. Set the Join type to Round.

16. Set Stepped to On.

17. Expand the Colors card and set different colors for the two series of data. You should see a chart like the one in Figure 8-8.

Figure 8-8. *Shape options in a line chart*

Note   If you are not displaying the marker, you can select a join type (the intersection where each line alters direction) from the Join Type pop-up in the Shapes card.

Series Labels

A fairly recent addition to the panoply of chart formatting options is the ability to add series labels to the data series in a line chart. To see this in action:

1. Create a new line chart using the CountryName (Axis), Gross Profit, and TotalDiscount fields.

2. In the Formatting pane, set the Legend to Off.

3. Set the Series labels to On.

4. Expand the Series labels card and ensure that the All option is selected for the Series pop-up.

5. Expand the Options card and set the Maximum width (this is a percentage of the whole line chart width) to **20**.

6. Ensure that the Series position is set to Right. You can see the result in Figure 8-9.

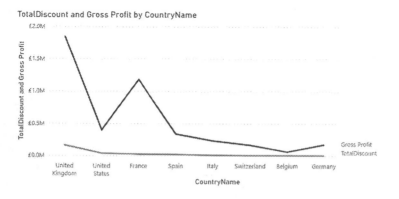

Figure 8-9. *Series labels in a line chart*

You can place the series labels either at the left or the right of the chart—and select the series you wish a label to be applied to.

Pie and Donut Charts

Pie and donut charts also have specific formatting possibilities. These consist of the ways that you can alter the detail labels for a pie or donut chart. Try out the following:

1. Create a new pie chart using the following fields:

   a. Color (from the Vehicle table)

   b. SpareParts (from the Sales table)

2. In the Visualizations pane, click the Format icon.

3. In the Visual section, set the Legend to On (should it be set to Off).

4. Expand the Legend card, and in the expanded Options card, place the legend at the left in the center.

5. Expand the Detail Labels card—and ensure that Detail labels are set to On.

6. Expand the Options card and set Overflow text to On (this allows data labels to appear even if this makes them cross pie chart segment borders).

7. Set the Position to Prefer outside.

8. Still in the Options card, select Data Value from the Label contents pop-up list.

9. In the Values card, choose a color for the text from the color palette (as well as a font and font attributes if you wish).

10. Enter, or select, a larger text size.

11. Select Millions as the display units from the Display Units pop-up list.

12. Enter **1** as the Value decimal places setting.

13. Set Background to On.

14. You will have a chart like the one in Figure 8-10.

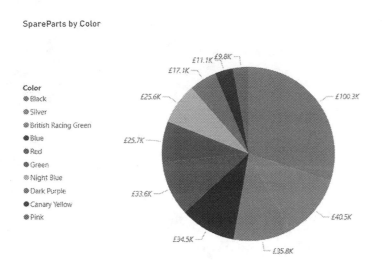

Figure 8-10. *Shape options in a pie chart*

Note   For a donut chart, you can also change the size of the inner "hole." This is altered by expanding the Shapes card of the Formatting pane and altering the Inner radius slider value.

The various options for positioning the detail labels are given in Table 8-3.

Table 8-3. *Detail Label Position Options*

Detail Label Position	Description
Outside	All detail labels will be positioned outside the pie slices.
Inside	All detail labels will be positioned inside the pie slices.
Prefer outside	All detail labels will be positioned outside the pie slices unless this would cause legibility issues in which case the detail label will be placed inside the pie chart.
Prefer inside	All detail labels will be positioned inside the pie slices unless this would cause legibility issues in which case the detail label will be placed outside the pie chart.

The various options for displaying the detail label contents are given in Table 8-4.

Table 8-4.   *Detail Label Content Options*

Detail Label Position	Description
Category	The category only will be displayed.
Data value	The data value only will be displayed.
Percent of total	The percent of total only will be displayed.
Category, percent of total	The category and percent of total will be displayed.
Data value, percent of total	The data value and percent of total will be displayed.
All detail labels	The data value, percent of total, and category will be displayed.

Note   If you select All detail labels as the Label contents, you will probably not need a legend as well as the label contents will display the category for each pie slice.

Ribbon Charts

Ribbon charts contain all the standard formatting options that you have seen applied to stacked column charts, so I will not reiterate all these possibilities here. There is, however, one formatting option that is specific to this chart type. This is the ribbon formatting.

To see this in action:

1. Create the ribbon chart that you made in Chapter 7 (you can see the original chart in Figure 7-7).

2. Click the Format icon in the Visualizations pane.

3. In the Visual section, expand the Ribbons card.

4. Expand the Spacing card and set the Spacing to **10**. This sets each ribbon apart from the others.

5. In the Colors card, set Connector color to Off. This sets the ribbon color to gray, rather than the color of the bar for each data point.

6. Set the Border to On. The result (which you can compare to Figure 7-7) is shown in Figure 8-11.

SalePrice by MonthYearAbbr and CountryName

CountryName ●Belgium ●France ●Germany ●Italy ●Spain ●Switzerland ●United Kingdom ●United States

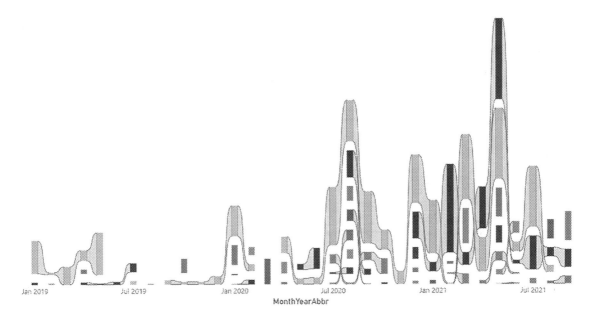

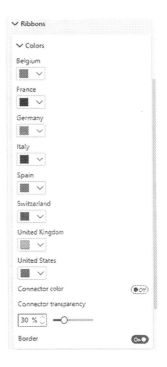

Figure 8-11. *A formatted ribbon chart*

Funnel Charts

Funnel charts allow you to display (or not) and format the one element that is specific to this kind of chart—the conversion rate. These are the percentage figures that appear above and below the funnel. This short walk-through explains how you can do this:

1. Create a new funnel chart using the following fields:

    a. Color (from the Vehicle table)

    b. SpareParts (from the Sales table)

2. In the Formatting pane (Visual section), expand the Conversion Rate Labels card.

3. Choose a color from the color palette.

4. Enter, or select, a larger text size and set any text attributes that you require. You will have a chart like the one in Figure 8-12.

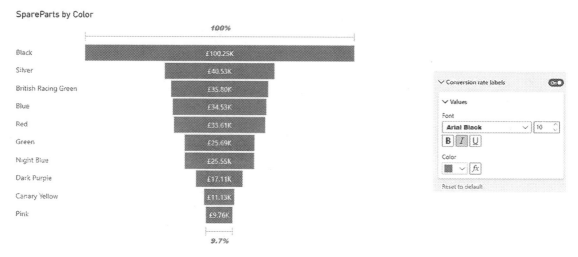

Figure 8-12. *Adjusting the conversion rate in a funnel chart*

Note   To prevent the conversion rate from being displayed, all you have to do is click the Conversion Rate Labels button.

Scatter and Bubble Charts

The next set of charts that allow you to apply some particular formatting are scatter and bubble charts. When you are creating these chart types, you can alter the following:

- Color by category

- Markers

- Shapes

To see these effects, we will create a new chart and then try out some of the available options. We will start with a scatter chart that we will then extend to make into a bubble chart:

1. Create a scatter chart using the following data elements:

   a. *Details*: Color (from the Vehicle table)

   b. *X Axis*: SalePrice (from the Sales table)

   c. *Y Axis*: Mileage (from the SalesInfo table)

   d. *Size*: CostPrice (from the Sales table)

2. Click the Format icon of the Visualizations pane.

3. Expand the Colors card and set both Color by category and Show all to On.

4. Set each vehicle color to the corresponding palette color.

5. Expand the Shape card.

6. Select a different shape type and set a larger shape size. The chart will now look like the one in Figure 8-13.

SalePrice. Mileage and CostPrice by Color

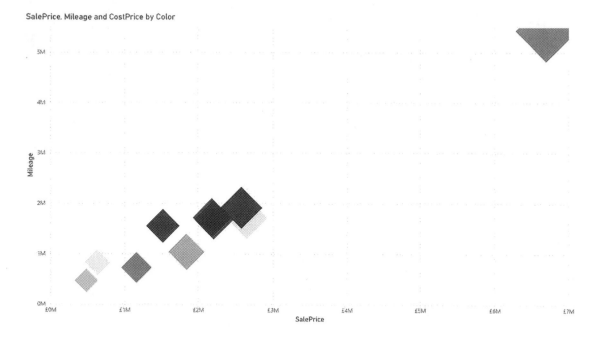

Figure 8-13. *Formatting a bubble chart*

There are a couple of points that need to be made at this juncture:

- You can, if you wish, customize each series just as you did for line charts.

Trellis Chart Formatting

The final chart type that allows you to apply some specific formatting is the trellis chart.

1. Re-create the trellis chart that you made for Figure 7-8.

2. Leaving the trellis chart selected, activate the Formatting pane.

3. In the Visual section, open the Small multiples title card.

4. Set the Position to Bottom.

5. Adjust the title font, attributes, and color to your taste.

6. Open the Small multiples grid card.

7. Set Rows to **3** and Columns to **4**. This will set the trellis chart to a matrix of four columns by three rows.

8. Set Customize options to On.

9. Set Inner column padding to **2**, Outer column padding to **2**, Inner row padding to **4**, and Outer row padding to **4**. This adjusts the inner spacing between each chart in the trellis.

10. The chart will now look like the one in Figure 8-14.

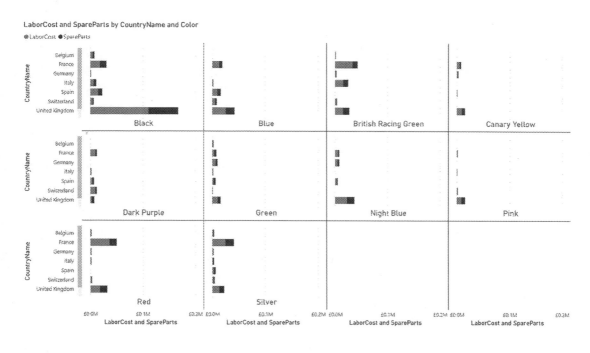

Figure 8-14. *Formatting a trellis chart*

Note   As you can see in Figure 8-14, a trellis chart may contain empty cells.

Conclusion

In this chapter, you learned how to enhance Power BI Desktop chart types by formatting them for added effect. This included modifying the colors of data series and data points as well as adding or removing titles. You also saw how to add legends and data labels to certain types of chart.

Once you had seen the formatting approaches that are common to most (if not all) chart types, you saw how to adjust the presentational aspects of specific chart types. This covered line, area, stacked area, pie, donut, funnel, bubble, and trellis charts.

You are now well on the way to becoming a Power BI Desktop dashboard maestro. All you need to look at now are a selection of the other visualization types that are available and you will have attained a complete mastery of high-impact dashboard presentation. So now, on to the next few chapters to finish your apprenticeship in Power BI visuals.

CHAPTER 9

Other Types of Visuals

While text-based visuals and "classic" charts can often make your point, there are times when you need to deliver your insights in ways that go beyond the more traditional data displays. This is where Power BI Desktop really comes to your aid. With the right data—and only a few clicks—you can revitalize your dashboards with

- Tree maps

- Gauges

- KPIs

- R visuals

- Python visuals

- Decomposition tree visuals

- Key influencers visuals

- Paginated reports

Most of these visualization types are as simple to create as the text-based visuals and charts that you saw in the preceding four chapters. What is more, all of them are built into Power BI Desktop and so are instantly available. Yet their very ease of use should not distract you from the clarity and power that they can bring to your reports and presentations.

This chapter will use the file C:\PowerBiDesktopSamples\ PrestigeCarsDataForDashboards-AdvancedVisuals.pbix as the basis for the visuals that you will create.

© Adam Aspin 2022
A. Aspin, *Pro Power BI Dashboard Creation*, https://doi.org/10.1007/978-1-4842-8227-4_9

Tree Maps

One type of visual that can really help your audience to see the way that individual values relate to a total is the tree map. While this is not a map in any geographical sense and does not resemble a tree, it can certainly assist users in giving a holistic overview of how the parts relate to the whole in an aggregated view of a dataset.

As, yet again, seeing is believing in the world of visuals, let's take a look at a tree map showing how the labor costs stack up for each make and model of car purchased:

1. Open the C:\PowerBiDesktopSamples\
    PrestigeCarsDataForDashboards-AdvancedVisuals.pbix file, or
    click an empty part of the dashboard canvas.

2. Click the Tree Map icon in the Visualizations pane. A blank tree
    map will appear.

3. Expand the Vehicle table and drag the Make field onto the
    Group area.

4. Drag the Model field onto the Details area.

5. Drag the LaborCost field onto the Values box in the field area. The
    tree map should look like the one in Figure 9-1.

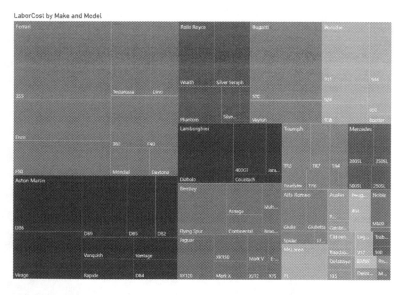

Figure 9-1. *A tree map showing labor cost for each make and model of car*

As you can see in Figure 9-1, the tree map has grouped each model of car by make and then displayed the labor cost as the relative size of each box in the tree map. This way, your viewers can get a rough idea of

- How the labor cost for each model compares to the total labor cost for the make

- How the labor cost for each make compares to the total labor cost

As you are probably expecting by now, you can hover the mouse over any box in the tree map and see a pop-up tooltip of the exact data.

Power BI Desktop will decide how best to organize the tree map. However, the final appearance will depend on how wide and how tall the visual is. So don't hesitate to resize this particular kind of visualization and see how it changes as you adjust the relative height and width.

There could be cases when a tree map cannot display all the available data, possibly because there are too many data points, or the range of values is too wide to be shown properly, or (as the case with the pie charts) because there are negative values in the data. In these circumstances, the tree map shows a warning information symbol in the top left of the visual. If you hover the mouse pointer over this icon, you will see a message like the one shown in Figure 9-2.

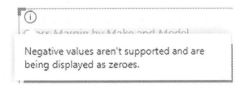

Figure 9-2. *The tree map data alert*

If you see this warning, then you could be advised to apply filters to the data (as described in Chapter 13) to filter out the data that is causing the problem.

Formatting Tree Maps

Tree maps can be formatted just like any other visual. The following are the primary available options in the Format icon in the Visualizations pane:

- Legend

- Data Colors

- Data Labels

- Category Labels

- Title

- Background

- Lock Aspect

- Border

Since applying all of these options was explained (for other types of visual) in previous chapters, I will not explain them in detail again, but I will provide a few comments about the available options.

Legend

In my opinion, a legend is superfluous as it duplicates the information about the grouping data that is already displayed in the tree map. You may find a legend necessary if you choose not to display the category labels, however.

Data Colors

This palette lets you choose a specific color for each grouping element.

Data Labels

You can display (or hide) the actual figures that are behind each segment of a tree map if you wish. This entails switching the Data Labels button to On or Off. If you expand the Data Labels card of the Formatting pane, you can also modify the color, units, number of decimals, and text size and font of the data labels.

Category Labels

This option lets you decide whether or not to display the grouping elements and the detail element information inside the tree map. If your tree map contains dozens (or hundreds) of data points, then you might want to hide the category labels. If you expand the Category Labels card of the Formatting pane, you can also modify the color, font, and size of the category labels.

Title

As is the case with most visuals, you can choose to show or hide the title, as well as alter its text, font size, and background color.

Background

You can apply a colored background to the kind of visuals that you can see in this chapter, too.

Lock Aspect

If you set Lock Aspect to On, then you can resize the visual while keeping it proportionally sized.

Border

As is the case with just about any visual, you can add or remove a border to tree maps, too.

Gauges

One extremely useful visual that is available out of the box is the gauge. These kinds of visuals are particularly effective when you want to compare actuals to targets or see how a metric compares to a key performance indicator (KPI), for instance. In this example, you will use a gauge to see how the total cost of purchases and spares compares to the threshold set by the finance department:

1. Open the C:\PowerBiDesktopSamples\ PrestigeCarsDataForDashboards-AdvancedVisuals.pbix file, or click an empty part of the dashboard canvas.

2. Click the Gauge icon in the Visualizations pane. A blank gauge visual will appear.

3. Expand the Sales table and drag the SalePrice field into the Values area. Alternatively, drag this field directly onto the gauge that you just created.

4. Drag the Target field from the GaugeTarget table into the Target value area.

5. Switch to the Formatting pane, and in the Visual section, expand the Gauge Axis card.

6. Enter **25000000** as the Max value. The gauge will look like Figure 9-3.

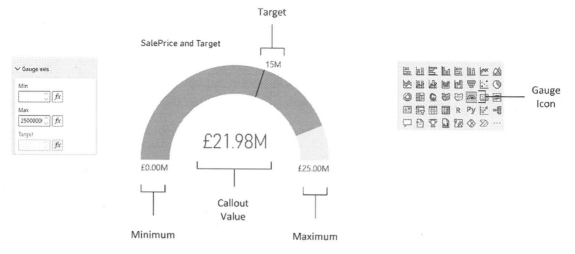

Figure 9-3. *A gauge in Power BI Desktop*

Gauges are designed to show progress against a target or a total. Consequently, you can set the elements described in Table 9-1 for a gauge.

Table 9-1. *The Specific Data Requirements for Gauges*

Element	Description
Value	The element that appears as a colored bar in the gauge
Minimum value	The minimum value to alter the perceptual effect of the gauge
Maximum value	The maximum value to alter the perceptual effect of the gauge
Target value	A metric that is defined as something to be attained

In fact, all that a gauge needs is a value. It will work without any of the other three elements. However, the real visual power of a gauge comes from the way that it uses the viewer's presumption of a target or value to be achieved. Consequently, it is usually best to apply a target at least and possibly a maximum value to convey an idea of success or failure for the reader.

Note It is worth noting that you can define a specific value in the data model. This can be extremely useful if you need to set the maximum, minimum, or target values for gauges. This way, you can modify a threshold once without having to change the attributes of multiple visuals independently.

Formatting Gauges

Many of the gauge formatting options are highly specific to gauge visuals. So here is a quick trip through the available presentation techniques that you need to know to enhance this type of visual:

1. Click the gauge that you created previously.

2. In the Visualizations pane, remove the Target value.

3. In the Visualizations pane, click the Format icon.

4. Expand the Gauge Axis card of the Visual section.

5. Enter **1000000** as the minimum value.

6. Expand the Data Labels card.

7. Ensure that the Data Labels switch is set to On and expand the Values card.

8. Choose a color from the pop-up palette for colors for the data labels and set a larger font size.

9. Expand the Target label card and switch target labels to On and expand the Values card.

10. Choose a color from the pop-up palette for colors for the target. Of course, you can modify the font attributes if you want.

11. Expand the Callout Value card.

12. Ensure that the Callout Value switch is set to On and expand the Callout Values card.

13. Choose a color from the pop-up palette for colors for the callout value.

14. Set the callout value decimals to **0**.

15. Expand the Gauge Axis card and add a target value of 15,000,000.

16. Expand the Data Colors card and select a color for the fill and the target. The gauge will look something like Figure 9-4.

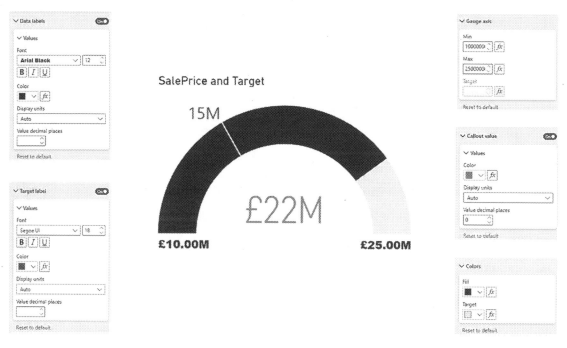

Figure 9-4. *A formatted gauge*

If you wish, you can also alter the background data labels, border, and title just as you did previously for other visuals. You can also choose not to display the data labels or the callout value (the value of the gauge) if you prefer. All you have to do is to set their respective switches to the Off position.

Note   When entering figures in the Formatting pane (referenced earlier in the chapter) of the Visualizations pane, you must not add any numeric formatting, such as thousands separators. If you do, the formatting will not work and Power BI will wait until you have entered the numbers in their raw form. You will have noticed that you cannot enter minimum, maximum, or target values if this data already comes from a table.

Gauges are a simple yet effective visual. A set of gauges can also be a truly effective way of displaying high-level key metrics on a dashboard.

The remaining gauge formatting options are common to most of the visuals that you have already seen.

KPIs

Power BI Desktop can also create key performance indicator visuals that illustrate how a data element is trending compared to a target value. Here is one example of this:

1. Click the KPI icon to add a clustered column chart visual to the dashboard. Leave the blank KPI visual selected.

2. Add the Mileage field (from the SalesInfo table) as well as the MonthYearAbbr field (from the Date table).

3. Add the KPI field from the KPITarget table to the Target Goals area of the Visualizations pane.

4. Click the Format icon in the Visualizations pane.

5. In the Visual section, expand the Callout Value card and tweak the font attributes to suit your taste.

6. Expand the Icons card and set the icon size to **55**.

7. Expand the Trend axis card and set the direction to Low is good. Select different colors for Good (color), Neutral (color), and Bad (color).

8. Expand the Target label card and then expand the Values card.

9. Set the font attributes for the target.

10. Set the Label as **Objective**.

11. Expand the Distance to goal card and set Distance direction as Decreasing is positive. Tweak any font attributes you want.

12. Set the Date to On and expand the Date card and set the font size to **14**. The KPI will look like the one shown in Figure 9-5.

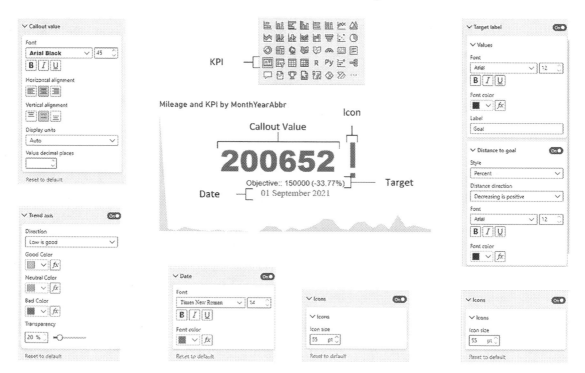

Figure 9-5. *A KPI visual*

R Visuals

Should you find that even the wide range of built-in visuals that Power BI Desktop has to offer are just not enough to make your point, then you can take visuals to another, higher level using the R language. "R" as it is known is a language that is used to analyze data and create visualizations of statistical data. It can be used inside Power BI Desktop reports and dashboards to extend the analysis that you are delivering using the data that you have prepared for your existing visuals.

R is not an intuitive language, but it is extremely powerful. So here is an example of how you can add an R visual to a dashboard using the CarSales data that you have already loaded:

Note   Creating R visuals implies installing an R engine on the PC that hosts Power BI Desktop. You can find one of the available R downloads at `https://mran.revolutionanalytics.com/download/`.

---

1. Open the Power BI Desktop file C:\PowerBiDesktopSamples\ PrestigeCarsDataForDashboards-AdvancedVisuals.pbix.

2. Click the R visuals icon in the Visualizations pane; the Enable Script Visuals dialog will be displayed, like the one shown in Figure 9-6.

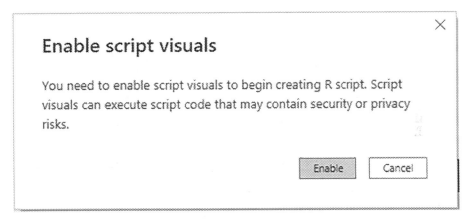

Figure 9-6.   *The Enable Script Visuals dialog*

3. Click Enable. An empty R visual will be added to the desktop canvas and a pane containing the R script editor will appear under the report. You can see this in Figure 9-7.

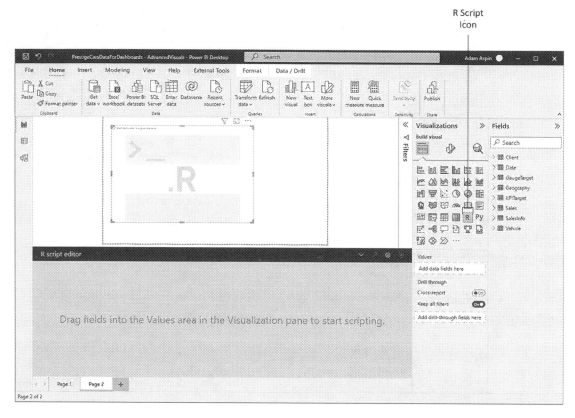

Figure 9-7. *Adding an R visual*

4. Drag the following fields onto the R visual or onto the Values area of the Visualizations pane if you prefer:

   a. Make

   b. SalePrice

5. Resize the R visual so that it is wider than it is tall.

6. Add the following script under the header lines in the R script editor (this script is available in the file C:\PowerBiDesktopSamples\Rscript.txt). Once you have done this, the script editor will look like Figure 9-8.

```
rdata <- table(dataset)
barplot(rdata
,axes=F
```

```
,main="Make"
,xlab="Cost Price"
,ylab = "Number Sold per Price Point"
,legend = rownames(rdata)
,col=c("darkblue","red", "green", "yellow", "pink",
"orange", "darkgreen") )
```

External
Editor

Minimize
Editor

Options

Run
Script

R script editor

⚠ Duplicate rows will be removed from the data.   ✕

```
 1 # The following code to create a dataframe and remove duplicated rows is always executed and acts as a
   preamble for your script:
 2
 3 # dataset <- data.frame(Make, SalePrice)
 4 # dataset <- unique(dataset)
 5
 6 # Paste or type your script code here:
 7 rdata <- table(dataset)
 8 barplot(rdata
 9 ,axes=F
10 ,main="Make"
11 ,xlab="Cost Price"
12 ,ylab = "Number Sold per Price Point"
13 ,legend = rownames(rdata)
14 ,col=c("darkblue","red", "green", "yellow", "pink", "orange", "darkgreen") )
```

Figure 9-8. *The R script editor with a functioning script*

7. Click the Run Script icon at the top right of the script editor.

8. The R visual will appear in Power BI Desktop.

9. Resize the R visual as necessary. The visual could end up looking
    like the one shown in Figure 9-9.

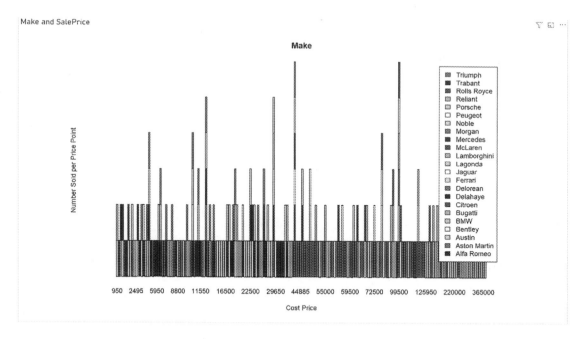

Figure 9-9. *An R visual*

You can, of course, only create R visuals if you are prepared to learn the R language. As this is the subject of entire tomes, I will not be describing the language here. Instead, I suggest that you refer to the many excellent resources that are already available on this subject.

Note   If you resize the R visual, you may have to rerun the R script (by clicking the Run Script icon in the R script editor) to force the visual to display correctly.

The R script editor icons are described in Table 9-2.

Table 9-2. *The R Script Editor Icons*

Icons	Description
Run Script	Runs—or reruns—the R script and re-creates the R visual in Power BI Desktop
R Script Options	Displays the dialog with available R script options
Edit script in external R IDE	Runs an external R editor, using the script from the Power BI Desktop R visual
Minimize the script pane	Hides (or redisplays) the R script pane

R Options

There are a couple of R options that you can adjust if this proves really necessary. You can find these by choosing File ä Options and Settings ä Options (or, more simply, by clicking the options icon at the top right of the R script editor) and then clicking R scripting in the left-hand pane of the Options dialog that you can see in Figure 9-10.

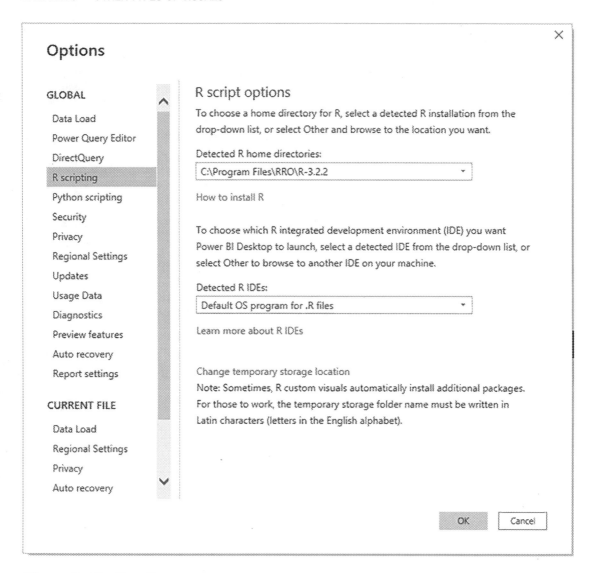

Figure 9-10. *R options*

There are, essentially, only a couple of possible tweaks that you could have to make:

- *R scripting engine*: Power BI Desktop should detect the R scripting engine that you have previously installed. Should it not do this, then you can browse to the directory containing the R scripting engine. Simply select Other in the pop-up list and click the Browse button.

- *IDE*: If you prefer to use a different external R integrated development environment (IDE), then simply click the Browse button to select a preferred R IDE. This will then be invoked the next time that you click the External Editor icon at the top right of the R script editor.

Note   The vast majority of formatting for an R visual is done inside the R script itself. You can, however, format the background, border, and title of the visual using the Power BI formatting options.

Python Visuals

Power BI Desktop also offers the possibility of creating your own visuals scripted in Python. While this is pretty similar to the approach that you just saw for R visuals, there are a few minor differences.

Firstly, you will need to install Python on your PC. There are several available approaches to doing this, and a quick search on the Web should provide you with the path to an up-to-date version of Python.

Secondly, you will probably need to install the pandas and possibly matplotlib libraries on your PC—unless they are already installed—as both these libraries are needed in the majority of cases when scripting Python charts as Power BI visuals.

To save you researching the techniques, all you have to do is to run the two following lines of code

```
pip install pandas
pip install matplotlib
```

in the Python script directory (on my laptop, this is C:\Users\Adam\AppData\Local\ Programs\Python\Python37-32\Scripts).

To create a Python chart as a Power BI visual:

1. Open the Power BI Desktop file C:\PowerBiDesktopSamples\ CarSalesDataForReports.pbix.

2. Click the Python visual icon in the Visualizations pane. You can see this in Figure 9-11. A pane containing the Python script editor will appear under the report.

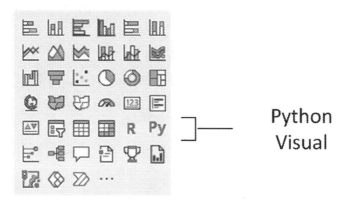

Python
Visual

Figure 9-11. *The Python visual icon*

3. Drag the following fields onto the Python visual (both are from the Stock table)—a dataframe is created automatically from the fields added to the Fields area:

    a. Make

    b. CostPrice

4. Add the following script under the header lines in the Python script editor:

```
import matplotlib.pyplot as plt
dataset.plot(kind='bar', x='Color', y='CostPrice')
plt.show()
```

5. Once you have done this, the script editor will look like the one in Figure 9-12.

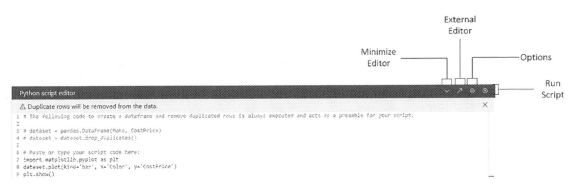

Figure 9-12. *The Python script editor*

6. Click the Run Script icon at the top right of the script editor. The Python visual will appear in Power BI Desktop.

7. Resize the Python visual as necessary. The visual could end up looking like the one shown in Figure 9-13.

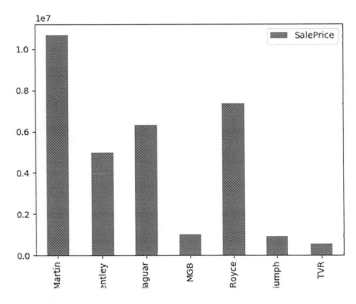

Figure 9-13. *A simple Python visual*

> **Note**   The vast majority of formatting for a Python visual is done inside the Python script itself. You can, however, format the background, border, and title of the visual using the Power BI formatting options.

This is quite possibly the simplest Python visual that you could make. However, the point is not to blind you with swathes of Python code, but rather to show you how easy it is to capitalize on your Python skills if you are moving to Power BI Desktop. Alternatively, you can use Power BI Desktop as an excellent training ground to learn Python for data visualization as you perfect your Python coding skills.

Python Options

As was the case with R visuals, you can tweak a couple of options to specify Python script options for Power BI Desktop. As these are essentially identical to those described earlier for R, I will not repeat these elements here. You can, however, see the available options in Figure 9-14.

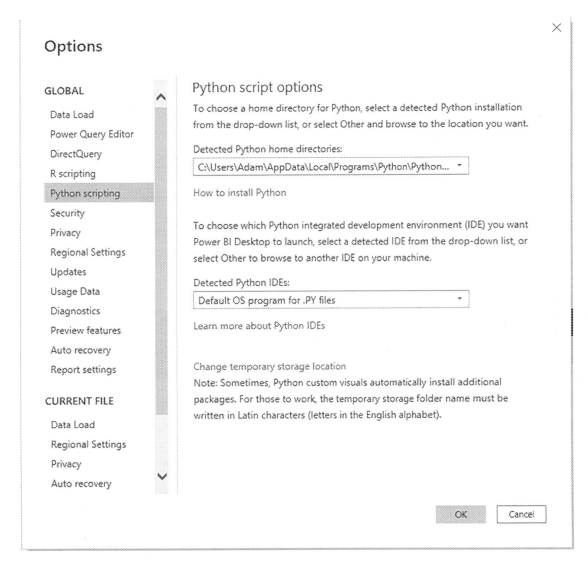

Figure 9-14. Python options

Decomposition Tree

One visual that has been added to the panoply of built-in visuals (accompanied by a huge cheer of welcome from the Power BI community) is the decomposition tree. This visual lets you drill down through multiple elements (that it calls dimensions) to see the path down to the lowest level of your analysis.

1. Open the file PrestigeCarsDataForDashboards.pbix.

2. Click the Decomposition Tree icon in the Visualizations pane. You can see this icon in Figure 9-18. Alternatively, go to the Insert menu and click the Decomposition Tree button.

3. Resize the blank visual that appears to make it larger.

4. Add the CostPrice field to the Analyze area.

5. Add the following elements to the Explain By area:

    a. Make (from the Vehicle table).

    b. Model (from the Vehicle table).

    c. Color (from the Vehicle table).

    d. CountryName (from the Geography table).

6. The resulting visual looks like the one in Figure 9-15.

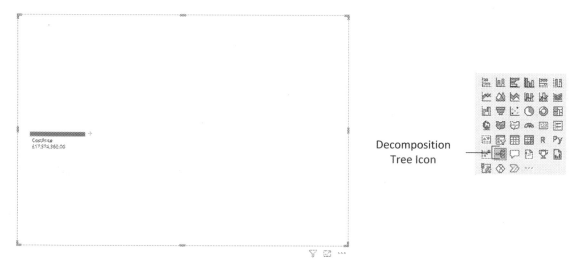

Figure 9-15. An initial decomposition tree

7. Click the cross to the right of the initial element in the decomposition tree (CostPrice). The pop-up menu displays the elements that you added previously to the Explain By area.

8. Click CountryName. Each country appears as a sublevel in the decomposition tree showing the relative values of the value that you initially selected.

9. Click the cross to the right of one of the countries. The pop-up menu displays the remaining elements that you added previously.

10. Select Color.

11. Click the cross to the right of one of the colors and select Make.

12. Click the cross to the right of one of the Makes and select Model. The decomposition tree should look something like the image in Figure 9-16.

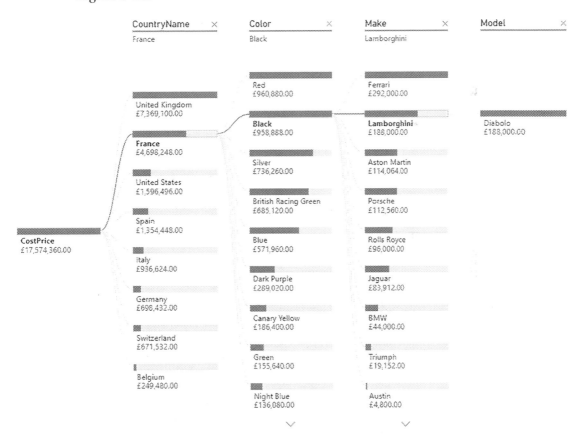

Figure 9-16. *A decomposition tree*

You can now see the path from the total cost price down through the country, color, and make to the models that are available. Clicking on *any* element in the dimensions (columns) will highlight a new path through the decomposition tree.

Formatting a Decomposition Tree

As you might expect, you can also format a decomposition tree to add extra pizzazz.

1. Select the decomposition tree that you just created and activate the Formatting pane.

2. In the Visual section, expand the Tree card and set

   a. The Primary color to dark blue (this indicates the drill-through path that you selected)

   b. The Deselected connectors color to light gray (this shows nonselected paths)

   c. The Connector shape to Round

   d. The Default action to Filter/highlight

3. Expand the Data bars card and choose a different color for the Positive Bar from the color palette.

4. Select a lighter color for the Bar background.

5. Set the Size to 85%.

6. Expand the Category Labels card and alter the Font family, size, and color.

7. Expand the Data Labels card and alter the Font family, size, and color. You could also alter the display units if you want.

8. Expand the Tree header card and set a Background color from the color palette, and then set Show subtitles to Off.

9. Add a border. The decomposition tree should look like the one shown in Figure 9-17.

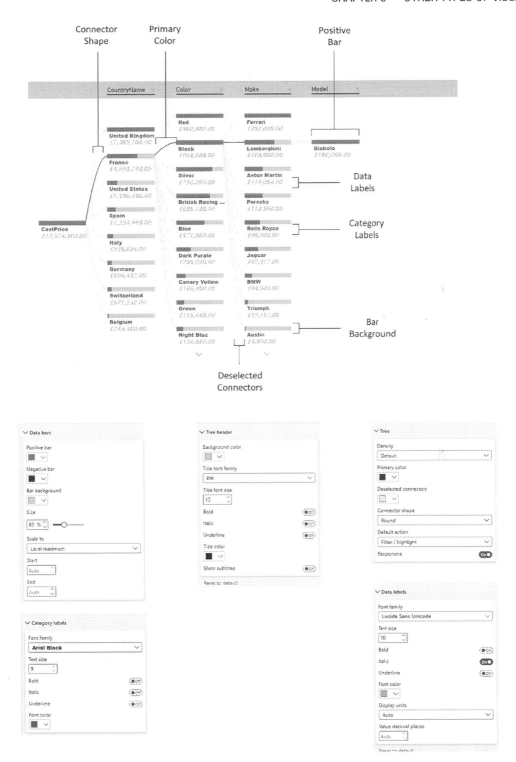

Figure 9-17. *A formatted decomposition tree*

Once a basic decomposition tree is set up, you can interact with it by clicking any element at any level to see, instantly, the composition of values at all the levels of the hierarchy that you have established.

There are several things that you need to know to get the best out of a decomposition tree:

- You can extend the hierarchy by adding further levels to the Explain By area at any time. These levels then appear in the pop-up menu.

- You remove a level from the hierarchy simply by clicking the cross at the top right of the element name. This does not remove the level from the Explain By area. In other words, you are altering the appearance—but not the underlying structure—of the visual.

- To alter the drill path down through the levels, simply remove any sublevels and then add them back in a different order.

- Clicking the lock icon in the level header temporarily locks the level and all levels to the left of the selected level. This avoids you removing it by mistake. Clicking a second time on the lock icon unlocks the level.

- Double-clicking on a value (say, the color Blue in this example) will hide all the sublevels. This allows you to rebuild a path down through the hierarchy in a few clicks.

- Selecting a node from the last level cross-filters the data in other visuals.

- The default action (for when you click on an element in a decomposition tree) can be to filter the data or to collapse the tree so that you can define a different path through the data.

- If there are too many elements at any level of the tree hierarchy, then you can scroll down vertically using the chevrons that appear at the bottom of the hierarchy.

Key Influencers Visual

The key influencers visual can be extremely useful when you want to examine the factors that influence a metric that you are analyzing and compare and contrast these factors. As with all visuals, it is probably easier to see it in action in order to understand it better.

1. Open the file CarSalesDataForReports.pbix.

2. Click the Key Influencers icon in the Visualizations pane.

3. Add the Weeks in Stock field (from the Stock table) to the Analyze area.

4. Add the following fields to the Explain By area:

   a. CostPrice

   b. TotalDiscount

   c. Mileage

5. With the key influencers visual selected, activate the Formatting pane.

6. Expand the Chart card and choose a different chart color.

7. Expand the reference line card and choose a different reference line color.

8. Expand the Bubble visual colors card and try out different color settings for the bubble visual (the elements on the left that explain the analysis of the data). The key influencers visual should look like the one shown in Figure 9-18.

Figure 9-18. *A key influencers visual*

You can now see which factors are considered to influence the time that a vehicle stays in stock.

There are, perhaps inevitably, several things that you need to know to use a key influencers visual efficiently:

- Clicking any of the influencers on the left of the visual shows the detail of the influencer in the chart on the right.

- You can select from the pop-up at the top of the visual whether to select influencers that potentially increase or decrease the element that you are analyzing.

- Clicking the Segments pane at the top of the visual switches to displaying a segmented population of the element that you are analyzing. You can see this in Figure 9-19.

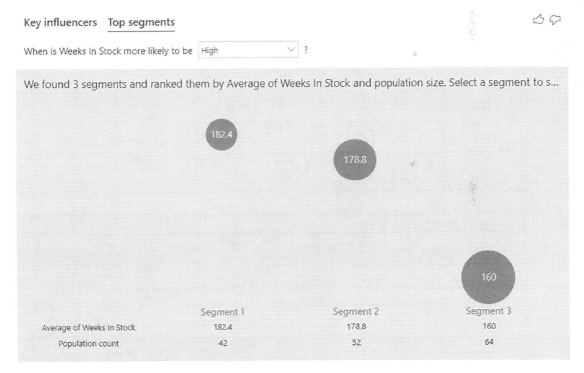

Figure 9-19. *Key influencers segments*

Paginated Reports

Paginated reports allow you to embed reports created with a separate Microsoft reporting technology—Reporting Services—inside Power BI dashboards.

Creating Reporting Services reports is a vast subject that has already been the subject of many books (including my book *Business Intelligence with SQL Server Reporting Services*—Apress 2015). So I cannot explain here all the details of Reporting Services report creation. However, if you are already acquainted with Reporting Services report creation, then you can leverage your skills to embed Reporting Services reports in Power BI dashboards.

Paginated reports are particularly useful if you need to export a complete, multipage list-style report. Such reports can print—or export—dozens of pages and hundreds or thousands of records. In the Power BI dashboard that contains a paginated report, you will only see a sample of the full output (as you do for a table). However, if you select Export from the paginated report toolbar, you can export the entire contents of the report to PDF, for example, and print the PDF file. Equally, if you select Open report from the paginated report toolbar, you can view the entire contents of the report in the Power BI Service.

To get an idea of what can be done, you will need to

1. Download the **Power BI Report Builder** (`www.microsoft.com/ en-us/download/details.aspx?id=58158`).

2. Upload the file PrestigeCarsDataForDashboards.pbix to the Power BI Service. This was explained in Chapter 1 if you need to revise the concept.

3. Open the Power BI Report Builder App and close the splash screen.

4. Right-click Data sources in the Report data pane on the left of Power BI Report Builder and select Add Power BI dataset connection.

5. Select the dataset in the dialog as shown in Figure 9-20. Of course, you will see only the datasets that you have loaded into your own Power BI workspace.

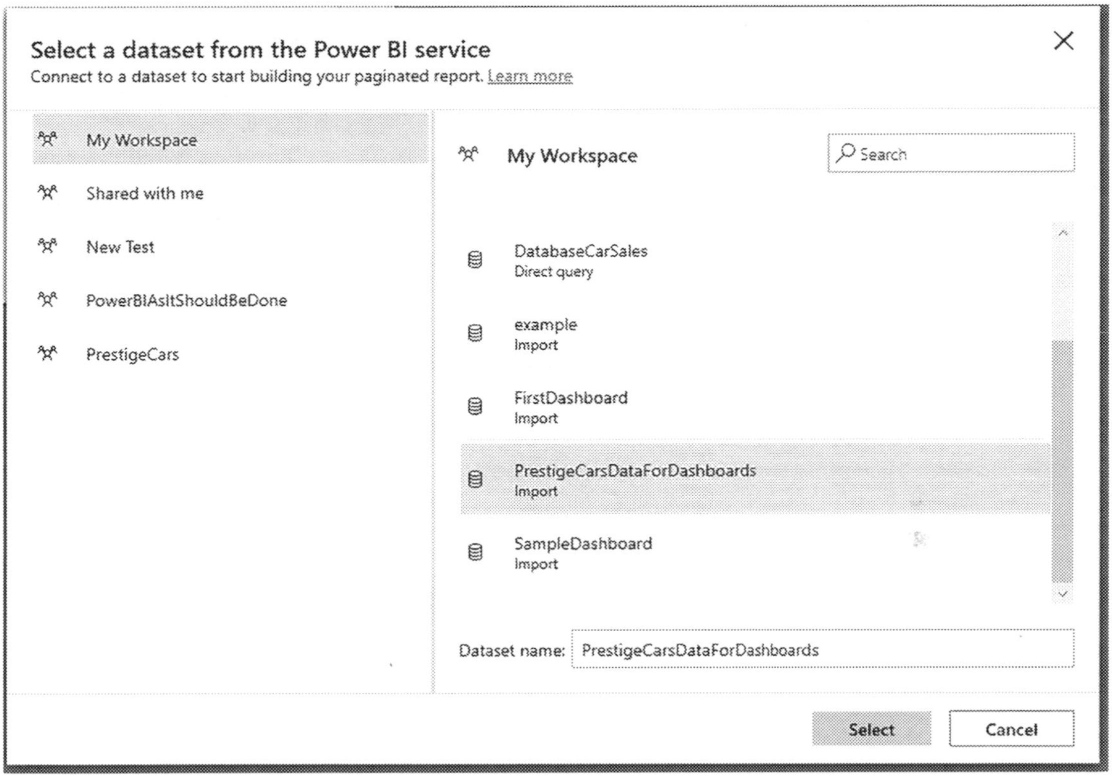

Select a dataset from the Power BI service   ✕

Connect to a dataset to start building your paginated report. Learn more

My Workspace		
Shared with me	
New Test	
PowerBIAsItShouldBeDone	
PrestigeCars	

My Workspace   🔍 Search

DatabaseCarSales
Direct query

example
Import

FirstDashboard
Import

PrestigeCarsDataForDashboards
Import

SampleDashboard
Import

Dataset name: PrestigeCarsDataForDashboards

                                                        Select   Cancel

Figure 9-20. *Connecting a paginated report to a Power BI dataset*

6. Click Select.

7. Right-click Datasets in the Report data pane on the left of Power BI
   Report Builder and select Add dataset.

8. Select the Data source that you created in step 5 from the Data
   source pop-up.

9. Enter the following DAX in the Query pane:

```
EVALUATE
SUMMARIZECOLUMNS
(
 Geography[CountryName]
,Geography[PostCode]
,Sales[DeliveryCharge]
)
```

10.   The dialog should look like the one in Figure 9-21.

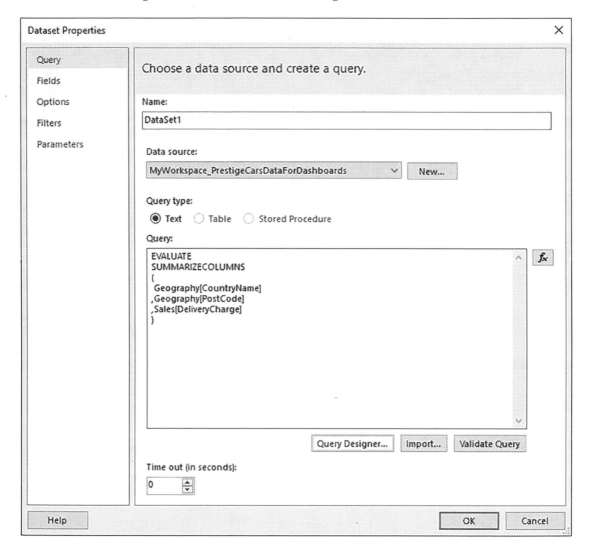

Figure 9-21. *A paginated report*

11.   Click OK.

12.   Switch to the Insert menu and click Table ➤ Insert Table.

13.   Click inside the report canvas to place the table.

14.   Click inside the table cell on the second row, first column, and
       then click the small table icon at the top right of the cell.

15. Select CountryName.

16. Add PostCode to the second column and DeliveryCharge to the third column. The Report Builder window will look like Figure 9-22.

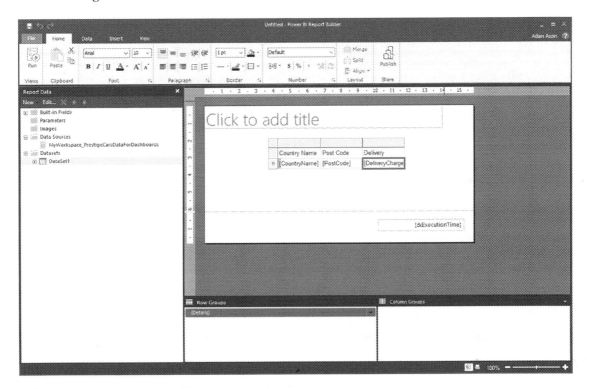

Figure 9-22. *A paginated report in Report Builder*

17. Save the Report Builder file. I suggest calling it PaginatedReport.

18. Click the Publish button in the Report Builder and select the Premium workspace that you wish to publish to.

19. Enter a file name (the name the paginated report will display in the Power BI Service).

20. Click OK. The paginated report is now finished. The dialog in Figure 9-23 will be displayed.

Publishing to Power BI
Success!
Open 'PaginatedReport' in Power BI
OK

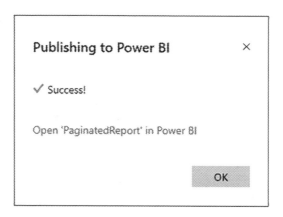

Figure 9-23. *Paginated report publishing successful*

21. Open a new, blank Power BI Desktop file.
22. Click Get data, and in the Power Platform section, select Power BI Datasets.
23. Connect to the Power BI dataset that you used in the paginated report.
24. Click the Paginated report icon in the Visualizations pane. An empty visual looking like the one shown in Figure 9-24 will appear.

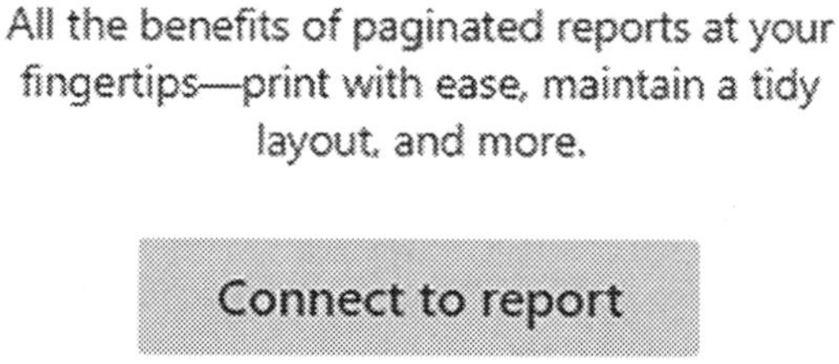

All the benefits of paginated reports at your fingertips—print with ease, maintain a tidy layout, and more.
Connect to report

Figure 9-24. *A paginated report in Report Builder*

25. Click Connect to report and select the report that you loaded previously. You will see all available paginated reports as shown in Figure 9-25.

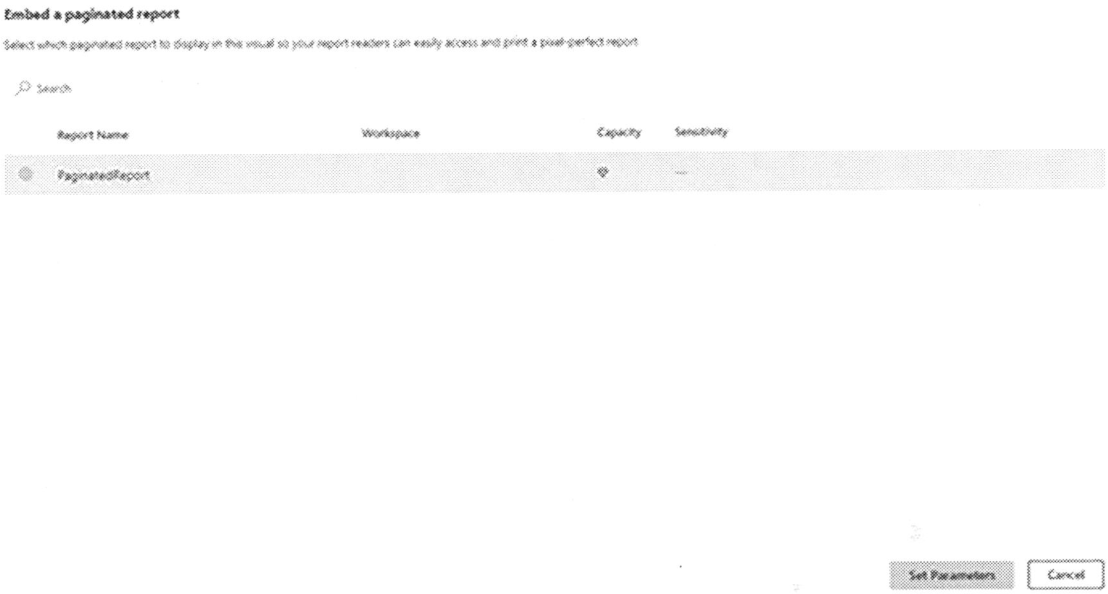

Embed a paginated report

Select which paginated report to display in the visual so your report readers can easily access and print a pixel-perfect report

🔍 Search

Report Name	Workspace	Capacity	Sensitivity
⚪ PaginatedReport		◈	—

Set Parameters   Cancel

Figure 9-25. *Available paginated reports in the Power BI Service*

26. The paginated reports visual will appear in Power BI Desktop and should look like the one shown in Figure 9-26.

Geography Country Name	Geography Post Code	Sales Delivery Charge
Germany		750
Belgium		750
Switzerland		750
France		750
Spain		750
Italy		750
United States	90009	750
United States	10001	750
United States	99301	750
Italy	120	750
Italy	129	750
Italy	175	750
Spain	8120	750
Spain	8400	750
Spain	8550	750
United Kingdom	B1 4BZ	750

Figure 9-26. *A paginated report in Power BI Desktop*

There are several points that you need to be aware of when adding paginated reports to Power BI Desktop:

- Paginated reports can contain parameters that filter the data in the report. Setting parameters would take us into the domain of complex paginated report development and so is outside the scope of this book. If you have set any parameters, you can link them to the Power BI dashboard file by clicking Set parameters in step 25.

- Paginated reports—unlike other Power BI visuals—will only be filtered on any fields that have been defined as paginated report parameters.

- You can choose not to display the paginated report toolbar at the top of the report visual by setting the Toolbar option to Off in the Formatting pane.

- Paginated reports can export the data they contain as Excel, CSV, PDF, PowerPoint, and Word documents. You can prevent this option being available to users by setting the Export toolbar option to Off in the Formatting pane.

- It can take some time to prepare a paginated report if it contains a lot of data. While paginated reports can be filtered on any parameters that they contain, you can choose not to have these parameters applied by setting the Auto-apply filters toolbar option to Off in the Formatting pane.

The sample files contain the paginated report file used in this section should you wish to use it. It is named PaginatedReport.rdl.

Conclusion

Over the course of five chapters, you have learned to apply a wide range of visuals that are built into Power BI Desktop which let you express the meaning hidden in your data. This chapter built on the previous chapters, by adding tree maps, gauges, R- and Python-based visuals to the mix, as well as decomposition trees and key influencers visuals.

To finish, you learned how to create paginated reports and embed these inside Power BI dashboards.

In the next chapter, you will see how to extend the already considerable range of visuals available "out of the box" with a selection of the extensive choice of third-party visuals that are currently available to download and use in Power BI Desktop.

CHAPTER 10

Third-Party Visuals

By now, you must surely have come to appreciate the sheer range of visual possibilities that Power BI Desktop has to offer. From a range of chart types to gauges, tables, cards, tree maps, and decomposition trees, it delivers a wealth of easy-to-use ways of delivering insight into your data clearly and effectively.

Yet Power BI Desktop does not stop with the built-in visualizations that you have seen so far. It has been designed to be a completely open and extensible business intelligence application that will allow third parties (and even Microsoft) to add other visuals. This means that the core elements that you have met so far are only a starting point. There are many other chart, text, and map visuals that you can add to Power BI Desktop in a few clicks—and then literally stun your audience with an eye-catching variety of dashboard elements.

As a freely extensible platform, Power BI Desktop also hosts a wide and growing variety of visuals developed by both Microsoft and third parties. This gallery of visual extensions is continually growing and incredibly easy to access and use. The final part of this chapter shows you some of the current visuals and how to find, add, and use them in your Power BI Desktop dashboards. This chapter will use the file C:\PowerBiDesktopSamples\ThirdPartyVisuals.pbix as the basis for the visuals that you will create.

Adding and using these enhancements is both quick and easy. This is because nearly all Power BI visualizations use the same interface and they are based on the underlying data model in exactly the same way. Consequently, learning to use a new visual will most likely only take a couple of minutes, as you are always building on the knowledge and techniques that you have already acquired.

Note You need to be aware that not all the custom visuals that are available are entirely bug-free. Also, they might not have all the formatting attributes or interactive capabilities available that you might wish for. However, this does

© Adam Aspin 2022
A. Aspin, *Pro Power BI Dashboard Creation*, https://doi.org/10.1007/978-1-4842-8227-4_10

not make them any less useful—or any less fun to use. In any case, we can reasonably expect them to be enhanced and improved over time.

The Power BI Visuals Gallery

The first thing to do is become acquainted with the Power BI visuals gallery. This is a central hub where you can find a range of free visuals, developed either by Microsoft or by third parties, that are ready to be added to your Power BI dashboards.

The following explains how to connect to the Power BI visuals gallery:

1. In the Insert ribbon, click the More visuals button and then select From AppSource in the pop-up menu. If you are not logged in to a Power BI account, you will see a dialog where you can log in.

2. Enter your password and sign in. You will see the dialog from Figure 10-1.

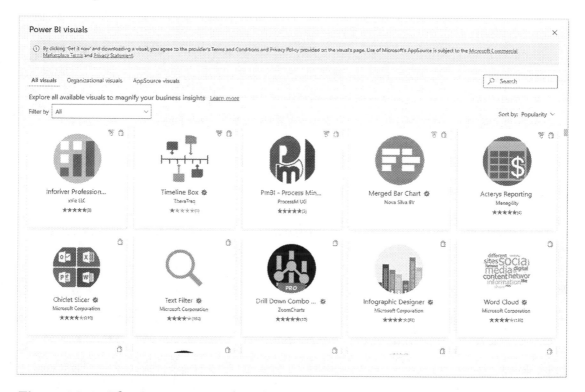

Figure 10-1. *The Custom Visuals gallery*

3. Click one of the visuals from among those available (you can search for a specific visual by entering a search term in the Search box or see them grouped and filtered by type if you click a type of visual on the left of the dialog). You will see a dialog like the one in Figure 10-2.

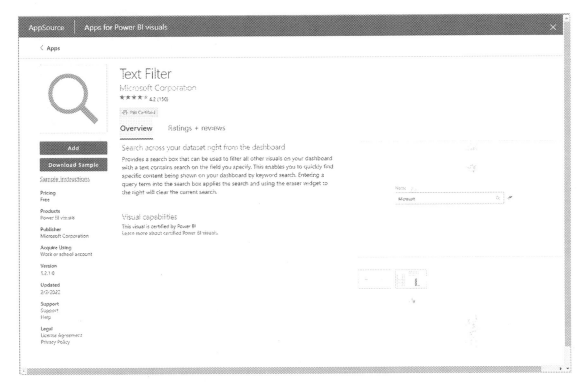

Figure 10-2. *Selecting a third-party visual*

4. Click Add. The visual will be added to the palette of available visualizations and the dialog that you can see in Figure 10-3 will be displayed.

Figure 10-3. *Confirmation dialog for visual import*

5. Click OK. The icon for the newly added visual will appear under the collection of built-in visuals in the Visualizations pane. You can now use the visual in the current Power BI Desktop report.

This selection of third-party visuals has undoubtedly evolved considerably since this book went to print, and so I imagine that what you are looking at now is very different. Hopefully, though, you should be excited to see lots of new and amazing types of data visualization that will allow you to add unparalleled pizzazz to your dashboards.

Loading Custom Visuals from Disk

Another way to access this treasure trove of extra presentation elements for your reports is to download them to your PC and then add them to Power BI Desktop as and when you need them. Here is how to do this:

1. In your web browser, navigate to `https://appsource.microsoft.com/en-us/marketplace/apps?product=power-bi-visuals`. You will see the Custom Visuals for Power BI web page. As things stand, it looks like Figure 10-4.

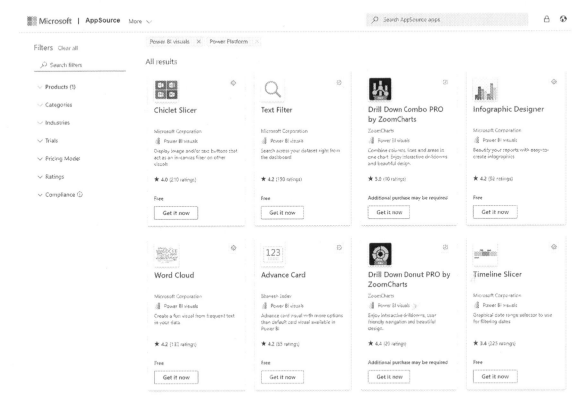

Figure 10-4. *The Custom Visuals for Power BI web page*

2. Click the Get it now button visual that you want to download. You may have to log in to AppSource. The visual will be downloaded. Depending on your browser (and any machine-specific configuration), it will be placed in a specific folder or give you the choice of a folder.

3. In Power BI Desktop, click More Visuals  From my files in the Insert ribbon. The Windows File Open dialog will appear.

4. Navigate to the folder where you downloaded the visual file in step 2. Click the visual file.

5. Click Open. The confirmation dialog will appear.

The icon for the visual will appear at the bottom of the visuals gallery in the Visualizations pane. You can then use this visual just like any other Power BI visual.

> **Tip**   Visuals are added as required to each individual Power BI Desktop file. So while you only download the visuals once, you have to load them into each Power BI Desktop (.pbix) file that you want to use them in. If you find yourself frequently using the same third-party visuals, you should create a Power BI Desktop file that contains all the visuals that you use, and then save it as a template for your future dashboard development. This is explained in Chapter 17.

Another way to import custom visuals that you have already downloaded is to click the ellipses in the gallery of visuals in the Visualizations pane. This will display a pop-up menu with the option to import visuals—either from the Power BI Store or from your collection of downloaded visuals.

Once you have added custom visuals to Power BI Desktop, you will see icons representing them in the Visualizations pane. As you can see in Figure 10-5, they are grouped underneath the built-in visuals.

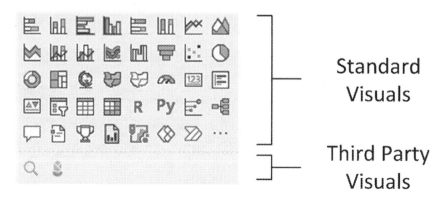

Figure 10-5. *Custom visuals in the Visualizations pane*

Removing Custom Visuals

If you wish to remove a third-party visual from the Visualizations pane:

1.   Click the ellipses in the gallery of visuals in the Visualizations pane.

2.   Select Remove a Visual. The dialog that you can see in Figure 10-6 will appear.

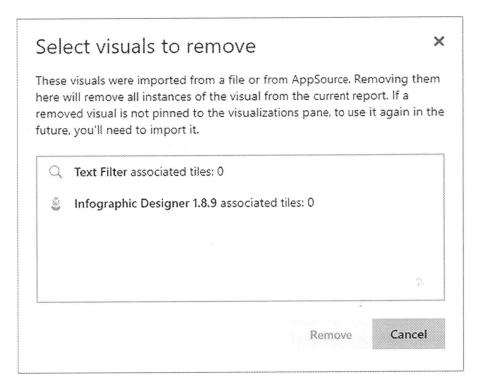

Figure 10-6. *Deleting a custom visual*

3. Select the visual(s) to remove from the current report. You can Ctrl-click several visuals in the dialog to select multiple visuals.

4. Click Remove. The dialog shown in Figure 10-7 will be displayed.

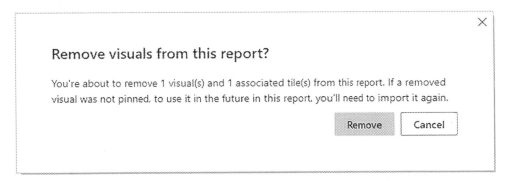

Figure 10-7. *The custom visuals delete dialog*

5. Click Yes, Delete.

Note   This will not remove any *files* that you have previously downloaded. You delete those as you would any standard file.

A Rapid Overview of a Selection of Custom Visuals

As the gallery of custom visuals is in a state of permanent flux, it is impossible to discuss all the currently available extensions to Power BI. However, to give you an idea of some of the possible enhancements that are available, the next few pages show *some* of the added visuals made available by Microsoft. Since there is no guarantee that these visuals will still be available in their current state by the time that you are reading this book, I do not explain how to create them, but merely show some examples of other chart types using the data available in the sample data that you have been using in this book.

In all the following examples, the visual title indicates the fields used to create the visual. Also, not all the makes are displayed in the visuals.

The file C:\PowerBiDesktopSamples\ThirdPartyVisuals.pbix contains all the visuals that you will see explained in the rest of this chapter.

Aster Plots

An *aster plot* is derived from the standard donut chart. However, it uses an extra data value to provide the "sweep" that you see in Figure 10-8.

SalePrice by Make

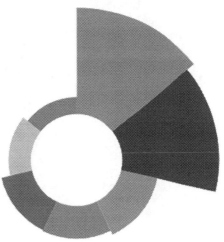

Figure 10-8. *An aster plot*

Radar Charts

Radar charts are often used in performance analyses to display metrics and how they compare. They allow you to show multiple values relative to a shared axis, as you can see in Figure 10-9.

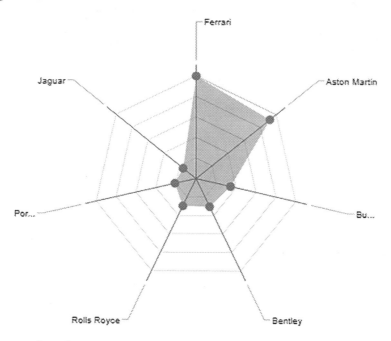

Figure 10-9. *A radar chart*

Bullet Charts

Bullet charts are extremely useful for tracking KPIs against targets. They frequently require you to add data that provides the thresholds against which performance is measured, either as absolute values or as percentages. However, they can be extremely effective at displaying how results compare to targets, as Figure 10-10 shows.

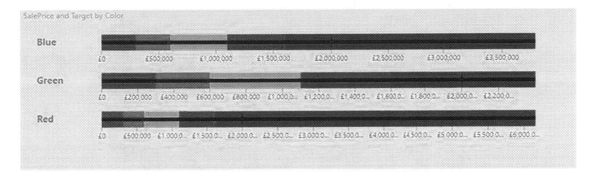

Figure 10-10. *A bullet chart*

Note   Be aware that a bullet chart can require you to extend and prepare the source data to add all the elements that this kind of chart requires—such as the various thresholds as well as minimum and maximum values.

Word Clouds

A *word cloud* shows the number of times that words in a dataset appear relative to each other. It can be a uniquely visual way to show relative weights of values, as you can see in Figure 10-11.

LaborCost by ClientName

Figure 10-11. *A word cloud*

Streamgraphs

A *streamgraph* is a smoothed, stacked, area chart. As you can see in Figure 10-12, a streamgraph is good at showing how values change over time.

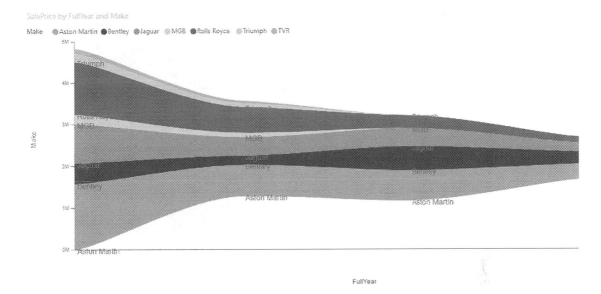

Figure 10-12. *A streamgraph*

Interestingly, a streamgraph has many more formatting options available than is the case for some other imported visuals.

Tornado Charts

A *tornado chart* is a variation of a bar chart; only the separation between two sets of values is made clearer by the vertical separation, as you can see in Figure 10-13. As was the case with bar charts, you can sort tornado charts by any of the data elements in the chart.

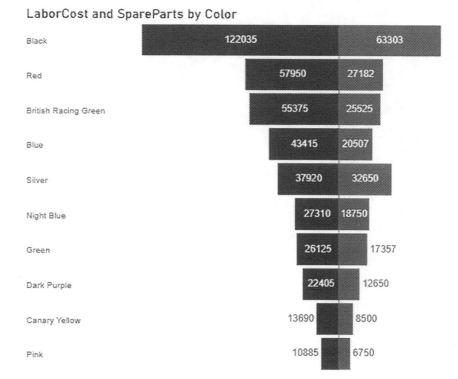

Figure 10-13. *A tornado chart*

Chord Charts

A *chord chart* is an interesting—and somewhat less traditional—way of displaying the relationship between values in a matrix structure. Figure 10-14 shows how colors and countries relate by sales.

SalePrice by CountryName and Color

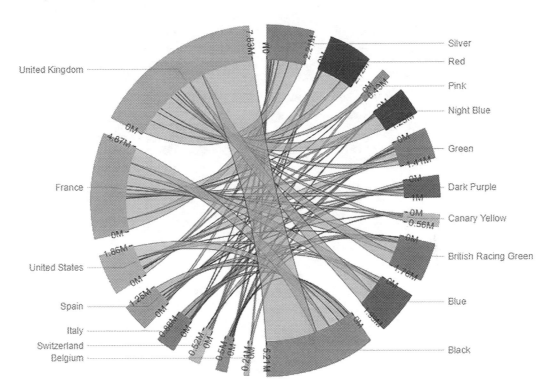

Figure 10-14. *A chord chart*

Sankey Diagrams

The *Sankey diagram* in Figure 10-15 also displays how colors and country sales relate.

SalePrice by CountryName and Color

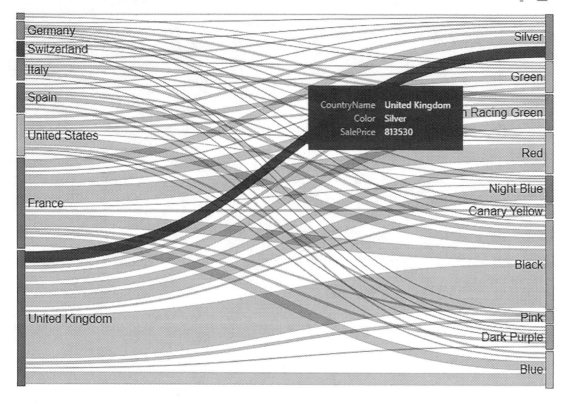

Figure 10-15. *A Sankey diagram*

Horizontal Bar Chart

The horizontal bar chart places the text for each bar inside the bars. This is essentially a space-saving technique. You can see this in Figure 10-16.

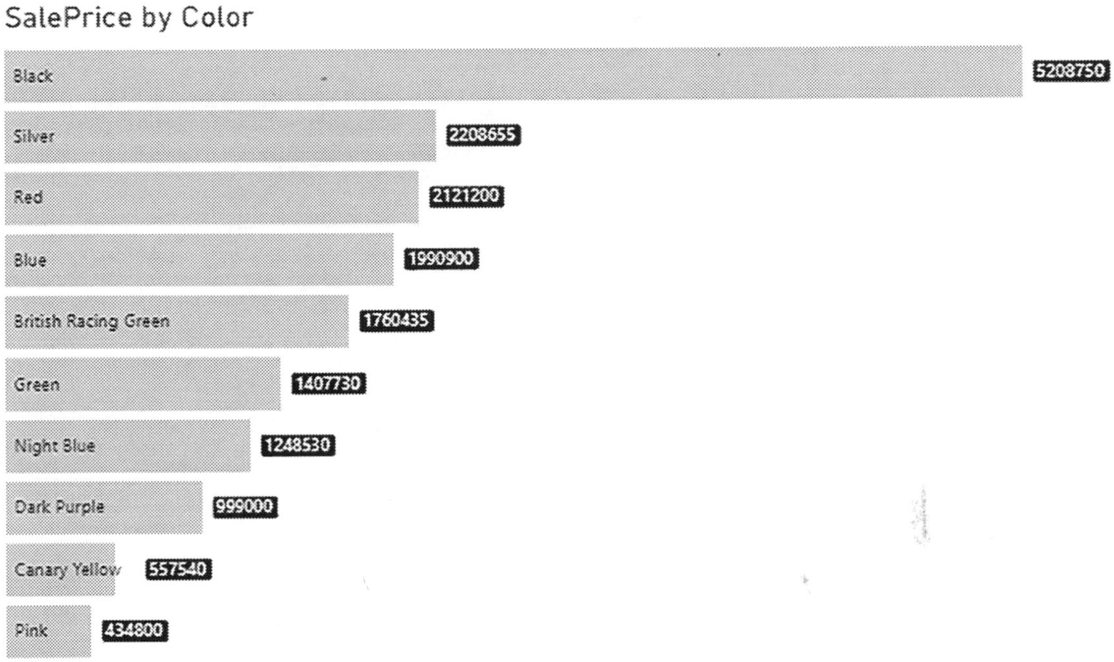

SalePrice by Color

Figure 10-16. *A horizontal bar chart*

It can also display lines, hammerheads, and lollipops.

Attribute Slicer

The attribute slicer displays lists of elements that you want to use to slice data. It is particularly useful when faced with long lists of potential slicer elements, as you can

- Search for the element(s) that interests you using the search bar—or, alternatively, click on a bar to remove it from the visual.

- See the actual values of each element when you hover over a bar.

You can see an example of this in Figure 10-17.

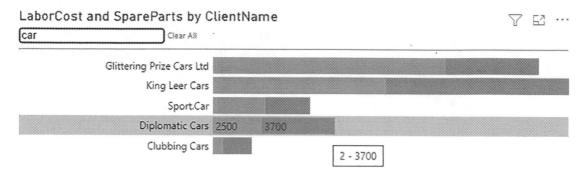

Figure 10-17. *An attribute slicer*

Histogram Chart

A histogram chart shows data grouped into bins and is an estimate of the probability distribution of a continuous variable. You can see an example of this in Figure 10-18.

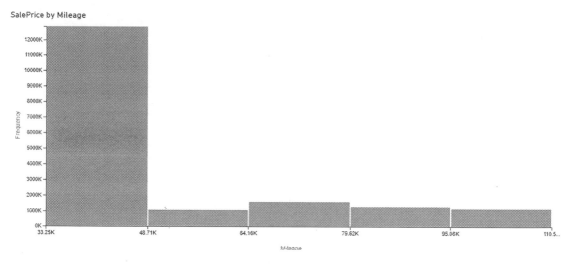

Figure 10-18. *A histogram chart*

Countdown Timer

The countdown shows the number of days, hours, minutes, and seconds in a "clock" that decrements in real time in any report. You can see an example in Figure 10-19.

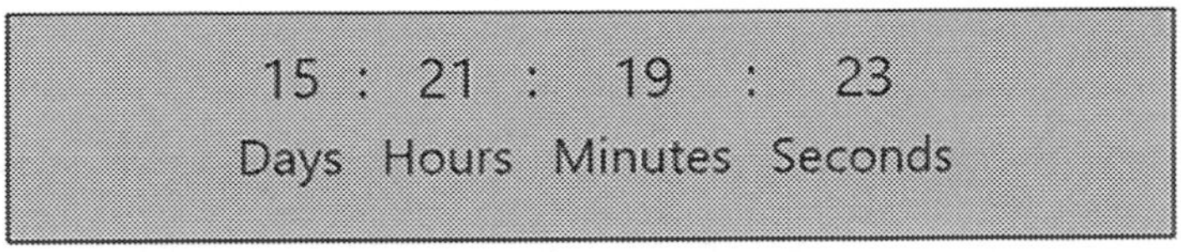

```
15  :  21  :  19  :  23
Days  Hours  Minutes  Seconds
```

Figure 10-19. *The countdown*

Infographic Designer

One addition to the collection of Microsoft-sourced third-party visuals that can set your dashboards apart from the crowd is the Infographic Designer. This visual allows you to create charts that use images for the chart elements. Moreover, it can layer multiple images to create extremely compelling infographics. The only initial drawback is that it uses a highly idiosyncratic interface that can take a while to master—and that is not at all intuitive, in my opinion. In any case, it is certainly worth a look.

1. Add the Infographic Designer to the Visualizations pane.

2. Add the following fields:

    a. Make to the Category area

    b. LaborCost to the Measure area

3. A fairly standard-looking column chart will appear.

4. Hover the pointer over the visual. The Edit Mark will appear top right. You can see an example in Figure 10-20.

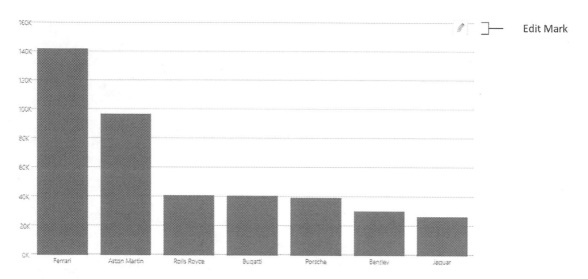

Figure 10-20. *Infographic Designer with Edit Mark*

5. Click the Edit Mark. The Mark Designer—which you can see in
    Figure 10-21—will appear. This is where you carry out virtually all
    your modifications to an infographic visual.

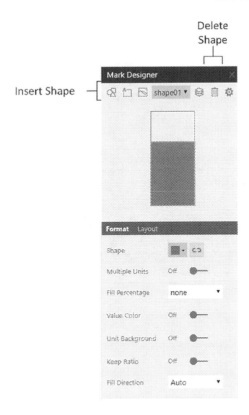

Figure 10-21. *Infographic Designer*

6. Click the Delete Element icon.

7. Click the Insert Shape icon and choose a shape type. I am selecting Transportation in this example.

8. Select a shape. I am selecting the Car shape in this example.

9. In the lower part of the Mark Designer, set Multiple Units to On. You can see an example of the output in Figure 10-22.

LaborCost by Make

Figure 10-22. *Infographic Designer output*

10.   Close the Mark Designer by clicking the cross at the top right.

You can redisplay the Mark Designer and continue formatting visuals simply by re-clicking the Edit Mark.

This is only the simplest of examples of what the Infographic Designer can deliver. You can add multiple shapes, change their colors, stretch or isolate them, and so much more. You can even create and add your own drawings. So, when you need a visual that breaks with the more traditional charts and tables that you are using, I suggest that you try it out. Just be aware that it requires a small investment in time to understand its myriad possibilities—and how its interface works.

Custom Slicers

There are also several excellent custom slicers available in the Microsoft App Store. I will introduce a few of these in Chapter 14.

Conclusion

In this chapter, just as you thought that it could not get any better, you discovered the jewel in the crown of Power BI Desktop: an extensive range of freely available extensions that you can add to your dashboards to deliver your insights in ways that leave other analytics tools in the dust. You have met some of the additional visuals that are available for download that let you express the trends hidden in your data, sometimes in surprisingly original ways.

You can now give free rein to your creativity and astound your audiences with a variety of ways of presenting your insights that will surely impress even the most jaded users.

CHAPTER 11

Drill down and Drill up

Delivering actionable analytics goes beyond just creating visuals. Interacting with the data in a dashboard can be a vital part of how users discover the salient information that the data may contain.

One fundamental way of analyzing data is to drill down into hierarchies of data to see how the data points that make up a visual are collated. This can help you to see "the wood for the trees" and to tease out the nuggets of vital information that a top-level view of the data may be concealing.

Drill down is built into the most standard Power BI Desktop visuals. These include matrices and most charts as well as certain other visuals such as tree maps.

For drill down to function correctly:

- The visual must be capable of being drilled into.

- The necessary levels of data must be created.

This chapter will introduce you to the use of drill down (which also covers drilling back up through the data). You will base the explanations in this chapter on a file called C:\PowerBiDesktopSamples\PrestigeCarsDataForDashboards.pbix. It is available on the Apress website as part of the downloadable material that accompanies this book.

Expanding and Drilling Down and Up

When creating a matrix in Chapter 4, you saw how to expand the matrix to include sublevels one at a time. However, Power BI Desktop offers a wide range of possibilities when it comes to navigating through layers of data in a matrix. These cover

- Displaying one or all sublevels of data in a hierarchy

- Displaying only a deeper level of data

- Drilling down to display only lower levels of a specific item

© Adam Aspin 2022
A. Aspin, *Pro Power BI Dashboard Creation*, https://doi.org/10.1007/978-1-4842-8227-4_11

- Drilling up to show the only previous level of a hierarchy

Navigating between levels of data is done using a combination of four interface elements:

- The Data/Drill ribbon

- The icons at the top of every matrix

- The context menu for a data element

- The +/- icons for each individual item in a level

It will probably help to get an overview of all of these before learning to move through levels of data.

The Data/Drill Ribbon

One important tool when drilling through hierarchical data is the Data/Drill ribbon. The buttons that this ribbon contains are shown in Figure 11-1 and explained in Table 11-1.

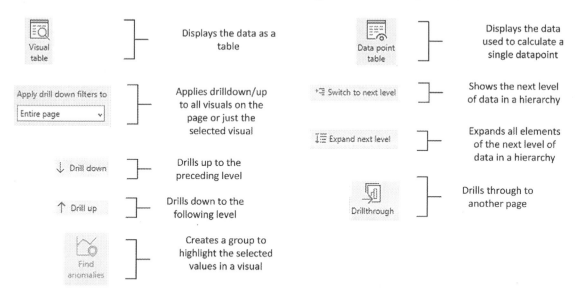

Figure 11-1. *The Data/Drill ribbon*

Table 11-1. *Data/Drill Ribbon Buttons*

Button	Description
Visual table	Displays the data as a table
Data point table	Displays the data used to calculate a single data point
Apply drill down filters	Chooses to drill down/up for a single visual or all the visuals on the page
Switch to next level	Displays the next level in the hierarchy
Expand next level	Expands the current level to show all next level elements
Drill up	Drills up one level
Drill down	Drills down one level
Drill-through	Drills through to a detail page
Find anomalies	Uses AI to find anomalies

The Drill Down and Up Icons

Any visual where drill down can be applied has a series of icons above the data. You can see these in Figure 11-2. I suggest that you familiarize yourself with these as they are fundamental when drilling through hierarchies of information. This applies not only to matrices but to most types of chart too.

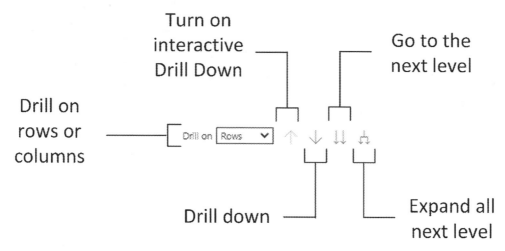

Figure 11-2. *The drill and expand icons for a matrix*

The Context Menu for Matrix Items

The final approach that you might need when navigating through hierarchies of data in matrices is the pop-up menu that appears when you right-click any row or column header in a matrix (that contains a hierarchy of data) or a data point in a chart. You can see this in Figure 11-3. The actual context menus vary slightly depending on the element you right-click on in a visual.

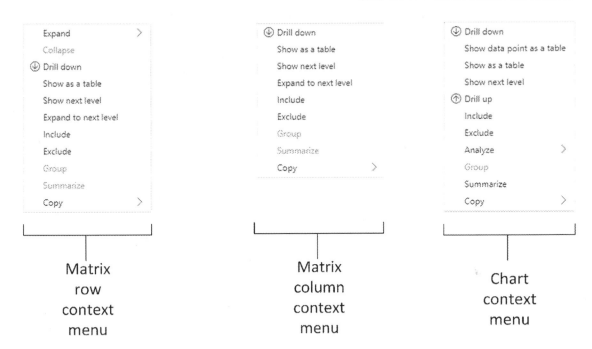

Figure 11-3. *The context menu for matrix items*

Matrix Drill down

Now that you have seen the various ways of invoking drill down, it is time to see how it is used in the real world. Let's begin with drill down applied to matrices. You will need a matrix to work on, and I suggest that you create a matrix (using the sample file C:\ PowerBiDesktopSamples\PrestigeCarsDataForDashboards.pbix) like this:

- *Rows*: Make and Model (in this order)

- *Columns*: CountryName and VehicleType (in this order)

- *Values*: SalePrice

The initial matrix should look like the one in Figure 11-4.

Make	Belgium	France	Germany	Italy	Spain	Switzerland	United Kingdom	United States	Total
Alfa Romeo	£23,000.00	£24,000.00	£17,550.00	£6,500.00	£5,690.00	£3,575.00	£111,245.00	£51,950.00	**£243,510.00**
Aston Martin	£211,500.00	£558,080.00	£206,000.00	£371,990.00	£156,050.00	£228,150.00	£2,653,965.00	£717,020.00	**£5,102,755.00**
Austin		£6,000.00	£23,600.00				£32,400.00	£2,500.00	**£64,500.00**
Bentley		£361,500.00	£165,390.00		£179,450.00	£112,250.00	£689,000.00	£181,650.00	**£1,689,240.00**
BMW		£55,000.00					£5,500.00		**£60,500.00**
Bugatti		£930,500.00					£985,000.00		**£1,915,500.00**
Citroen		£30,500.00			£65,890.00	£2,350.00	£2,340.00		**£101,080.00**
Delahaye		£25,500.00		£12,500.00	£29,500.00		£39,500.00		**£107,000.00**
Delorean							£99,500.00		**£99,500.00**
Ferrari		£1,750,450.00	£99,500.00	£330,000.00	£601,500.00		£2,154,900.00	£604,500.00	**£5,540,850.00**
Jaguar		£335,715.00		£79,500.00			£347,740.00	£120,000.00	**£882,955.00**
Lagonda							£218,000.00		**£218,000.00**
Lamborghini		£404,500.00	£330,000.00	£245,000.00	£145,000.00	£220,500.00	£382,150.00		**£1,727,150.00**
McLaren		£295,000.00							**£295,000.00**
Mercedes		£134,225.00			£56,890.00	£22,500.00	£195,400.00	£62,100.00	**£471,115.00**
Morgan							£18,500.00		**£18,500.00**
Noble	£29,500.00				£45,950.00		£131,450.00		**£206,900.00**
Peugeot	£4,900.00	£3,200.00		£1,250.00		£2,350.00	£9,345.00		**£21,045.00**
Porsche		£380,850.00	£31,000.00		£198,340.00	£17,850.00	£482,800.00	£58,400.00	**£1,169,240.00**
Reliant							£1,900.00		**£1,900.00**
Rolls Royce		£554,950.00		£99,500.00	£119,600.00	£165,000.00	£515,450.00	£182,500.00	**£1,637,000.00**
Trabant							£8,440.00		**£8,440.00**
Triumph	£42,950.00	£32,840.00		£24,540.00	£89,200.00	£64,890.00	£126,850.00	£15,000.00	**£396,270.00**
Total	£311,850.00	£5,882,810.00	£873,040.00	£1,170,780.00	£1,693,060.00	£839,415.00	£9,211,375.00	£1,995,620.00	**£21,977,950.00**

Figure 11-4. *A matrix ready for drill down*

Expand All Levels

In Chapter 4, you saw how to expand and collapse a single row at a single level using the +/- icons in a multilevel matrix. However, it can become laborious (to say the least) if you need to do this for more than a couple of rows. So Power BI Desktop provides the option to expand down all the elements of the next level in a row hierarchy.

1. Select the matrix with three levels of data displayed that you can see in Figure 11-4.

2. Click the Expand down one level in the hierarchy icon. You should see the matrix looking like the one in Figure 11-5.

Make	Belgium	France	Germany	Italy	Spain	Switzerland	United Kingdom	United States	Total
⊟ Alfa Romeo	£23,000.00	£24,000.00	£17,550.00	£6,500.00	£5,690.00	£3,575.00	£111,245.00	£51,950.00	£243,510.00
1750		£9,950.00				£3,575.00			£13,525.00
Giulia	£10,500.00	£2,550.00	£6,000.00				£58,145.00	£12,500.00	£89,695.00
Giulietta			£11,550.00	£6,500.00	£5,690.00		£29,000.00	£39,450.00	£92,190.00
Spider	£12,500.00	£11,500.00					£24,100.00		£48,100.00
⊟ Aston Martin	£211,500.00	£558,080.00	£206,000.00	£371,990.00	£156,050.00	£228,150.00	£2,653,965.00	£717,020.00	£5,102,755.00
DB2		£45,000.00		£61,500.00	£52,500.00		£247,940.00	£49,500.00	£456,440.00
DB4		£36,500.00		£59,400.00			£185,800.00		£281,700.00
DB5		£69,500.00		£45,000.00			£149,340.00	£36,500.00	£300,340.00
DB6		£196,080.00		£82,590.00	£45,950.00		£580,885.00	£113,590.00	£1,019,095.00
DB9		£134,000.00	£99,500.00			£124,500.00	£309,650.00	£291,850.00	£959,500.00
Rapide	£86,500.00		£61,500.00				£154,500.00		£302,500.00
Vanquish		£122,000.00			£57,600.00		£124,450.00	£56,990.00	£361,040.00
Vantage	£125,000.00						£218,500.00		£343,500.00
Virage				£123,500.00		£103,650.00	£682,900.00	£168,590.00	£1,078,640.00
Total	£311,850.00	£5,882,810.00	£873,040.00	£1,170,780.00	£1,693,060.00	£839,415.00	£9,211,375.00	£1,995,620.00	£21,977,950.00

Figure 11-5. *A matrix with the second level of data expanded*

The other ways of expanding an entire level are

- In the Data/Drill ribbon, click Expand next level.

- Right-click any row header and select Expand to next level.

- Right-click any row header and select Expand  Entire level.

Displaying Data at the Previous Level

What if you are currently showing, say, two levels of a data hierarchy and want to return to displaying only the top level? This is also known as collapsing a level of data.

1. Select the matrix with three levels of data displayed that you can see in Figure 11-5.

2. Click the Drill Up icon at the top right of the matrix.

The matrix will show only two levels of data and look, once again, like the image in Figure 11-4.

The other ways of collapsing an entire level are

- In the Data/Drill ribbon, click Drill Up.

- Right-click any row header and select Drill Up.

Displaying Data for a Sublevel

A matrix does not oblige you to display all levels of data at once. You can, if you prefer, display only the data for a lower level of the matrix hierarchy, as follows:

1. Select or re-create the matrix that you began with in Figure 11-5, showing only the top-level data.

2. Click the "Go to the Next Level in the Hierarchy" icon at the top of the matrix (alternatively, in the Data/Drill ribbon, click Switch to next level). Only the second level of data (model information) will be displayed in the matrix. You can see an example of this in Figure 11-6.

Model	Coupe	Saloon	Total
135		£25,500.00	£25,500.00
145		£69,000.00	£69,000.00
175		£12,500.00	£12,500.00
1750		£13,525.00	£13,525.00
203		£3,200.00	£3,200.00
205	£950.00	£3,950.00	£4,900.00
250SL		£35,550.00	£35,550.00
280SL		£270,290.00	£270,290.00
350SL	£66,275.00	£23,500.00	£89,775.00
355	£500,450.00	£691,000.00	£1,191,450.00
360	£135,000.00	£228,000.00	£363,000.00
400GT		£145,000.00	£145,000.00
404		£12,945.00	£12,945.00
500	£2,500.00	£1,150.00	£3,650.00
500SL		£75,500.00	£75,500.00
Total	£2,370,985.00	£19,606,965.00	£21,977,950.00

Figure 11-6. *Displaying a different level of data from a matrix*

As you can see, the totals are identical. Only the data segmentation has changed.

To return to the previous level in the data hierarchy, simply click the Drill Up button in the Data/Drill ribbon—or the Drill Up icon at the top left of the matrix.

As an alternative to using the "Go to the Next Level in the Hierarchy" icon, you can click Switch to next level in the Data/Drill ribbon.

Drilling Down at Row Level

Another completely different option when navigating hierarchies of data is to drill up and down into a *specific element* of a hierarchy. The key difference between expanding and drilling is as follows:

- Expanding a hierarchy will display the next level of data for *all* top-level elements.

- Drilling down will only display the next sublevel for the *selected* data element.

To see this in practice, try the following:

1. Right-click any top-level data element in a matrix (I will take Aston Martin in the matrix that you can see in Figure 11-4).

2. Select Drill Down from the context menu. The matrix will now look like the one in Figure 11-7.

Make	Coupe	Saloon	Total
⊟ **Aston Martin**	**£830,850.00**	**£4,271,905.00**	**£5,102,755.00**
DB2	£107,450.00	£348,990.00	**£456,440.00**
DB4	£29,500.00	£252,200.00	**£281,700.00**
DB5		£300,340.00	**£300,340.00**
DB6	£170,000.00	£849,095.00	**£1,019,095.00**
DB9	£269,900.00	£689,600.00	**£959,500.00**
Rapide		£302,500.00	**£302,500.00**
Vanquish	£12,500.00	£348,540.00	**£361,040.00**
Vantage	£169,000.00	£174,500.00	**£343,500.00**
Virage	£72,500.00	£1,006,140.00	**£1,078,640.00**
Total	**£830,850.00**	**£4,271,905.00**	**£5,102,755.00**

Figure 11-7. *Drilling down in a matrix*

If the matrix contains further levels of a hierarchy, you can continue to drill down into further levels of data simply by right-clicking any data element at the second level and selecting Drill Down from the context menu.

To return to a previous level, all you have to do is click the Drill Up button in the Data/Drill ribbon—or the Drill Up icon at the top left of the matrix. Alternatively, you can right-click a data item and select Drill Up from the context menu.

Drill Down Using Click-Through

If you find it a little wearing to right-click and select the Drill Down option, then you have an alternative solution. You can switch a matrix to drill down with a simple click on a data item. Here is how you can do this:

1.   At the top right of a matrix, click the "Click to turn on drill down" icon. This will become a light arrow on a dark background.

2.   Click any data element (a country, for instance). You will drill down to the next level.

You can turn off this option at any time by re-clicking the "Click to turn on drill down" icon. It will return to being a dark arrow on a clear background, indicating that this form of drill down is deactivated.

Drilling Down at Column Level

The same drill down and drill up logic applies to columns as to rows.

1.   Take the column matrix that you created previously (and that you can see in Figure 11-4). This contains the Drill on icon at the top right of the matrix.

2.   Click the Drill on pop-up and select Columns.

3.   Click the "Expand All Down One Level in the Hierarchy" icon. You will see something like Figure 11-8, where the vehicle type has appeared under Country in the column header.

CountryName Make	Belgium Coupe	Saloon	Total	France Coupe	Saloon	Total
⊟ Alfa Romeo		£23,000.00	**£23,000.00**		£24,000.00	**£24,000.00**
⊟ Aston Martin		£211,500.00	**£211,500.00**	£102,000.00	£456,080.00	**£558,080.00**
⊟ Austin					£6,000.00	**£6,000.00**
⊟ Bentley					£361,500.00	**£361,500.00**
⊟ BMW					£55,000.00	**£55,000.00**
⊟ Bugatti					£930,500.00	**£930,500.00**
⊟ Citroen					£30,500.00	**£30,500.00**
⊟ Delahaye					£25,500.00	**£25,500.00**
⊟ Delorean						
⊟ Ferrari					£1,750,450.00	**£1,750,450.00**
⊟ Jaguar				£94,990.00	£240,725.00	**£335,715.00**
⊟ Lagonda						
⊟ Lamborghini					£404,500.00	**£404,500.00**

Figure 11-8. *Drilling down in a multilevel column hierarchy*

As you can see, a hierarchy can be applied equally to columns and rows. This boils down to

- Adding the field to the correct area in the Build tab of the Visualizations pane (Rows or Columns)

- Selecting the appropriate drill down mode from the pop-up at the top of the matrix (Columns or Rows)

Including and Excluding Matrix Elements

Some matrices can swamp you in data. So you might need to focus on a few selected elements. This is really simple in Power BI Desktop:

1. Re-create the matrix from Figure 11-4.

2. Click the "Expand All Down One Level in the Hierarchy" icon to see the complete hierarchy of makes and models.

3. Ctrl-click any element (make, model, or a value) for

    a. Alfa Romeo Giulia

    b. Aston Martin DB4

    c. Aston Martin DB9

4. Right-click one of the selected elements and select Include from
    the pop-up menu. All other elements will be removed from the
    matrix. The result is shown in Figure 11-9.

Make	Belgium	France	Germany	Italy	Switzerland	United Kingdom	United States	Total
⊟ Alfa Romeo	£10,500.00	£2,550.00	£6,000.00			£58,145.00	£12,500.00	£89,695.00
Giulia	£10,500.00	£2,550.00	£6,000.00			£58,145.00	£12,500.00	£89,695.00
⊟ Aston Martin		£170,500.00	£99,500.00	£59,400.00	£124,500.00	£495,450.00	£291,850.00	£1,241,200.00
DB4		£36,500.00		£59,400.00		£185,800.00		£281,700.00
DB9		£134,000.00	£99,500.00		£124,500.00	£309,650.00	£291,850.00	£959,500.00
Total	£10,500.00	£173,050.00	£105,500.00	£59,400.00	£124,500.00	£553,595.00	£304,350.00	£1,330,895.00

Figure 11-9. *Including selected elements from a matrix*

Note   As an alternative to including certain elements, you can select all the
elements that you wish to *exclude*, and choose Exclude from the pop-up menu.

To reset the matrix to its original state:

1. Expand the Filters pane.

2. Click the Remove filter icon for the Included filter. You can see this
    in Figure 11-10.

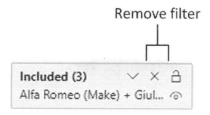

Figure 11-10. *Removing the Included filter to reset a matrix*

Note   Filters are explained in detail in Chapter 13.

Drilling into and Expanding Chart Data Hierarchies

An extremely useful aspect of Power BI Desktop charts is that you can use them as an interactive presentation tool. One of the more effective ways to both discover what your data reveals and deliver the message to your public is to drill into, or expand, layers of data. All the standard Power BI chart types let you do just this.

Drill down works with all the standard chart types. This means that you can drill into

- Stacked bar charts

- Stacked column charts

- Clustered bar charts

- Clustered column charts

- 100% stacked bar charts

- 100% stacked column charts

- Line charts

- Area charts

- Stacked area charts

- Line and stacked column charts

- Line and clustered column charts

- Waterfall charts

- Scatter charts

- Bubble charts

- Pie charts

- Funnel charts

- Donut charts

- Tree map charts

The key point to remember when you are creating drill down charts is that you *must* place the fields that you wish to drill into in the *Axis* area (the Shared Axis area for dual-axis charts) of the field area, *not* in the Legend area (and not in the Details area for a pie chart).

Drill Down

Fortunately, you use the same techniques that you saw previously in this chapter when navigating data hierarchies to drill down into charts. So extending this approach from tables and matrices to charts is really easy. Here, then, is a simple example of how you can analyze the hierarchy of makes, models, and colors of vehicles sold in a drill down chart:

1. Click the Clustered Column Chart icon in the Visualizations pane. An empty chart visual will be created on the dashboard canvas.

2. Drag the following fields into the Axis area of the field area in this order:

   a. Make (from the Vehicle table)

   b. Model (from the Vehicle table)

   c. Color (from the Vehicle table)

3. Drag the SalePrice (from the Sales table) and the CostPrice (from the Sales table) fields onto the chart. The chart will look like the one in Figure 11-11. As you can see, it only displays the top-level element from the Axis field area—the *make* of vehicle.

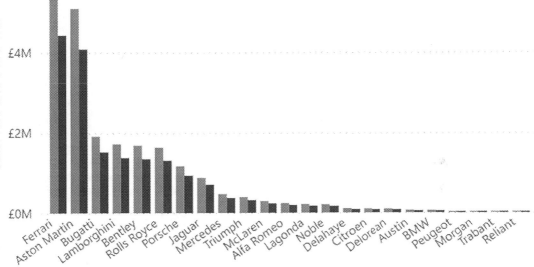

Figure 11-11. A column chart displaying the top level of data in a hierarchy

4.   Click the Turn on Drill Down icon at the top right of the chart. This icon will become a white arrow on a dark background.

5.   Click either of the columns for Ferrari. The chart will now display the models of Ferrari sold, as you can see in Figure 11-12.

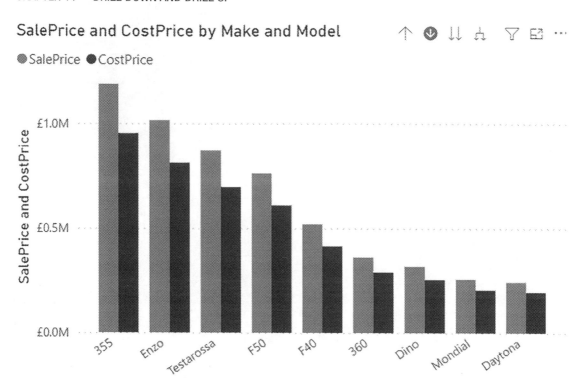

Figure 11-12. *A column chart displaying the second level of data in a hierarchy*

6. Click on one of the columns for F50. The chart will now display
    the colors of Ferrari F50 sold. Once you have drilled down to a
    lower level in a chart, you can always return to the previous level
    (and from there continue drilling up until you reach the top level)
    by clicking the Drill Up icon at the top right of the chart.

Expand All Down One Level in the Hierarchy

The "Expand All Down One Level in the Hierarchy" icon produces a different result
to drilling down by clicking a bar in the chart. If you click the "Expand All Down One
Level in the Hierarchy" icon, you see *all* the elements at the next level down, not just the
elements in the hierarchy that are a subgroup. To see this, try out the following steps:

1. Re-create the chart from the previous section (follow steps 1 through 3) until you can once again see the chart from Figure 11-11.

2. Click the "Expand All Down One Level in the Hierarchy" icon.

3. Resize the chart to enhance its visibility. You will see a chart that looks like the one shown in Figure 11-13.

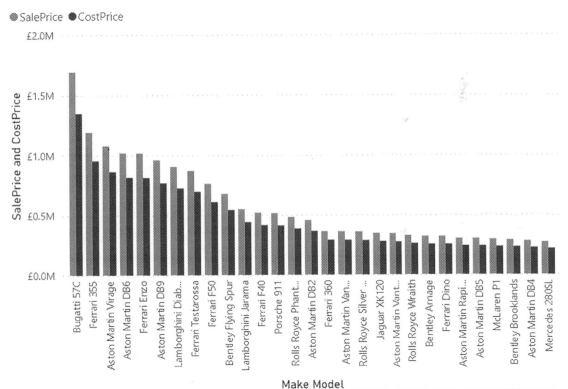

Figure 11-13. *Expanding a chart down one level*

4. Click the "Expand All Down One Level in the Hierarchy" icon a second time.

5. Resize the chart if necessary, as there will now be one column for each combination of make, model, and color.

Note   You can use any of the techniques that you previously applied to matrices to drill down and up in chart data. So you can right-click and select drill down options from the context menu or apply any of the options in the Data/Drill menu if you prefer.

Go to the Next Level in the Hierarchy

The final hierarchy navigation technique that you can apply is to Go to the Next Level in the Hierarchy. To test this, try out the following steps:

1. Re-create the chart from Figure 11-11.

2. Click the "Go to the Next Level in the Hierarchy" icon.

3. Resize the chart to enhance its visibility. You should see a chart like the one shown in Figure 11-14.

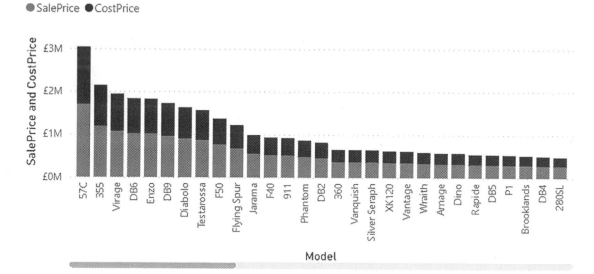

Figure 11-14. *Going to the next level in a chart*

4. Click the "Go to the Next Level in the Hierarchy" icon one more time. You will see a chart of vehicle colors. To resume, the three options that you can use to navigate a chart hierarchy are

- *Drill Down*: This will only show the data at the next level for the *specific element* that you clicked.

- *Expand All Down One Level in the Hierarchy*: This will show the data at the next level for *all* elements.

- *Go to the Next Level in the Hierarchy*: This will display data *only for the lower level* in the data hierarchy.

Note   Whichever technique you used to display a lower level of data, you can always go up to the previous level by clicking the Drill Up icon.

Including and Excluding Data Points in Charts

You saw earlier in this chapter that you can include and exclude records from a matrix. Well, you can apply this technique to charts as well. This can help you to remove clutter, discard outliers, or simply focus on a selected set of data points. Here's an example of how to exclude data points:

1. Create a clustered column chart using the following data elements:

    a. *Axis*: Make (from the Vehicle table)

    b. *Legend*: Model (from the Vehicle table)

    c. *Value*: SalePrice (from the Sales table)

2. Ctrl-click to select the four tallest columns.

3. Right-click any of the selected columns and choose Include from the pop-up menu. The chart will look like the one shown in Figure 11-15.

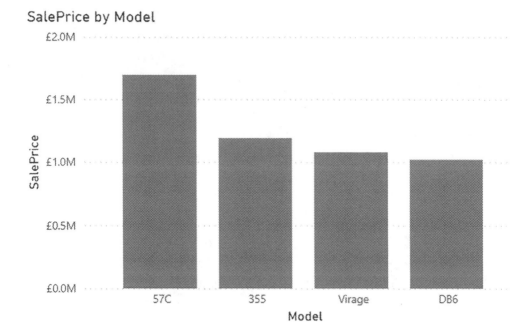

SalePrice by Model

Figure 11-15. *A column chart after including data points*

The remaining data is exactly the same as before, but removing the very tall columns allows you to see more clearly any differences among the remaining data elements.

Note   To revert to displaying all the source data points, you need to display the Filters pane and delete the "Included" filter.

Drill Down and Tree Maps

The same drill down and expand lower-level logic that you have already seen for matrices, charts, and maps also applies to tree maps. As you are used to the concept by now, I will only show a short example of drill down using a tree map:

1. Create a tree map by placing the Make and Model fields (in this order) in the Group area. Add SalePrice to the Values area. The Field Area and the tree map will look like those shown in Figure 11-16. You can see that the sale price by model is no longer visible.

SalePrice by Make

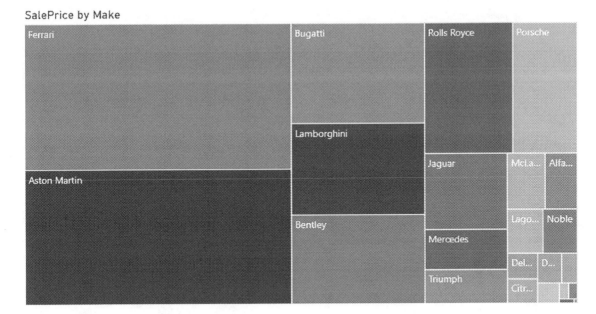

Figure 11-16. *Drilling down into a tree map visual*

2. Activate Drill down by clicking the "Click to turn on drill down" icon at the top right of the visual.

3. Click on Aston Martin. You will drill down to the next level (color), and the visual will look like the one shown in Figure 11-17.

SalePrice by Make and Model

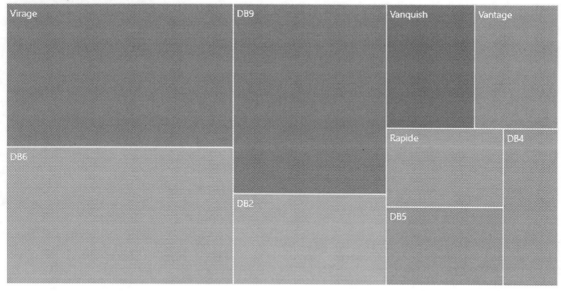

Figure 11-17. *Drilling down into a tree map visual*

Conclusion

This chapter introduced you to data drill down in Power BI visuals. You saw how to delve deep into layers of data (which are, in fact, hierarchies that you define) in order to tease out information and discover meaning as well as highlighting potential anomalies that may not be immediately visible at first sight.

CHAPTER 12

Maps in Power BI Desktop

Another powerful technique that you can use to both analyze and present your insights is to display the data in map form. All that this requires is that your source data contains information that can be used for geographical representation. So if you have country, state, town, postal (or ZIP) code, or even better latitude and longitude in the dataset, then you can get Power BI Desktop to add a map to your report and show the selected data using the map as a background.

Better yet, a Power BI Desktop map behaves just like any other visual. This means that you can filter the data that is displayed in a map, as well as highlighting it, just as you can do for charts, tables, and matrices. Not only that, but a map is an integral part of a Power BI Desktop report. So if you highlight data in a chart, a map in the same report will be cross-filtered. However, you will have to wait for Chapter 14 to discover about cross-filtering.

Power BI Desktop provides you with four types of map visuals:

- Maps
- Filled maps
- Shape maps
- ArcGIS maps

The first three map types are simple and expressive. The fourth type (ArcGIS maps) requires a little more effort to master, but is capable of delivering some truly stunning output. However, it can require additional licensing costs.

The aim of this chapter is to show you some of the ways in which you can add real spice to your reports by using maps. Then, when presenting your analyses, you can interact with the maps and *really* impress your audience.

This chapter will use the file C:\PowerBiDesktopSamples\ PrestigeCarsDataForDashboards.pbix as the basis for the visuals that you will create.

© Adam Aspin 2022
A. Aspin, *Pro Power BI Dashboard Creation*, https://doi.org/10.1007/978-1-4842-8227-4_12

Working with Bing Maps

Before adding the first map, I want to explain how mapping works in Power BI Desktop. The geographical component is based on Bing Maps. So, in order to add a map, you need to be able to connect to the Internet and use the Bing Maps service. Secondly, the underlying dataset must contain fields that are recognized by Bing Maps as geographical data. In other words, you need country, state, town, or other information that Bing Maps can use to generate the plot of the map. Fortunately, Power BI Desktop will indicate if it recognizes a field as containing data that it can use (hopefully) to create a map, as it will display a tiny icon of a globe in the field area for every field in the underlying dataset that apparently contains geographical data.

To avoid the risk of misinterpreting data, you can add metadata to the underlying data model, which defines geographical field types. By applying data categories to fields, Power BI Desktop maps will then use these categories to interpret geographical data for mapping. Preparing data so that any fields used by Bing Maps are not only recognizable as containing geographical data, but also uniquely recognizable, is vital. You must help Bing Maps so that if you are mapping data for a city named Paris, Bing can see whether you mean Paris, France, or Paris, Texas. The companion volume *Pro DAX and Data Modeling in Power BI* explains some of the ways in which you can prepare your data for use by Bing Maps, and consequently, use it to enable map visuals in Power BI Desktop.

Note   There are some areas of the world that cannot use Bing Maps. So if you attempt to use Power BI Desktop mapping in these geographical zones, you will not see any map appear when you attempt to create a map.

Creating Maps in Power BI Desktop

Let's begin by creating a map of Sales by Country. Fortunately, the sample dataset contains the country where the sale was made. This means that we can use this data to make Power BI Desktop display a map of our worldwide sales. Here is how to create an initial map:

1.   Open the C:\PowerBiDesktopSamples\
       PrestigeCarsDataForDashboards.pbix file.

2. On a new, blank page, click the Map icon in the Visualizations pane (this is the largely empty globe that you can see in Figure 12-1). A blank map will appear (even if it looks a little peculiar, it is meant to be a map).

3. Expand the Geography table and drag the CountryName field onto the map visual. The visual will display a map showing points in all the countries for which there are values.

4. Expand the Sales table and drag the SalePrice field onto the map visual. The visual will change the size of each data point to reflect the sales value.

5. Place the cursor over the map and drag Europe to the center of the map.

6. Using the mouse wheel, zoom in to fit the countries with sales in the center of the visual. Hover the mouse pointer over a data "bubble" to display a pop-up showing the exact data that is represented. The map will look something like Figure 12-1.

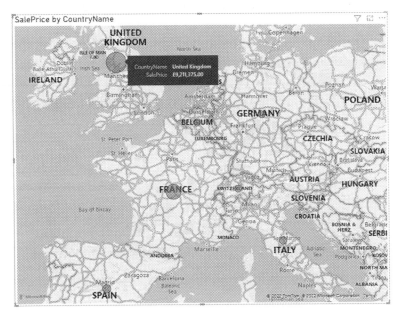

Figure 12-1. A map of sales

It is probably worth clarifying a few points about maps in Power BI Desktop before we go any further. The following are the essential points to note:

- A map is a visual like any other. You can resize and move it anywhere on the Power BI Desktop canvas.

- The map will apply any filters that have been set for the report (you will learn more about filters in the next chapter).

- Each data point (or bubble) in a map is proportional to the relative size of the underlying data.

Using Geographical Data

While it might seem obvious, you need geographical data if Power BI Desktop is to display your insights overlaid upon a map. So you really, absolutely must ensure that your underlying dataset contains columns of data that can be interpreted as geographical information. In the examples so far, you have seen how Power BI Desktop is capable of interpreting country names and using these to display data in maps. However, it is not limited to displaying only countries. You can use any of the following to generate map visuals:

- Country
- Zip (postal) code
- State
- County
- Town
- Latitude and longitude

As an example, take a look at Figure 12-2, where the Town field in the Clients table was used in the Location box in the field area. The map was then adjusted to display only the United Kingdom using the techniques described in steps 5 and 6 of the initial example.

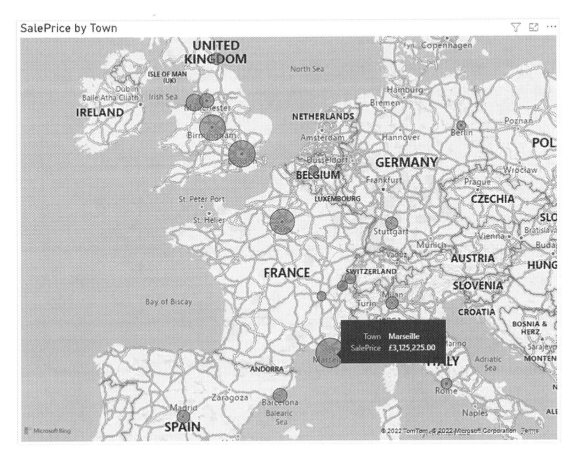

Figure 12-2. *Displaying relative sales per town*

Geographical Data Types

Power BI Desktop really is exceptionally helpful and forgiving when it comes to creating maps. If the data that you have can be interpreted geographically, then Power BI Desktop will do its best to display a map. However, you will almost certainly have to mold the dataset into a coherent data model before you start using Power BI Desktop.

In the first Power BI Desktop example, we added a single geographical data field. What is more, this field was recognized instantly for what it was—country names. In the real world of mapping data, however, you may have to not only add several fields but also specify which type of geographical data each field represents. Put simply, Power BI Desktop needs to know what the data you are supplying represents. Not only that, it needs to know what it is looking at without ambiguity. Consequently, it is up to you to define the source data as clearly and unambiguously as possible. This can involve one or more of several possible approaches.

Define the Data Category in the Data Model

If you have read *Pro DAX and Data Modeling*, you will have learned that you can define a data category for each column of data in Power Pivot. Although this is not an absolute prerequisite for accurate mapping with Power BI Desktop, it can help reduce the number of potential anomalies.

Add Multiple Levels of Geographical Information

The Power BI Desktop data model lets you add several levels of geographical information to a table. For instance, you can add not just a country but also a county and a town to a record in a table. The advantage of adding as many relevant source data fields as possible is that by working in this way, you are helping Power BI Desktop dispel possibly ambiguous references. For instance, if you only had a Town field, Power BI Desktop might not know if you are referring to Birmingham, Alabama, or England's second city. If the data source has a Country field *and* a Town field, however, then Power BI Desktop has a much better chance of detecting the correct geographical location. This principle can be extended to adding states, counties, and other geographical references.

Drilling Down in Maps

Power BI Desktop lets you drill into geographical data just as you can drill into other data hierarchies in other types of visualization. To see this, you can carry out the following steps:

1. Create a new map visual, and place the following fields (and in this order) in the Location box:

    a. CountryName (from the Geography table)

    b. Town (from the Geography table)

    c. SalePrice (from the Sales table)

2. Click the Drill Down icon at the top right of the map visual to activate drill down You can see this in Figure 12-3.

3. Click the bubble for the United Kingdom. The map visual will display data at the next level (town) for the selected country. You can see this in Figure 12-3, which shows both levels of data.

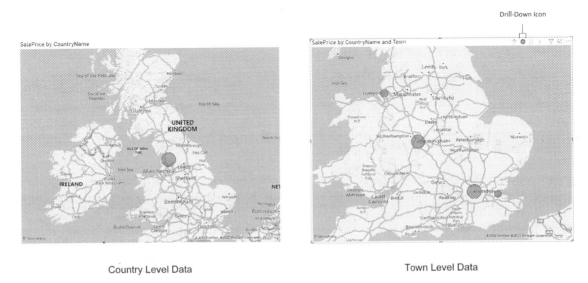

Country Level Data   Town Level Data

Figure 12-3. *Drilling down into a geographical hierarchy*

Fortunately, the techniques that you use to drill down and up in maps are identical to those that you have already seen in the previous chapter for matrices and charts. To resume, briefly:

- Click the Drill Up icon at the top left to go up one level.

- Click the "Go to the Next Level in the Hierarchy" icon to see data from the next level down.

- Click the "Expand All Down One Level in the Hierarchy" icon to see all data from the next level down.

Note   As you might expect, Power BI Desktop will zoom into a country to show the detail at town level if you are drilling down from the country. The map will stay at its original resolution if you decide to show all data from a lower level.

Adjusting the Map Display in Power BI Desktop

As you have seen, creating a map is extremely easy. However, the initial map is not necessarily the finalized version that you wish to show to your audience. You may wish to

- Position the map elements more precisely inside the visual

- Zoom in or out of the map

In the next few sections, we will look at the various modifications that you can make to Power BI Desktop maps. Hopefully, you will find these tweaks both intuitive and easy to implement. In any case, with a little practice, you should find that these modifications take only a few seconds to accomplish.

Positioning the Map Elements

If the area displayed in a map is not quite as perfect as you would prefer, then you can alter the area (whether it is a country or a region) that appears in the map visual. You can do this as follows:

1. Place the mouse pointer over the map. The pointer icon may become a hand icon.

2. Click and drag the pointer around to move the map elements.

Zooming In or Out

It is conceivable that the map that is displayed is not at a scale, which you would prefer. Fortunately, this is extremely easy to fix. All you have to do is the following:

1. Place the mouse pointer over the map.

2. Roll the mouse scroll wheel forward to zoom in to see part of the map in greater detail. Alternatively, roll the mouse scroll wheel backward to zoom out of the map.

Note   There are currently no keyboard shortcuts for moving around in maps or zooming in and out of maps.

Multivalue Series

So far, you have seen how you can add a single data series to a map and have the data represented as a data point. Power BI Desktop can extend this paradigm by allowing you to display the data bubble as a pie that contains a second data series—and consequently display the data broken down by a specific dataset per geographical entity.

As an example of this (and to revise some of the map creation techniques that we have seen so far), let's try to analyze European car sales by color:

1.   Keep the map that you created in the previous section (or create it if you have not yet done so).

2.   Expand the Vehicle table and drag the Color field into the Legend area.

3.   Resize the map visual.

The map now contains a legend for the colors of vehicles sold. Each bubble is now a pie of data. The overall size of the pie represents, proportionally, the sum total data for each country compared to the other pies. The map should now look like Figure 12-4.

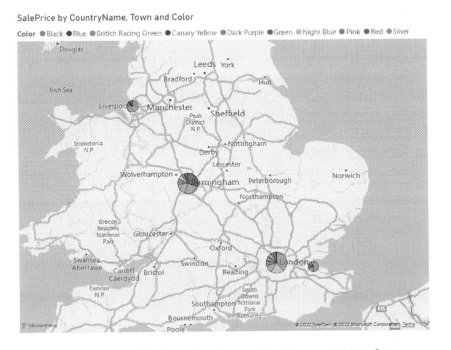

Figure 12-4. *Displaying pie charts in a Power BI Desktop map*

It is worth remarking that if you hover the mouse pointer over the data representation (the pie) for a country, as you pass the pointer over each pie segment, you will see a tooltip giving the details of the data, including which car color it refers to.

Note   When displaying maps, you nearly always need to filter data in some way. You will discover all the details about filtering data in the next chapter.

Cross-Filtering Data

If you have added data to the Legend box of the field area, and a legend is displayed, you can cross-filter segments of data in a map. This allows you to draw the audience's attention to specific trends in your data.

Using the map that you created previously and can see in Figure 12-5, click Blue (the second element) in the legend. The pie segments that correspond to blue cars sold are highlighted, as shown in Figure 12-5 (this only works if drill mode is not activated).

SalePrice by CountryName, Town and Color

Color ⊚ Black ● Blue ⊚ British Racing Green ⊚ Canary Yellow ⊚ Dark Purple ⊚ Green ⊚ Night Blue ⊚ Pink ⊚ Red ⊚ Silver

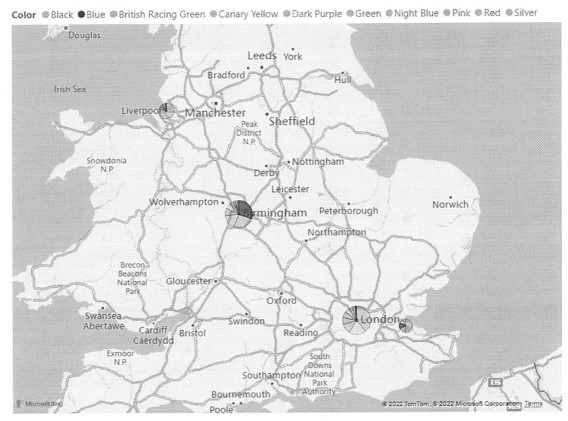

Figure 12-5. *Highlighting map data*

To remove cross-filtering from a map, all you have to do is click the legend element that you are using to cross-filter data, or simply click the title of the legend. Alternatively, click any of the cross-filtered elements on the map.

This is just a preview of how Power BI Desktop applies highlighting to visuals. You will learn more about this technique in Chapter 14.

Note   Cross-filtering a map will also apply cross-filtering to other visuals on the dashboard page.

Filled Maps

Another way to display data is to fill a geographical area with color rather than to display a bubble. Power BI Desktop lets you do this, too.

1. Click in an empty part of the dashboard canvas in the C:\
    PowerBiDesktopSamples\PrestigeCarsDataForDashboards.
    pbix file.

2. Click the Filled Map icon in the Visualizations pane. A blank map
    will appear.

3. Expand the Geography table and drag the CountryName field
    onto the map visual. The visual will display a map shading in the
    countries for which there are values. For the moment, all countries
    will be the same color. The map will now look like Figure 12-6.

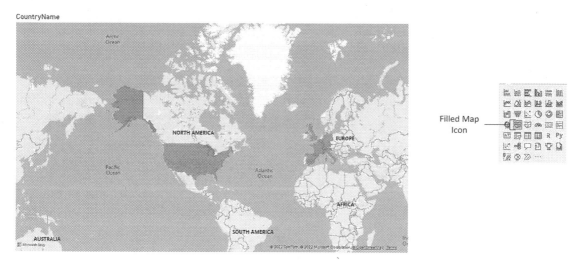

Figure 12-6. *An initial filled map*

4. Switch to the Formatting pane and expand the Fill colors card.

5. Set Show all to On.

6. Choose a color for each country. The map will now look like
    Figure 12-7.

CountryName

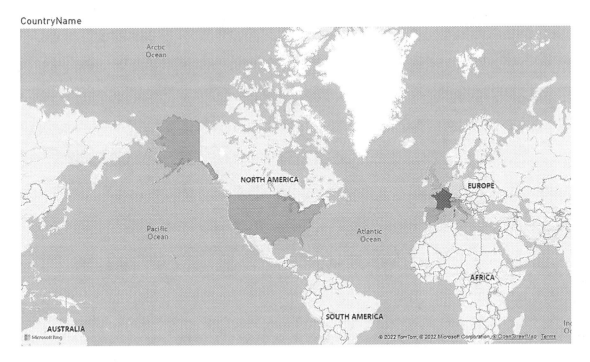

Figure 12-7. *A formatted filled map*

Shading in Filled Maps

Power BI Desktop can colorize the countries based on a value if you prefer. Here is how you can add colors to the filled map based on the total sales for each country:

1. Select the map that you created previously, and in the Formatting pane, expand the Fill colors card and set Show all to Off.

2. Click the Fx icon to display the Fill colors dialog.

3. Select Gradient as the format style.

4. Select SalePrice in the "What field should we base this on?" pop-up.

5. Check the Add a middle color check box.

6. Select colors for Minimum, Center, and Maximum. The dialog will look like the one shown in Figure 12-8.

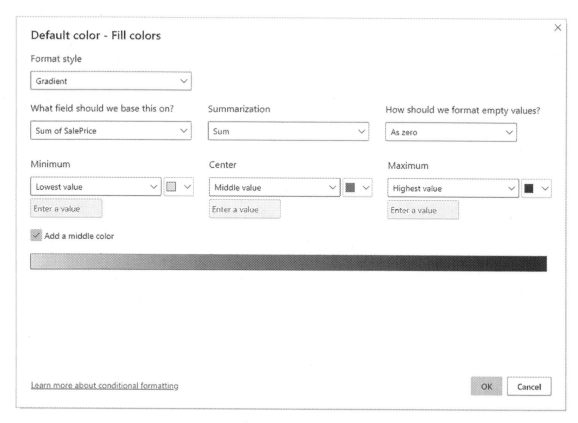

Figure 12-8. *The Fill colors dialog for shape maps*

7.   Click OK. The map will now look like Figure 12-9.

CostPrice by CountryName

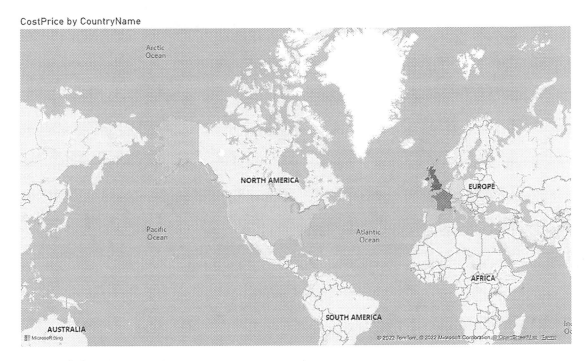

Figure 12-9. *A shaded filled map*

The fill colors can be defined using rules or colors specified in a data table just as was the case when applying conditional formatting to tables. As this was explained in Chapter 3, I will not repeat the explanation here.

Shape Maps

Another way to visualize geographical data is by state or region. This option implies that the source data contains the standard codes that are used to define states and regions. To create a shape map:

1. Click the Shape Map icon in the Visualizations pane.

2. Drag the PostCode field (from the Geography table) into the Location area (or onto the map).

3. Drag the SalePrice field (from the Sales table) into the Color Saturation area (or onto the map). The shape map will look like the one in Figure 12-10.

SalePrice by Postal

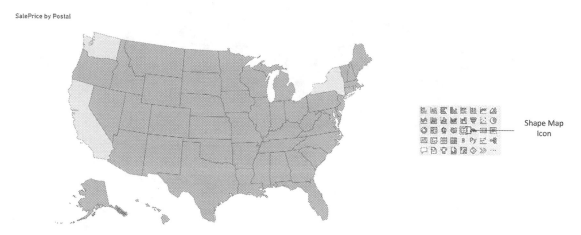

Figure 12-10. *A shape map*

Map Keys

You will probably need to find the map keys (the region codes) that Power BI Desktop uses to display data in a shape map. This way, you can add them to your source data or tweak the source data to include the appropriate geographical codes.

1. Select the shape map that you created in Figure 12-10.

2. In the Formatting pane, expand the Map settings card and then expand the interior Map settings card.

3. Click View Map Keys. A dialog containing the map keys will be displayed, as you can see in Figure 12-11.

Figure 12-11. *Map keys for a specific country*

This is the list of the data elements that Power BI Desktop will use to allocate data to a geographical area. It follows that you will need to have this data—or to be prepared to add it—in your source data. So at least one column in the source data must correspond to one of the values shown in Figure 12-11.

Adding Shape Maps

If you have specific map shapes (and this can include everything from towns to floor plans), then you can load these by clicking the Add Map button in the Shape card of the Formatting pane for shape maps.

Shape map definitions must be created in a specific .json format. Unfortunately, looking at creating these is outside the scope of this book.

Formatting Maps

As you would probably expect, there are numerous formatting options that you can apply to maps. Indeed, the way that you can format maps is virtually identical to the way that you apply formatting to other visuals. Given that the five previous chapters covered many of these options in detail, I will only explain the possibilities in this section and refer you back to previous chapters if you want all the details.

As far as maps and filled maps are concerned, you can modify the following:

- *Title*: This includes displaying or hiding the title, as well as setting the title text, font color, and background color.

- *Background*: This covers applying a background, setting its color, and defining its transparency.

- *Lock Aspect*: If you set Lock Aspect to On, then you can resize the map while keeping it sized proportionally.

- *Border*: You can add or remove a border for a map just as you can with just about any Power BI Desktop visual.

All map types allow you to adjust the data colors. However, the way that the colors are modified is slightly different, depending on the map type. We will now look at the individual formatting options by map type.

Maps

Map visuals allow you to adjust the following aspects of their formatting:

- Data colors
- Category labels
- Bubbles
- Map controls
- Map styles

Some of these elements are similar to formatting options that you have seen before, so I will not re-explain them here. However, other elements of formatting are handled either in completely new ways or in a manner so different from how a similar format option is dealt with in other types of visual that they need a fresh explanation.

Data Colors

Selecting a data color for a map allows you to select the color that will be used for the data bubble. As is the case with so many chart-based visuals, you can also set specific colors for each data point.

1. Select (or re-create) the map from Figure 12-1.

2. Switch to the Formatting pane.

3. Expand the Bubbles card and then the Colors card.

4. Set Show all to On.

5. Select a color for each country.

Category Labels

If you need to supply the name of the geographical element that is currently displayed in a map (the town or the country, say), then you can set the Category Labels button to On. If you expand the Category Labels card, then you can also choose the font family, size, and color for the category labels. Expanding the Background card lets you define a background color for the category labels.

As you have seen this earlier in the book, I will not re-explain it all here. Figure 12-12, however, shows the Formatting pane with some of these options applied.

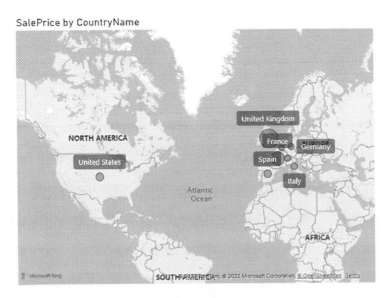

Figure 12-12. *Formatting category labels*

Bubbles

Expanding the Bubbles card in the Formatting pane allows you to adjust the Size slider to set the relative size of the bubbles. You can see an example of this in Figure 12-13.

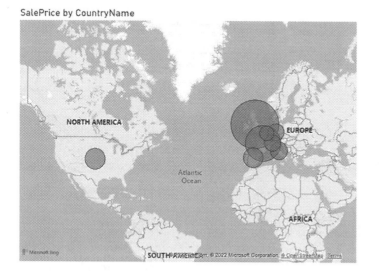
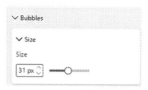

Figure 12-13. *Formatting bubble sizes*

Map Controls

There are currently only two map controls that can be tweaked, and they are

- Auto zoom

- Zoom buttons

You access these options by expanding Map settings followed by Controls in the Formatting pane.

The default (Auto Zoom set to On) means that filtering the map data will cause only relevant geographical areas to appear in the map. If you switch this option to Off, then the map will display the same area until you alter this manually.

Adding Zoom buttons displays two large zoom buttons at the top right of the map as shown in Figure 12-14. You can use these to zoom in and out of the map.

SalePrice by CountryName

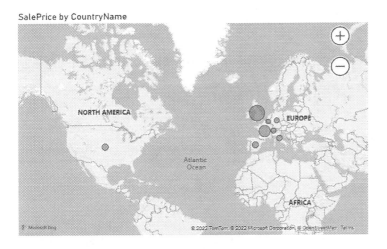

Figure 12-14. *Formatting map controls*

Map Styles

There are currently five map styles in the version of Power BI Desktop that was available as this book went to press:

- Road (the default)

- Aerial

- Dark

- Light

- Grayscale

All the maps that you have created thus far in the chapter have been in the "Road" style. You can see the other map styles in Figure 12-15.

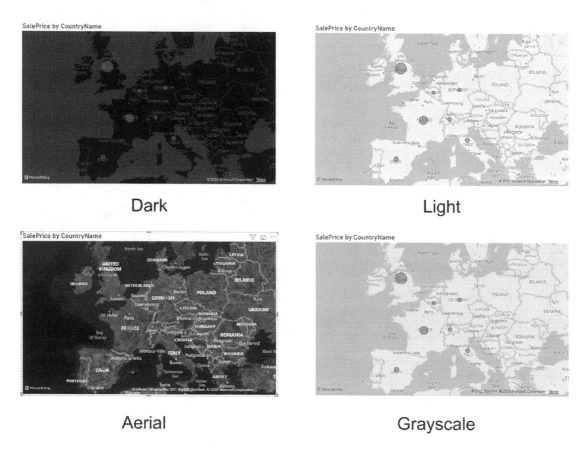

Figure 12-15. *Map styles*

Tooltips

Just as was the case for charts, you can add extra data fields to the Tooltips area in the
Visualizations pane. Then, when you hover the pointer over a map data point (which
could be a country in a shaded map like the one in Figure 12-12), you will see the extra
data information for the map point in the tooltip.

Shape Maps

The essential thing that you can change in a shape map is the color—or colors—of
the actual shapes. Apart from this—which you have already seen—you have one
main option:

- Set a color range for each geographical area for which there is data.

Also, you can select a color for any parts of the map for which there is no data.

ArcGIS Maps

Microsoft has collaborated with ESRI (an international supplier of geographic information system [GIS] software) to include ArcGIS mapping in Power BI Desktop. Quite simply, this feature allows you to take geospatial representation of data to a whole new level. Using ArcGIS maps, you can

- Perform spatial analysis by adding heat maps and aggregating data.

- Add demographic and reference data.

- Make any map look great.

Creating an ArcGIS Map

In this section, you will see a couple of examples of how using ArcGIS maps can add real pizzazz to your dashboards.

1. Open the file C:\PowerBiDesktopSamples\ PrestigeCarsDataForDashboards.pbix.

2. In the Visualizations pane, click the ArcGIS maps for Power BI icon.

3. A blank ArcGIS map will be added to the report canvas. You can see this in Figure 12-16. If you have an ArcGIS account, you can log in at this point.

Sign in to ArcGIS

◉ ArcGIS Online   ○ ArcGIS Enterprise

https://www.arcgis.com

Sign in

————————————————OR————————————————

To start, drag data to the Location or Latitude
and Longitude field wells. Learn more.

Figure 12-16. *The ArcGIS map visual placeholder*

4. Add the following fields to the ArcGIS map:

    a. Town (from the Geography table)

    b. SalePrice (from the Sales table)

5. Enlarge the visual to get a clearer view. The ArcGIS map will look
    like the one in Figure 12-17.

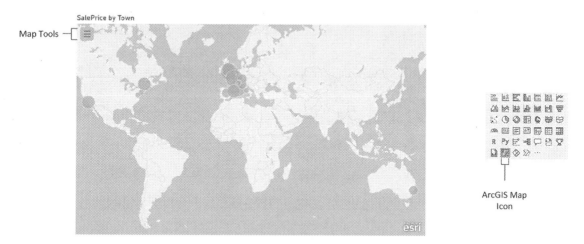

Figure 12-17. *An initial ArcGIS map*

So far so easy—and in all honesty, this is not so very different from what you have
done already using the traditional Power BI Desktop mapping tools. However, things
are about to get much more interesting as you learn to use the added options in
ArcGIS maps.

Note   You can move the display area in an ArcGIS map or zoom in and out just as you can for any other map in Power BI Desktop.

Selecting a Basemap Type

Once you have created an ArcGIS map, you can extend it with some powerful effects. One option is to change the appearance of the map itself:

1.   Select the ArcGIS map and click the Map tools icon to display all the map tools.

2.   In the Formatting pane, expand the Map tools card.

3.   Set Basemaps to On. The Basemaps icon will be added to the ArcGIS tools.

4.   Click the Basemaps tool icon. The Basemaps window will open. You can see this in Figure 12-18.

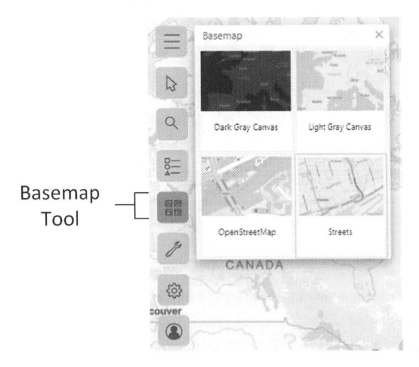

Figure 12-18.   *The ArcGIS basemap tool*

5. In the ArcGIS map, select a basemap from the palette of
    available types.

6. Close the Basemap window by clicking the close button at the top
    right of the window. The map display will change to reflect your
    choice, as you can see in Figure 12-19.

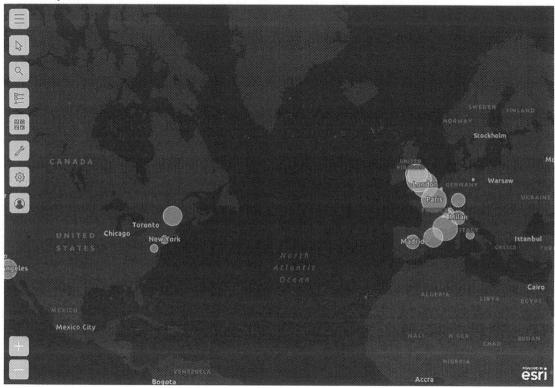

Figure 12-19. *Changing the basemap type of an ArcGIS map*

7. Click Collapse map tools at the top left of the ArcGIS map to return
    to the report canvas.

Note   To close the palette of basemaps and display only the map itself, simply
click the small cross at the top right of the basemap type palette. This will, of
course, only apply to ArcGIS editing mode.

Adding a Reference Layer

ArcGIS maps allow you to access certain statistical geographical datasets and add them to maps. You could, for instance, add the per capita income data to a map and see how (if at all) that relates to car sales:

1. Re-create the initial ArcGIS map that you used at the start of this section.

2. Expand the ArcGIS map tools and click the context icon. A subset of reference layer icons will appear as shown in Figure 12-20.

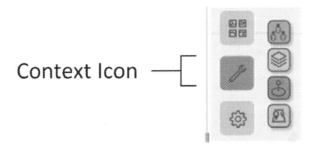

Figure 12-20. *Accessing the ArcGIS reference layer*

3. Click the Reference Layer icon (the second from the top).

4. Select the 2020 USA Per Capita Income reference layer from the reference layer pane. You can see this in Figure 12-21.

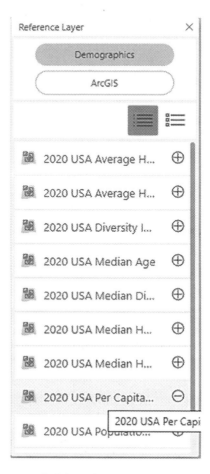

Figure 12-21. *Some of the available reference layers in ArcGIS maps*

5.   Close the Reference layer window.

6.   Adjust the map display to zoom in on the United States. You can
     see the resulting map with reference data in Figure 12-22.

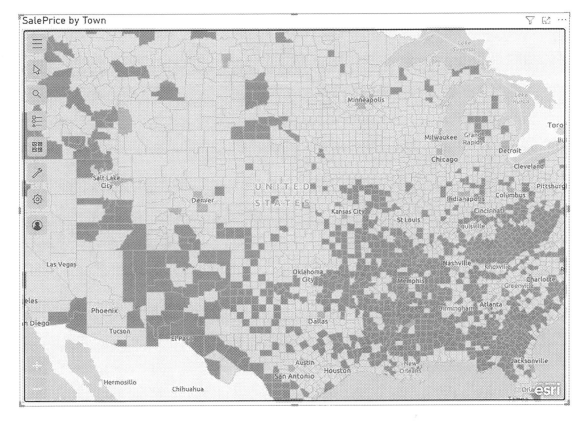

Figure 12-22. *A USA map with reference data added*

Tip   You can only add one layer of reference data at a time.

Adding Infographics

ArcGIS maps also come with access to data relating to demographics. You can add reference data like this:

1.   Re-create and then edit the initial ArcGIS map that you used at the start of this section.

2.   Click the context icon and select the Infographics icon (the top icon).

3.   Select the following options:

a. Expand Population and then expand 2021 Key demographic indicators and select 2021 total population.

b. Click Back and then expand Age and then expand 2021 Age dependency and select 2021 child population.

4. You can see the additional reference data that is displayed in Figure 12-23.

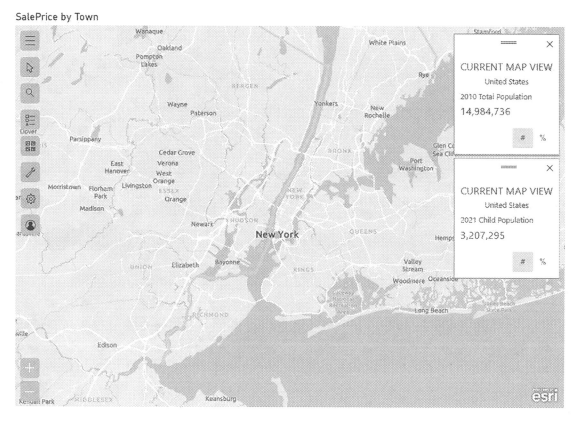

Figure 12-23. *ArcGIS reference data*

There is, of course, much more that ArcGIS can do, but I hope that this brief explanation will incite you to delve deeper into this extremely powerful addition to the Power BI toolkit.

Conclusion

In this chapter, you saw how to display geographical data in a variety of map types, from filled maps, where the data is represented by the intensity of an area's shading, to bubble maps, where the size of data points on a map lets the data speak for itself. You also saw how to add truly expressive ArcGIS map visuals to your reports, where you were able to add extra geographical data to enhance your analysis.

You have now explored all the essential visualization techniques that Power BI Desktop places at your disposal. It is now time to learn how to "slice and dice" your data to discover the meaning behind the figures. This is the subject of the next two chapters.

CHAPTER 13

Filtering Data

Power BI Desktop is built from the ground up to enable you, the user, to sift through mounds of facts and figures so that you can deliver meaningful insights. Consequently, what matters is being able to isolate fundamental data elements and highlight the information it contains quickly, easily, and accurately. This way, you can always explore a new idea or simply follow your intuitions without needing either to apply complex processes or to struggle with an impenetrable interface. After all, Power BI Desktop is there to help you come up with new analyses that could give your business an edge on the competition.

Power BI Desktop provides two main approaches to assist you in focusing on the key elements of your data:

- *Filters*: Structurally restrict the data displayed in a report, page, or visual. This is the subject of the current chapter.

- *Slicers*: Allow you (or your users) to highlight key information instantly, visually, and interactively. We will look at these in the next chapter.

The people who developed Power BI Desktop recognize that your data is the key to delivering accurate analysis. This is why you can filter on any field or set of fields in the underlying data model to extract its real value. This approach is not only intuitive and easy, it is also extremely fast, which ensures that you almost never have to wait for results to be returned.

You can add filters before, after, or during the creation of a Power BI Desktop report. If you add filters before creating a table, then your table will only display the data that the filter allows through. If you add a filter to an existing report, then the data visualization will alter before your eyes to reflect the new filter. If you modify a filter when you have visualizations on a Power BI Desktop report, then (as you probably guessed by now) all the visualizations affected by the filter will also be updated to reflect the new filter criteria—instantaneously.

© Adam Aspin 2022
A. Aspin, *Pro Power BI Dashboard Creation*, https://doi.org/10.1007/978-1-4842-8227-4_13

You can filter any type of data:

- Text

- Numeric values

- Dates

- Logical values

Each data type has its own ways of selecting elements and setting (where possible) ranges of values that can be included—or excluded. This chapter will explain the various techniques for isolating only the data that you want to display. You will then be able to create Power BI Desktop reports based only on the data that you want them to show.

We will see all how these approaches work in detail in the rest of this chapter. In any case—and as is so often the case with Power BI Desktop—it is easier to grasp these ideas by seeing them in practice than by talking about them, so let's see how tiles, slicers, and highlighting work. This chapter uses the C:\PowerBiDesktopSamples\ PrestigeCarsDataForDashboards.pbix sample file as the basis for all the filters that you will learn to apply.

Filters

Subsetting data in Power BI Desktop is based on the correct application of filters. Consequently, the first thing that you need to know about filters is that they work at three levels. You have

- Report-level filters (these apply to all pages)

- Page-level filters

- Visualization-level filters

The characteristics of these three kinds of filter are described in Table 13-1.

Table 13-1. *Power BI Desktop Filters*

Filter Type	Application	Comments
All pages	Applies to every visualization in the current report	Filters data for every visual in the current file
Page-level	Applies to every visualization in the active page	Filters data for every visual in the current page
Visual-level	Only applies to the selected visualization	Applies only to the selected visual (table, chart, etc.)

Filters are always applied in exactly the same way. What matters is the *extent* that they affect the visuals in a Power BI Desktop presentation. In practice, this makes your life much easier because you only have to learn how to apply a filter once and then you can use it in the same way at different levels in separate files.

Saying that there are three types of filter available in Power BI Desktop is a purely descriptive distinction. For Power BI Desktop, any filter is a filter, and all filters work in the same way. However, as there is a clear hierarchy in their application, I will begin with visual-level filters and then move on to their ascendants—page-level filters and report-level filters (filters on all pages). Given the general similarity between the three, it is probably worth noting that it is important you ensure that you are creating or modifying the appropriate filter. As this is not always obvious, not least when you are starting out with Power BI Desktop, I will try to make it clear as we proceed how exactly you can distinguish at what level you are applying a filter, as the effects can have wide-ranging consequences for the message that you are trying to convey.

Collapsing and Expanding the Filters Pane

The first thing to note is that all filters are applied in the Filters pane. This is a collapsible pane immediately to the right of the report canvas. The Filters pane takes up a significant amount of screen real estate. This can be mitigated by collapsing the Filters pane when you do not need it and expanding it when you need either to add filters or modify existing filters.

To collapse the Filters pane, simply click the collapse icon (the right-facing chevron) at the top right of the Filters pane. The pane will become a thin vertical bar on the right of the screen. To make the Filters pane reappear, click once again the same icon (which is now a left-facing chevron). You can see the collapse/expand button in Figure 13-1.

Adding Filters

Let's now look at how to use filters, beginning at the lowest level of the filter hierarchy: visual-level filters. The Filters pane automatically adds any fields that you use as the basis for a visualization. To see this, create the following visual:

1. Open the C:\PowerBiDesktopSamples\ PrestigeCarsDataForDashboards.pbix file.

2. Create a clustered bar chart using these fields:

   a. Make (from the Vehicle table)

   b. SalePrice (from the Sales table)

Expand the Filters pane. It will look like Figure 13-1.

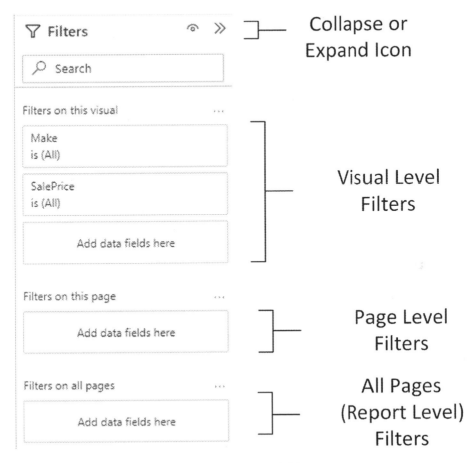

Figure 13-1. *Automatic creation of visual-level filters*

Figure 13-2 shows that adding a data field to a visual automatically adds the same field to the Visual Level Filters pane.

Note   The Filters pane only shows visual-level filters if a visual is selected.

Applying Filters

To see the filter working, let's limit the chart to displaying only a few makes of vehicle:

1. Select the clustered bar chart that you created previously.

2. In the Filters pane, hover the pointer over the Make filter in the Filters pane. A downward-facing chevron will appear at the right of the field that is being used as a filter. You can see this in Figure 13-3. This will be a visual-level filter.

3. Expand the Make filter by clicking the chevron. The Filters pane will display all the makes that appear in the visual.

4. Select the following makes in the Filters pane by selecting the check box to the left of each of the following elements:

    a. Jaguar

    b. Rolls-Royce

    c. Triumph

You will see that data is only displayed for the makes of car that were selected in the filter. The resulting chart should look like Figure 13-2.

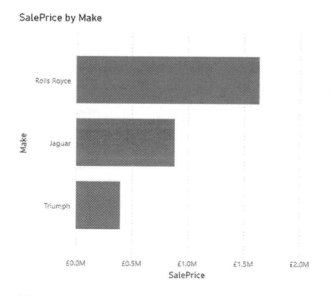
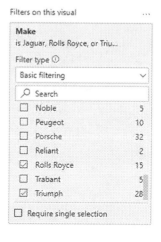

Figure 13-2. *A simple filtered chart*

You will have noticed that when the filter was first applied, every check box was empty, including the Select All check box. The default is (fairly logically) to set up a filter ready for tweaking, but not actually to filter any data until the user has decided what filters to apply. Once you start adding filter elements, they will be displayed in the Filters pane just below the name of the field that is being used to filter data. Another point to note is that once a filter has been modified, it will normally be displayed in a different color in the Filters pane.

You modify filters the same way you apply them. All you have to do to remove a selected filter element is to click the check box with a check mark to clear it. Conversely, to add a supplementary filter element, just click a blank check box.

One final thing to note is that if you subsequently minimize the filter for a field (by clicking the upward-facing chevron that has replaced the downward-facing chevron to the right of the field name), you will now see not only the field name in the Filters pane but also a succinct description of the filter that has been applied. You can see an example of this in Figure 13-3.

Figure 13-3. *Filter description*

Note   You can also add fields to the Filters pane before adding data fields to the visual. Simply create a blank visual and then leave it selected while you add the filter fields to the Filters pane.

The Select All Filter

The only subtlety concerning simple filters is that you also have the Select All check box. This acts as a global on/off switch to select, or deselect, all the available filter elements for a given filter field. The Select All filter field has three states:

- *Blank*: No filters are selected for this field.

- *Checked*: All filters are selected for this field.

- *Partially filled*: Some filters are selected for this field.

Checking or unchecking the Select All filter field will select or deselect all filter elements for this field, in effect rendering the filter inactive. The Select All filter field is particularly useful when you want not only to remove multiple filter selections in order to start over but also want to select all elements in order to deselect certain elements individually (and avoid manually selecting reams of elements).

Note   When selecting multiple elements in filter lists, you may be tempted to apply the classic Windows keyboard shortcuts that you may be in the habit of using in, for instance, Excel or other Windows applications. Unfortunately, Ctrl- or Shift-clicking to select a subset of elements does not work at the moment. Neither can you select and deselect a check box using the spacebar. It is not possible to use the cursor keys to pass from one element to another in a filter list either.

Clearing Filters

Setting up a finely honed filter so that you are drilling through the noise in your data to the core information can take some practice. Fortunately, the virtually instantaneous application of filters means that you can see almost immediately if you are heading down the right path in your analysis. However, there are frequent occasions when you want to start over and remove any settings for a particular filter. This can be done in one of two ways. The first is a single step:

1. With the filter contents expanded, click the small eraser icon to the right of the filter, as shown in Figure 13-4.

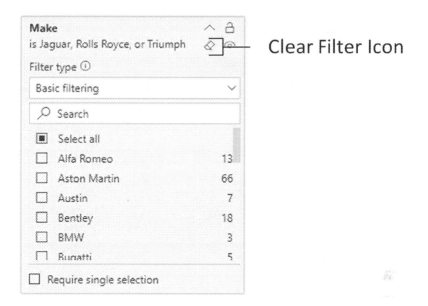

Figure 13-4. *The Clear Filter icon*

Alternatively, you can do the following, but *only* for basic filters:

1. Expand the filter in the Filters pane by clicking the downward-facing chevron.

2. Click the Select All option to remove all filter selections.

3. Minimize the filter.

Once a filter has been cleared, the only way to get it back to its previous state is to press Ctrl+Z immediately. Otherwise, you will have to reapply the requisite criteria.

Adding Filters

You are not restricted to filtering visuals on the data fields that you used to create the visual. You can, in fact, filter a visual on any field in the data model. As an example of this:

1. Select the bar chart that you created previously.

2. Drag the Color field into the Add data fields here area in the Filters on this visual section of the Filters pane.

3. Apply the filter as you saw in previous sections.

Removing Filters

When working with filters, at times, you may want to clear the decks and start over. The fastest way to do this is to delete a filter; once a filter is deleted, it no longer has any effect on the data in the Power BI Desktop report. This can be done as follows:

1. Click the Remove Filter icon to the right of the selected filter. This icon is shown in Figure 13-5.

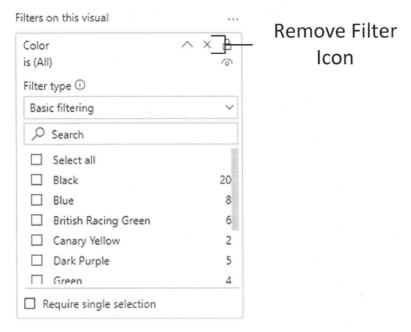

Figure 13-5. *Removing a filter*

The art here is to ensure that you have selected the correct filter to remove. The technique, however, is the same for all report- and page-level filters, as well as for visual-level filters that are not used to display data.

Once a filter has been removed, the only way to get it back is to click Undo (or press Ctrl+Z) immediately; otherwise, you will have to rebuild it from scratch. Interestingly, although you can add filters by dragging elements into the Filters pane, you cannot drag them out of the Filters pane to remove them.

However, you *can* remove visualization-level fields (that are not used as data for the visual) from the Filters pane by clicking the cross at the right of the field name.

Note   Visual-level filters that are based on fields used to create the visual cannot be removed, only reset to empty so that no filters are applied.

Filtering Different Data Types

So far, you have only seen how Power BI Desktop can filter text elements. Although text-based elements are a major part of many data filters, they are far from the only available type of data. There are also

- Numeric data

- Date and time data

- Logical (true/false) data

Filtering Numeric Data

You can filter on numeric elements just as you can filter on text-based elements in Power BI Desktop. However, when filtering on numbers, you likely want to select ranges of numbers as precise figures.

Range Filter Mode

The first trick worth knowing is that, when filtering on numeric data, the default option is to use a *threshold selector*, which is the only filter for numeric filters. The threshold selector allows you to set the lower and/or upper limits of the range of numbers that you want to display in a Power BI Desktop report, page, or visual.

The following explains how to set the range of figures for which data is displayed:

1. Select the chart that you created previously.

2. Clear any existing filters.

3. Remove any filters (except the visual filters for Make and SalePrice that cannot be removed as they relate to the fields used to create the visual).

4. In the Filters pane, hover the pointer over the SalePrice filter in the Filters pane. A downward-facing chevron will appear at the right of the field that is being used as a filter.

5. Expand the SalePrice filter by clicking the chevron. The Filters pane will display two pop-ups that will enable you to set the upper and lower range thresholds.

6. Click the upper pop-up and select the "Is greater than or equal to" option.

7. In the box under the upper pop-up, enter the value **1000000** (without any thousands separators or currency units).

8. Ensure that the And radio button is selected under the pop-up.

9. Click the lower pop-up and select the "Is less than or equal to" option.

10. In the box under the lower pop-up, enter the value **8000000** (without any thousands separators or currency units).

11. Click Apply Filter. The chart will change to show only values in the range that you set in the filter.

That is it. You have set a range for all data in the Power BI Desktop report corresponding to the selected field. It should look like Figure 13-6. It is worth noting that in this figure I have widened the Filters pane so that you can see the entire text that Power BI Desktop adds to a range filter to explain what the filter does. If you leave the Filters pane at its default width, you will only see an abbreviated version of the filter definition.

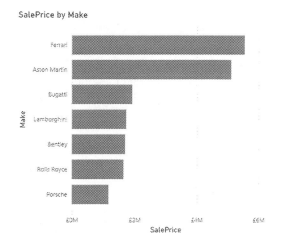

Figure 13-6. *A filter range*

When selecting a range of numeric data, you do not have to set both upper and lower bounds. You may set either one or both.

Note   Should you want to select a precise number from those available in a dataset, you can switch a numeric filter's filter type to basic filtering. This will show all the individual numbers in the selected field, as well as the number of times that each value occurs.

Numeric Filter Options

Numbers cannot be filtered exactly the same ways as text; the filtering options are slightly different. These filter options are described in Table 13-2.

Table 13-2. *Numeric Filter Options*

Filter Option	Description
Is Less Than	The selected field is less than the number you are searching for.
Is Less Than Or Equal To	The selected field is less than or equal to the number you are searching for.
Is Greater Than	The selected field is greater than the number you are searching for.
Is Greater Than Or Equal To	The selected field is greater than or equal to the number you are searching for.
Is	The selected field matches exactly the number you are searching for.
Is Not	The selected field does not exactly match the number you are searching for.
Is Blank	The selected field is blank.
Is Not Blank	The selected field is not blank.

If you are using both threshold levels to define a range of values to include or exclude, or even specific values to include or exclude, then you need to apply one of the logical filter options. These are shown in Table 13-3.

Table 13-3. *Logical Filter Options*

Filter Type	Description
And	Applies both filter elements to *reduce* the amount of data allowed through the filter
Or	Applies either of the filter elements separately to *increase* the amount of data allowed through the filter

When applying a numeric filter, you must—not altogether surprisingly—enter a numeric value. If you enter text by mistake, you will see a yellow lozenge appear at the right of the box to alert you to the fact that you entered a text by mistake, and the Apply filter text will remain grayed out.

In this case, you have to delete the characters that you entered and enter a numeric value in the place of the text.

Filtering Date and Time Data

At its simplest, date and time data is merely a list of elements or a range of numeric data. Consequently, dragging a field from a date dimension into the Filters pane allows you to select one or more elements (such as years or months) or to define a range (of weeks, for instance). Take the following steps to see this in action:

1. Select the chart that you created earlier using the Make and SalePrice fields.

2. Clear any existing filters.

3. Expand the Date table in the Fields list.

4. Drag the FullYear field into the Add data fields here area in the Filters on this visual section of the Filters pane. Since Power BI Desktop assumes that the years are numbers, it switches to advanced filtering.

5. Select Basic Filtering from the Filter Type pop-up list to revert to a list of years.

6. Select **2020** in the filter list. Figure 13-7 demonstrates this. The chart will be updated to show only data for the chosen years.

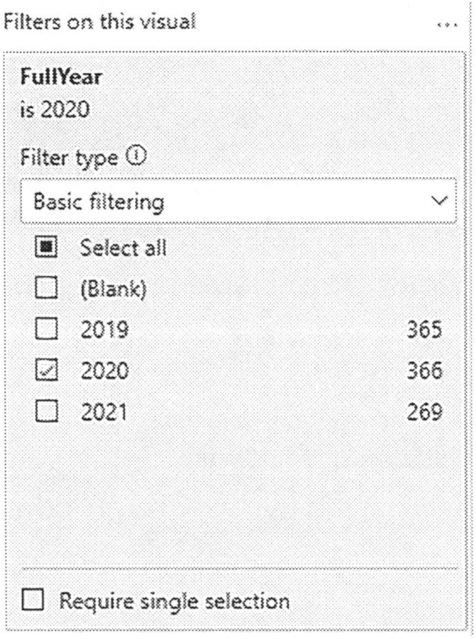

Figure 13-7. *A year filter*

One of the reasons that I created a date dimension is to allow you to filter on date elements this simply. So you can now use any of the fields in the Date table to restrict the data that is in a visualization. In my opinion, the following are very useful fields in this dimension:

- FullYear

- MonthAndYearAbbr

- QuarterAndYear

- YearAndWeek

However, you need to remember that you can combine multiple elements in a filter to get the correct result. So there is nothing to stop you from filtering on a specific year, and then adding the day of the week and calculating all the sales for the Saturdays in the year, for instance. By combining different filter elements from a properly constructed data dimension, you can look at how data varies over time incredibly easily.

This means that, when filtering by dates, you could need to apply multiple filters, where you can select elements from each of the different filters: Year, Quarter, and/or Month. Alternatively, if you will be filtering on successive elements in a date hierarchy (Year, followed by Month, for instance), you may find it more intuitive to drag the filter elements from the date hierarchy to the Filters pane in the temporal order in which you will be using them (i.e., Year followed by Month). This way, you can proceed in a logical manner, from top to bottom in the Filters pane, to apply the date criteria that interest you.

Note   Whatever the data type, you cannot add hierarchies to a filter. Instead, you must expand the hierarchy in the Fields list and drag each element of a hierarchy into the required Filters pane.

Date and Time Filters

If you are filtering on a Date or DateTime field, then you quickly notice that Power BI Desktop adapts the filter to help you select dates and times more easily. In essence, Power BI Desktop lets you select from four ways of filtering date and time data:

- Select one or more exact dates or times (basic filtering).

- Define a range of dates or times (advanced filtering).

- Specify a range of dates relative to the current day (relative date filtering).

- Select a top few dates (top N filtering).

Moreover, the filter area for a date adds

- A calendar pop-up that lets you click a day of the month (and scroll through the months of the year, forward and backward)

- A time series scroll filter that lets you select times to every minute throughout the day

To see this in action, imagine that you want to see all sales for a range of dates:

1. Select the chart that you created previously.

2. Delete the FullYear filter from it, as described earlier.

3. Leaving the chart selected, expand the DateDimension table and drag the DateKey field into the Add data fields here area in the Filters on this visual section of the Filters pane. You will see a list of all the dates in the DateDimension table in the filter.

4.   Click Advanced Filtering.

5.   From the "Show items when the value" pop-up list, select "is on or after."

6.   Click the calendar icon beneath the pop-up. The calendar pop-up is shown in Figure 13-8.

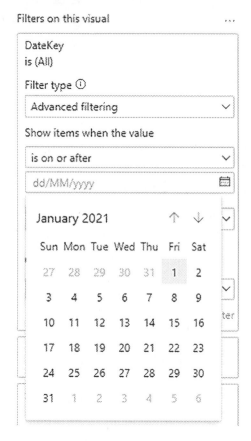

Figure 13-8. *The calendar pop-up*

7.   Select a date from the calendar (I suggest 1/1/2020). This date will appear in the box under the calendar icon.

8.   Click the And radio button.

9.   In the second pop-up, select "is on or before."

10. Click the calendar icon beneath the pop-up and select a date from the calendar. I suggest the 31st of December 2021. This date will appear in the box under the second pop-up.

11. Click Apply Filter. The Filters pane will look like Figure 13-9—and the chart will be filtered to display data where the saledate is inside the range that you entered.

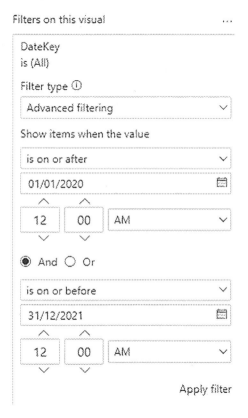

Figure 13-9. *A date range filter*

There are a couple of tricks that may save you time when you are selecting dates from the calendar pop-up (you may be familiar with these techniques in other desktop packages):

- When using the calendar pop-up, clicking the right-facing chevron to the right of the month and year displays the following month.

- When using the calendar pop-up, clicking the left-facing chevron to the left of the month and year displays the previous month.

- When using the calendar pop-up, clicking the month and year displays a Year pop-up, in which you can click the right-facing chevron to the right of the year to display the following year (or click the left-facing chevron to the left of the year to display the previous year), and then you can select the month from those displayed. You can see this in Figure 13-10.

‹	2012	›
January	February	March
April	May	June
July	August	September
October	November	December

Figure 13-10. *The calendar pop-up for months*

- If you have already clicked the month and year and are looking at the months for a year, you can click the year to see ranges of years. You can use the left- and right-facing chevrons to scroll through previous and successive ranges of years, and then select the year that you want to filter on. You can see this in Figure 13-11.

‹	2001 - 2020			›
2001	2002	2003	2004	2005
2006	2007	2008	2009	2010
2011	2012	2013	2014	2015
2016	2017	2018	2019	2020

Figure 13-11. *The calendar pop-up for years*

- When using the time pop-up, clicking inside any constituent part of the time (hour, minute, or second) and then clicking the up and down scroll triangles above and below the time field allows you to scroll rapidly through the available options.

- Clicking AM or PM to the right of the time box lets you switch from AM to PM.

If you do not want to select a date using the calendar pop-up, then you can enter a date directly in the date box of the advanced filter for a Date (or DateTime) field. Just remember that you must enter the date in the date format corresponding to the environment that you are using and that can be understood by Power BI Desktop.

Note   If you enter a date where the format does not correspond to the system format, or if the date is purely and simply invalid (the 30th of February, for instance), then Power BI Desktop will not let you apply the filter. To correct this, merely select a correct date using the calendar pop-up. Similarly, if you enter a nonexistent time, then Power BI Desktop will refuse to accept it and will revert to the previous (acceptable) time that was chosen.

Date Filter Options

Dates cannot be filtered in exactly the same ways as text or numbers. Consequently, the advanced filtering options for date filters are slightly different from those used when filtering other data types. They are described in Table 13-4.

Table 13-4. *Advanced Date Filter Options*

Filter Option	Description
Is	The selected field contains the date that you are searching for.
Is Not	The selected field does not contain the date that you are searching for.
Is After	The selected field contains dates after the date that you entered, that is, later dates that do not include the date you entered.
Is On Or After	The selected field contains dates beginning with the date that you entered or later.
Is Before	The selected field contains dates before the date that you entered, that is, earlier dates, not including the date you entered.
Is On Or Before	The selected field contains dates on or before the date that you entered, that is, earlier dates, up to and including the date you entered.
Is Blank	The selected field is blank.
Is Not Blank	The selected field is not blank.

Relative Date Filtering

Another way of finding data for a range of dates applies specifically to the current date. Power BI Desktop can help you find, for instance, sales in the past days, weeks, months, or even years. Here is how:

1. Select the chart that you created previously.

2. Clear all filters from it, as described earlier.

3. Leaving the chart selected, expand the Date table and add the DateKey field to the Filters pane for the visual.

4. In the Filter Type pop-up list, select Relative Date Filtering.

5. In the pop-up for "Show items when the value," select "Is in the last."

6. In the empty area in the filter, enter **3**.

7. In the second pop-up for "Show items when the value," select Years. The Filters pane will look like the one in Figure 13-12.

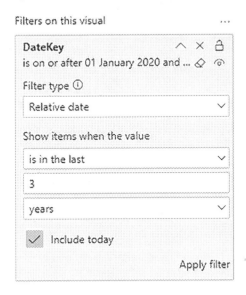

Figure 13-12. *Applying a relative date filter*

8. Click Apply Filter to filter the data in the visual.

There are several options available for relative date filtering. These are described in Table 13-5.

Table 13-5. *Relative Date Filter Options*

Filter Option	Filter Definition	Description
Is In The Last	Relative positioning	Takes a range of dates before the current date
Is In This	Relative positioning	Specifies the current time period to be used
Is In The Next	Relative positioning	Takes a range of dates after the current date
Days	Time element	Sets days as the number of time periods
Weeks	Time element	Sets weeks (rolling seven-day periods) as the number of time periods
Calendar Weeks	Time element	Sets full calendar weeks as the number of time periods
Months	Time element	Sets months (rolling periods from date to date) as the number of time periods
Calendar Months	Time element	Sets full months as the number of time periods
Years	Time element	Sets years (rolling periods from date to date) as the number of time periods
Calendar Years	Time element	Sets full years as the number of time periods

Note   Selecting "Is in the last" or "Is in the next" relative date filter options will display an additional field in the Filters pane where you can enter the number of days, weeks, months, etc. to be used to filter the data.

Filtering True or False Data

There are other data types in the source data that you are likely to be handling. You might have Boolean (True or False) data, for instance. However, for Power BI Desktop, this is considered, for all intents and purposes, to be a text-based filter. On the other hand, there are data types that you cannot filter on and that do not ever appear in the Filters pane. Binary data (such as images) is a case in point.

So if you filter on Boolean data, Power BI Desktop displays True and False in the expanded filter for this data type. The following explains how to see this:

1. Create a clustered bar chart using the following fields:

    a. IsCreditRisk (from the Clients table)

    b. SalePrice (from the Sales table)

2. Expand the IsCreditRisk field in the Filters pane.

3. Select True. The chart and Filters pane will look like they do in Figure 13-13.

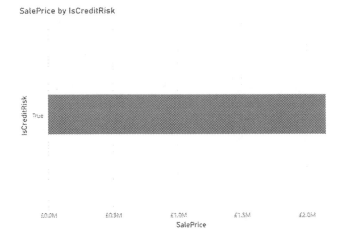

Figure 13-13. *Applying a Boolean filter*

Advanced Text Filters

In many cases, when you are delving into your data, merely selecting a "simple" filter will be enough to highlight the information that interests both you and your audience. There will inevitably be cases when you need to filter your data more finely in order to return the kinds of results that sort the wheat from the chaff. This is where Power BI Desktop's advanced filtering capabilities come to the fore. Advanced filtering lets you search inside field data with much greater precision, and it is of particular use when you need to include, or exclude, data based on parts of a field if it is text.

Applying an Advanced Text Filter

Let's begin with a simple example of how to apply an advanced filter to a text field:

1. Click the visual that you want to filter. Once again, we will use the chart that you created earlier in this chapter using Make and SalePrice as the data fields.

2. Clear any existing filters.

3. Expand the Make field in the Filters pane (unless it has already been done).

4. Select Advanced Filtering from the Filter Type pop-up. The body of the filter switches to show the advanced filter pop-ups and boxes, and the text under the filter title now reads "Show items when the value."

5. Select Contains from the pop-up.

6. Click inside the filter text box (under the box displaying Contains) and enter the text to filter on (**aston** in this example).

7. Click Apply Filter. All objects in the Power BI Desktop report will only display data where the client contains the text *aston*. The result is shown in Figure 13-14; the advanced filter used to produce it is also shown.

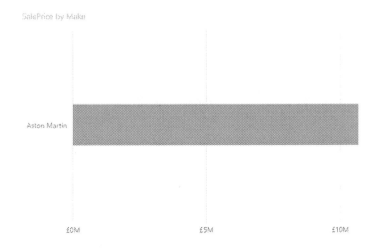

Figure 13-14. *The results of applying an advanced filter*

Here are several comments that it is important to make at this stage:

- Advanced filtering is *not case sensitive*. You can enter uppercase or lowercase characters in the filter area; the result is the same.

- Spaces and punctuation are important, as they are taken literally. For instance, if you enter *A* (with a space after the A), then you only find elements containing an A (uppercase or lowercase) followed by a space.

- Advanced filters, just like standard filters, are cumulative in their effect. So if you have applied a filter and do not get the results you were expecting, be sure to check that no other filter at another level is active that might be narrowing the data returned beyond what you want.

- If your filter excludes all data from the result set, then any table in the Power BI Desktop report displays This Table Contains No Rows.

- Similarly, if your filter excludes all data, charts will be empty.

In any case, if you end up displaying no data, or data that does not correspond to what you wanted to show, just clear the filter and start over.

Clearing an Advanced Filter

Inevitably, you will also need to know how to remove an advanced filter. The process is the same as for a standard filter; all you have to do is click the Clear Filter icon at the top of the filter for this field (just under the chevron for the field in the field area). The filter elements are removed for this filter.

Reverting to Basic Filtering

If you decide that you no longer wish to define and use a complex filter, but you wish to revert to basic filtering, then all you have to do is select Basic Filtering from the Filter Type pop-up list for the selected filter. The Filters pane will switch to basic filtering for the selected field.

Text Filter Options

When filtering on the text contained in a data field, you can apply the string you are filtering onto the underlying data in several ways. These are the same for both the upper and lower of the two advanced filter options for a text field. They are described in Table 13-6.

Table 13-6. *Advanced Text Filter Options*

Filter Option	Description
Contains	The selected field contains the search text anywhere in the field data.
Does Not Contain	The selected field does not contain the search text anywhere in the field data.
Starts With	The selected field begins with the search text, followed by any data.
Does Not Start With	The selected field does not begin with the search text, followed by any data.
Is	The selected field matches the search text exactly.
Is Not	The selected field does not match the search text exactly.
Is Blank	The selected field is blank.
Is Not Blank	The selected field is not blank.

You are not limited to setting a single advanced text filter. Just as was the case for numeric values, you can set two filters and apply either of them (by setting the logical operator to Or). Alternatively, you can set two complementary text filters by setting the logical operator to And.

Top N Filtering

One of the reasons to filter data is to extract meaning from the mass of available information. One easy way to deliver meaningful analysis is to isolate the best-performing (or worst-performing) elements. Suppose, for instance, that you want to see the top three best-selling makes of car:

1. Click the visual that you want to filter. Once again, we will use the chart that you created earlier in this chapter using Make and SalePrice as the data fields.

2. In the Filters pane, expand the Make card of the Visual Level Filters pane.

3. Select Top N from the Filter Type pop-up list.

4. Ensure that Top is selected from the available elements in the Show Items pop-up list.

5. Enter 3 in the field to the right of the Show Items pop-up list.

6. Drag the SalePrice field into the By Value field.

7. Click Apply Filter. You will see the chart and filter looking like they do in Figure 13-15.

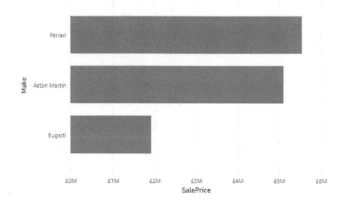

Figure 13-15. *Applying a top N filter*

What has happened here is that the SalePrice field has been aggregated for each make in the background. Then the highest three values have been used to filter the data.

Note   Filtering on the bottom N elements merely means selecting Bottom in the Show Items list.

Specific Visualization-Level Filters

So far in this chapter, we have looked at filters where the fields that were used to filter a visual were *also* visible in the actual visual—be it a chart, map, or table. Inevitably, there will be times when you will want to filter on a field that is *not* displayed in a visual. Although we touched on this earlier, it is worth explaining the concept in greater detail.

The following example explains how to apply a visualization-level filter:

1. Create a clustered bar chart of SalePrice by ClientName.

2. Display the Filters pane (unless it is already visible).

3. Expand the Vehicle table and drag the Color field into the Filters pane in the Add data fields here well for the *visual*. The list of colors will be expanded automatically in the Filters pane. The Color field will *not* be displayed in the visual, however.

4. Select a couple of colors, such as Night Blue and Silver. The result
    is shown in Figure 13-16.

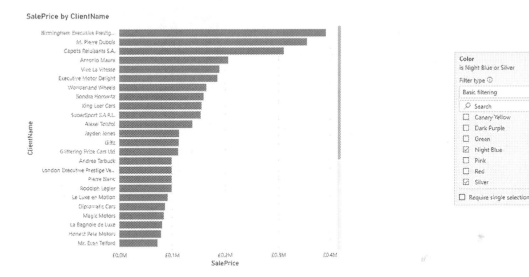

Figure 13-16. *A visualization-level filter without using the data field*

You will notice right away that the filters that you have applied only affect the
selected visualization (the chart in this example). When you create complex reports that
contain several visualizations, you will see that no other visualizations in the report have
their underlying data modified in any way.

You can clear any filter at the visualization level by clicking the Clear icon at the top
right of the filter name. Moreover, you can add multiple fields to the Filters pane for a
visual *and* you can add them in any order.

Note   Removing a field from the field area will not remove this field from the
Filters pane if the filter is active. This can be deceptive because the field is no
longer displayed in the visual; however, its effects can still be seen.

Multiple Filters

So far, we have treated filters as if only one was ever going to be applied at a time. Believe me, when dealing with large and intricate datasets, it is unlikely that this will be the case. As a matter of course, Power BI Desktop will let you add multiple filters to a report. This entails some careful consideration of the following possible repercussions:

- All filters are active at once (unless you have cleared a filter) and their effect is cumulative. That is, data will only be returned if the data matches *all* the criteria set by all the active filters. So, for example, if you have requested data between a specified date range and above a certain sales figure, you will *not* get any data in which the sales figure is lower than the figure that you specified or with a sales date before or after the dates that you set.

- It is easy to forget that filters can be active. Remember that all active filters in the Filters pane remain operational whether the Filters pane itself is expanded or collapsed. If you are going to collapse filters to make better use of the available space on the screen, then it is worth getting into the habit of looking at the second line below any filter title that will give you a description of the current filter state. It will display something like Contains Rolls. Of course, the exact text varies according to the filter that you have applied.

Page-Level Filters

Now that you have seen what filters are and how you can apply them to visuals, it is time to extend the concept and see how filters can be applied to multiple visuals.

The good news is that all filters are configured in exactly the same way whatever the level at which they are applied. Consequently, applying filters at page level or report level is simply a question of choosing where in the Filters pane to place a filter.

As an example, suppose that you want to filter all the visuals on a page to display data for a specific year:

1. In an open Power BI Desktop file (such as the one containing the chart that you can see in Figure 13-15), click the dashboard canvas outside any existing visuals.

2. Expand the Date table.

3. Drag the FullYear field onto the field area into the Filters on this
    page area. The advanced filtering options for this field will be
    displayed.

4. Select Basic Filtering as the filter type.

5. Check 2019 in the list of available years. All visuals on the current
    page will be filtered to display only data for this year.

Figure 13-17 shows you the Filters pane for this operation. You can see that a
page-level filter looks identical to a visual-level filter. The only difference (apart from the
effect that it produces) is the position in the Filters pane.

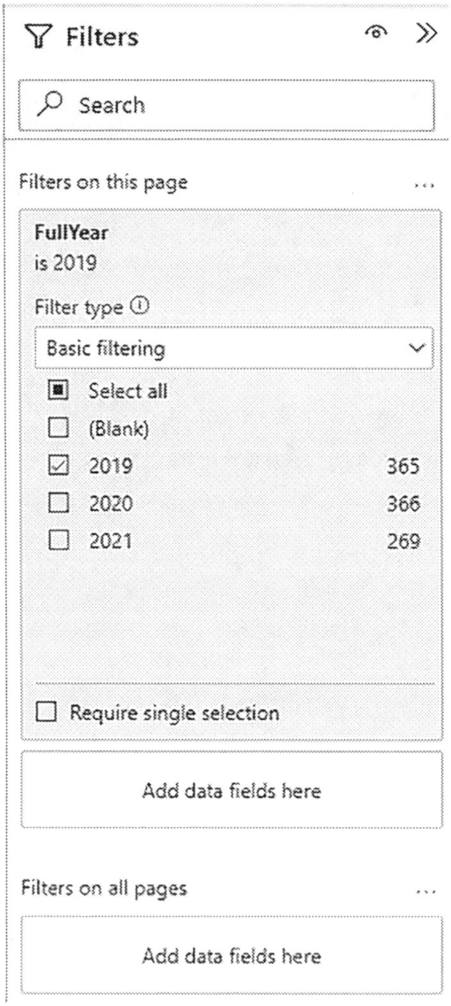

Figure 13-17. *Applying a page-level filter*

You can add multiple page-level filters if you wish simply by dragging further fields into the field area and into the Page Level Filters box. The order in which the fields are added is unimportant. You will notice that the page-level filters remain visible whether you have selected a visual or not.

Filters on All Pages

The highest level of filtering is applied at report (or all pages) level. This means that any filter set here will apply to every page (or dashboard) in a report and consequently also to every visual in the file. Applying report-level filters is virtually identical to the application of page-level filters. So let's suppose that your entire report covers a single country. Here is how to set a filter that will apply to every page in the Power BI Desktop report:

1. Take the report that you created with SalePrice by ClientName and then filtered by color at visual level (Night Blue and Silver) and FullYear at page level (2019).

2. Click the dashboard canvas outside any existing visuals.

3. Expand the Geography table and drag the CountryName field onto the field area into the Filters on all pages box. The basic filtering options for this field will be displayed.

4. Select United Kingdom from the list of available countries. All visuals in the current report (on every page) will be filtered to display only data for this year.

Figure 13-18 shows you the Filters pane for this operation.

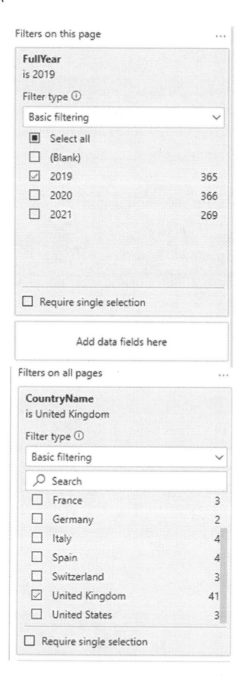

Figure 13-18. *Applying filters to all pages*

You can add multiple report-level filters if you wish simply by dragging further fields into the field area and into the Report Level Filters pane. Once again, the order in which the fields are added is irrelevant. You will notice that the report-level filters remain visible whether you have selected a visual or not.

Filter Field Reuse

Although it may seem counterintuitive, you can reuse the same field at the same filter level to assist you in certain cases.

As an example of this, imagine that you want to see all the mileage for vehicles between clearly defined thresholds. Take a look at the following example:

1. Take the report that you created with SalePrice by ClientName and then filtered.

2. Remove all filters.

3. Expand the Vehicle table.

4. Drag the Mileage field into the field area and place it in the Filters on all pages area.

5. Select "is greater than" from the first pop-up.

6. Enter **50000** in the box for the first threshold.

7. Ensure the And radio button is selected.

8. Select "is less than" from the second pop-up.

9. Enter **70000** in the box for the first threshold.

10. Click Apply Filter.

11. Drag the Mileage field once more into the field area and place it in the Filters on all pages area under the filter that you just created.

12. Ensure that Basic Filtering is selected for this filter. A list of available mileage for vehicles in stock (as well as the number of cars for each mileage figure) for the *previously selected mileage range* will appear. You can see this in Figure 13-19.

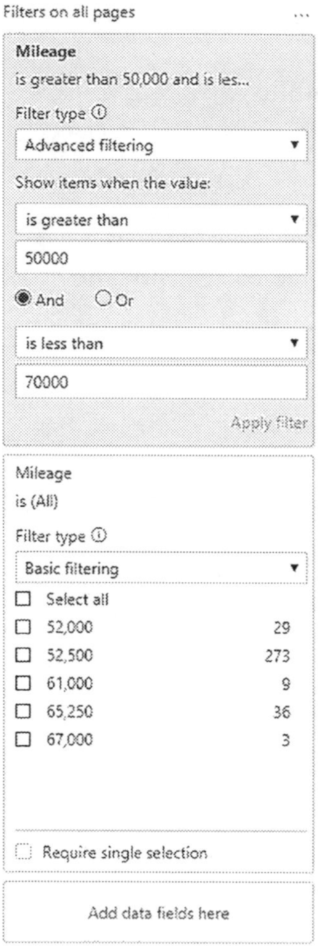

Figure 13-19. *Combining multiple iterations of the same field in a filter*

You can now use the more detailed filter to filter the visuals on the current page.

The interesting thing to note is that a hierarchy of filters is applied, even inside a filter box in the Filters pane. Put simply, a filter that is placed above another filter will filter the available elements in the lower filter. This only applies, however, to reuse of the same filter.

Note This example was set to filter at page level. It could equally well have been applied at report level.

Requiring Single Selection

Some filter choices will allow you to select multiple options from a list. You may want to force either yourself or an end user to select only one element from this list.

In such cases, all you have to do is check the Require Single Selection check box under the list. This will deselect any existing selected elements from the list both once this option is active and (possibly more importantly) when a new selection is made in the filter.

Note   Choosing the Require Single Selection option will also hide the Filter Type pop-up list. To switch to a different filter type, you will have to deactivate the Require Single Selection option by unchecking the check box.

Using the Filter Hierarchy

Given the multiple levels of filters that can be applied, a hierarchy of filters is applied in Power BI Desktop:

- First, at the data level, any selections or choices you apply to the underlying data restrict the dataset that Power BI Desktop can use to visualize your information.

- Second, at the report level, any report-level filters that you apply affect all visualizations in the report using the (possibly limited) available source data.

- Third, at the page level, any page-level filters that you apply will affect all visualizations on the view, using the (possibly limited) available source data filtered by any report-level filters.

- Finally, for each visualization, any visualization-level filters that you apply will further limit the data that is allowed through the report- and page-level filters—but only for the selected visualization.

It is worth noting the following points:

- You have no way to apply a completely different selection to a visualization filter if it has been filtered out at a higher (report or page) level. Clicking Select All will *only* select from the subset of previously filtered elements.

- If you apply a filter at visualization level and then reapply the same filter at report or page level, but with different elements selected, you will still be excluding all nonselected elements from the filter at visualization level. I stress this because Power BI Desktop will remember the previously selected elements at visualization level, and leave them visible even if they cannot be used in a filter, because they have already been excluded from the visualization-level filter by being ruled out at view level. In my opinion, this adds a certain visual confusion, even if the hierarchical selection logic is applied.

Hopefully, this shows you that Power BI Desktop is rigorous in applying its hierarchy of filters. Should you need to apply a filter at visualization level when the filter choice is excluded at report or page level, you have no choice but to remove the filter at the higher level and then reapply visualization-level filters to all necessary visualizations.

Filtering Tips

Power BI Desktop makes it incredibly easy to filter data and to exclude any data that you feel is not helpful in your data analysis. However, like many powerful tools, this ability to apply filters so quickly and easily can be something of a double-edged sword. So here are a few words of advice and caution when applying filters to your data.

Searching for Filters

There could be cases when you have applied dozens of filters to a dashboard—and you need to find one of the filters in order to modify it. In cases like these, it is good to know that Power BI Desktop allows you to search for specific filters.

1. In the Filters pane, enter all or part of the field name that corresponds to a filter you want to locate. The filter will be displayed as shown in Figure 13-20.

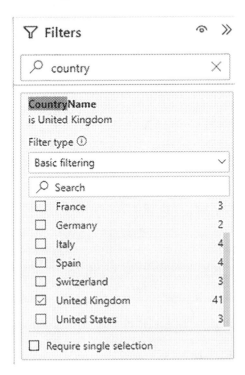

Figure 13-20. *Searching for filters*

Don't Filter Too Soon

As an initial point, I would say that a key ground rule is "Don't filter too soon." By this, I mean that if you are examining data for trends, anomalies, and insights, you have to be careful not to exclude data that could contain the very insights that can be game changing.

The problem is that when you first delve into a haystack of data in search of needles of informational value, you have no idea what you could be looking for. So I can only suggest the following approaches:

- Begin with no filters at all and see what the data has to say in its most elemental form.

- Apply filters one at a time and remember to delete a filter before trying out another one.

- Try to think in terms of "layers" of filters. So once you have defined an initial set of filters, add further filters one by one.

- Go slowly. The temptation is to reach a discovery in order to shout about it from the rooftops. This can lead to excessive filtering and unreliable data.

- Always remove any filters that are not absolutely necessary.

- Be careful if you hide the Filters pane. It is too easy to forget that there are active filters if they are not visible in some way.

- Remember that you can have filters specific to a visualization that might not be immediately visible in the Filters pane without scrolling. So always check if any visualization filters are active for each table and chart in a report.

Annotate, Annotate, Annotate

If you are presenting a key finding based on a dataset, then it can save a lot of embarrassment if you make it clear in every case what the data does and does not contain. For example, you could be so pleased with the revelatory sales trend that you have discovered that you forget to note an important exclusion in the underlying data. Now, no one is suggesting that you are doing anything other than making a point, but your audience needs to know what has been excluded and why—just in case it makes a difference. After all, you don't want a workplace rival pointing this out to invalidate your findings in the middle of a vital meeting, do you?

Annotation techniques are described in Chapter 15 if you need to jump ahead to check this out now.

Avoid Complex Filters

Power BI Desktop filters are designed to be intuitive and easy to use. A consequence of this is that they can prove to be a little limited when you need to apply very complex filters—be they text, numeric, or date filters.

If you need to create a complex filter, it's probably best *not* to create one in the report. Instead, consider trying to filter source data using Power Query. Should you need a more interactive way of switching between complex filter settings in a report, then use DAX to define columns that display a text as the result of a filter, and then use the result of the filter as a selection.

Note   As DAX is a vast subject in its own right, this book will not provide an introduction to this language. You can, however, find an introduction to DAX in the companion volume *Pro DAX and Data Modelling in Power BI.*

Conclusion

This chapter has shown you how to apply and fine-tune a series of techniques to enable you to select the data that will appear in your Power BI Desktop reports. The main thing to take away is that you can filter data at three levels: the overall report, each page, and each visualization on a page.

You have also seen a variety of selection techniques that allow you to subset data. These range from the avowedly simple selection of a few elements to the specification of a more complex spread of dates or values. Finally, it is worth remembering that you can filter data using any of the fields in the underlying dataset, whether the field is displayed in a visual in a report or not.

Filters are, however, not the only technique that you can apply to sift through the data. Another approach is to use slicers. These are explained in detail in the next chapter.

CHAPTER 14

Slicers and Cross-Filtering

With your filters in place, you now have some extremely powerful and insightful dashboards ready to be paraded in front of your colleagues, bosses, and clients. Yet static illustrations can only tell a story in a certain way. What you need to clinch the deal or convince an audience is some truly telling *interaction* with your facts and figures. Once again, Power BI Desktop is the tool of choice, as it highlights the key metrics in your presentation with a single click—and consequently makes your point, simply and elegantly.

Put less breathlessly, you can interact with your filtered data in Power BI Desktop reports to subset or isolate metrics. These elements have the following characteristics:

- Always visible in the Power BI Desktop report
- Instantly accessible
- Interactive
- Clearly indicate which selections are being applied

So what are the effects that you can add to a Power BI Desktop report to select and project your data? Essentially, they boil down to two main approaches:

- Slicers
- Cross-filtering

These interactive elements can be considered to function as a supplementary level of filtering. That is, they take the current filters that are set in the Filters area (at any level) and then provide *further fine-grained interactive selection* on top of the dataset

© Adam Aspin 2022
A. Aspin, *Pro Power BI Dashboard Creation*, https://doi.org/10.1007/978-1-4842-8227-4_14

that has been allowed through the existing filters. Each approach has its advantages and limitations, but used appropriately, each gives you the ability not only to discover the essence of your data but also to present your analyses clearly and effectively.

You will use the C:\PowerBiDesktopSamples\PrestigeCarsDataForDashboards.pbix sample file as the basis for all the slicers that you create in this chapter.

Slicers

A key form of interactive filter in Power BI Desktop is the *slicer*. This is, to all intents and purposes, a standard multiselect filter, where you can choose one or more elements to filter data in a report. The essential difference is that a slicer *remains visible* on the Power BI Desktop report, whereas a filter is normally hidden. So this is an overt rather than a covert approach to data selection that makes the selection criteria immediately visible. Moreover, you can add multiple different slicers to a Power BI Desktop report and consequently slice and dice the data instantaneously and interactively using multiple, cumulative, criteria. Slicers can be text based, or indeed, they can be simple charts, as you will soon see. You can even add third-party slicers to your dashboards if you require even more advanced—or visually interesting—ways to slice your data.

Adding a Slicer

To appreciate all that slicers can do, we need to see one in action. This means having at least one standard visual in a page so that you can see the result of applying a slicer. To test a slicer:

1. Create a table (to show the effect of using a slicer) using the following fields:

    a. CountryName (from the Geography table)

    b. SalePrice (from the Sales table)

2. Resize the table so that it fits the data.

3. In the Fields list, expand the Vehicle table.

4. Drag the Color field to an *empty* part of the dashboard canvas. It will become a single-column table.

5.   Click the Slicer icon in the Visualizations pane. The table of colors
     will become a slicer. The Slicer icon is shown in Figure 14-1.

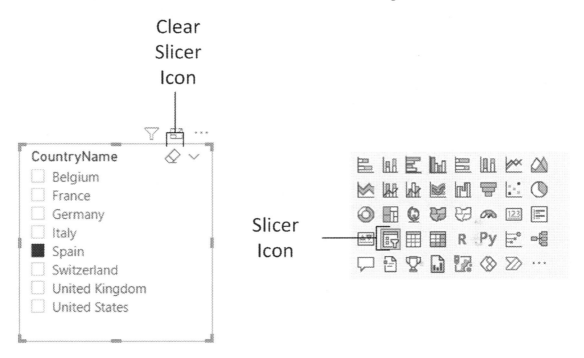

Figure 14-1. *A slicer in action*

6.   Adjust the size of the slicer to suit your requirements using the
     corner or lateral handles. If the slicer contains many elements,
     Power BI Desktop will add a vertical scrollbar to indicate that
     there are further elements available.

You can recognize a slicer by the small squares (or in some cases circles) to the left
of each element in the list. This way, you know that it is not just a single-column table.
Figure 14-2 shows a slicer using the CountryName field.

Tip   If the Slicer icon is grayed out, then ensure that the table that you are trying
to convert to a slicer has only *one* column (i.e., one field in the Values box of the
field area for this visual).

You can create *multiple* slicers for each page. All you have to do is repeat steps 3
through 6 for adding a slicer using a different field as the data for the new slicer.

You can also create slicers by

1. Clicking in an empty area of the report canvas

2. Clicking the Slicer icon

Hierarchical Slicers

Slicers can be made more powerful—and more interesting—by making them
hierarchical. This is probably best appreciated by looking at a simple example:

1. Click in an empty area of the report canvas and click the Slicer
    icon. A blank slicer will appear.

2. Add the Make and Model fields to the slicer.

3. Expand a make in the slicer by clicking the down-facing chevron
    to the left of the required make. The slicer should look something
    like the one shown in Figure 14-2.

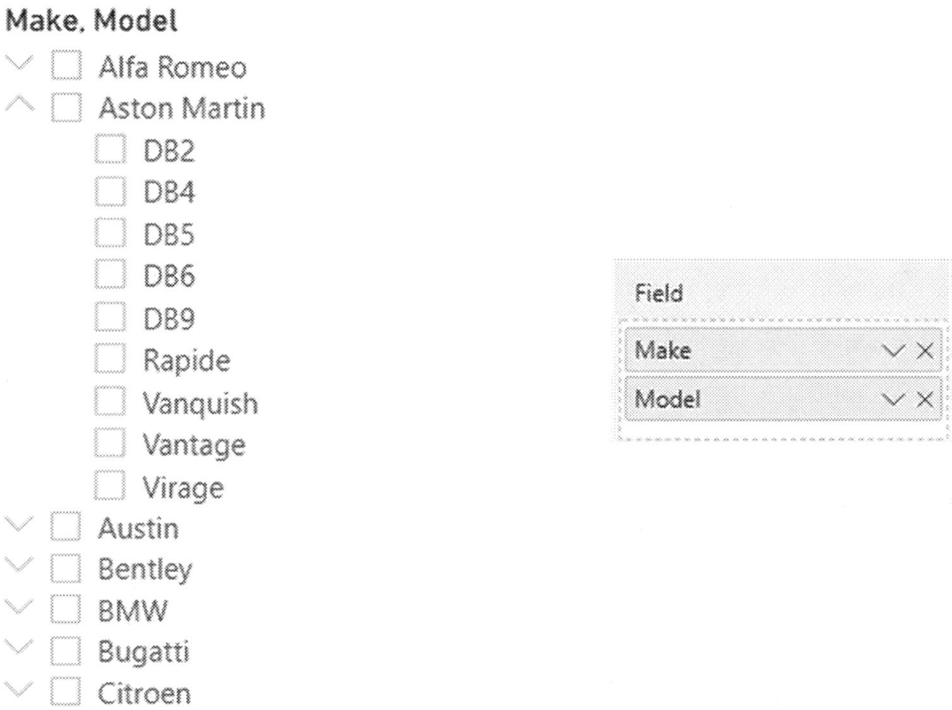

Make, Model
- ⌄ ☐ Alfa Romeo
- ⌃ ☐ Aston Martin
  - ☐ DB2
  - ☐ DB4
  - ☐ DB5
  - ☐ DB6
  - ☐ DB9
  - ☐ Rapide
  - ☐ Vanquish
  - ☐ Vantage
  - ☐ Virage
- ⌄ ☐ Austin
- ⌄ ☐ Bentley
- ⌄ ☐ BMW
- ⌄ ☐ Bugatti
- ⌄ ☐ Citroen

Field		
Make	⌄	✕
Model	⌄	✕

Figure 14-2. *A hierarchical slicer*

Applying Slicers

To apply a slicer and use it to filter data on a page, click a single element in the slicer or Ctrl-click multiple elements.

All the objects in a Power BI Desktop page are filtered to reflect the currently selected slicer list. In addition, each element in the slicer list that is active (and consequently used to filter data by that element) now has a small rectangle to its left, indicating that this element is selected.

When you apply a slicer, think filter. That is, if you select a couple of elements from a slicer based on the CountryName field, as well as three elements in another slicer based on the Color fields, you are forcing the two slicers (filters) to limit all the data displayed in the page to two countries that have any of the three colors that you selected. The core difference between a slicer and a filter is that a slicer is always visible—and that you have to select or unselect elements, not ranges of values.

If you experiment, you will also see that you cannot create a slicer from numeric fields in the source data. A slicer has to be based on a text field. If you need slicers based on ranges of data, then you will need to prepare these ranges in the data model. The CarAgeBucket field is an example of this.

Tip   If you Ctrl-click all the selected elements in a slicer, you can unselect all the data it represents. This will not clear the Power BI Desktop report, however. Unselecting everything is the same as selecting everything—despite the fact that the selection squares are no longer visible to the left of each element in the slicer. Using Shift-click is no different from clicking a slicer element, however.

In a hierarchical slicer, selecting a filter element at a higher level selects all the child elements lower in the filter hierarchy for the selected level.

Clearing a Slicer

To clear a slicer and stop filtering on the selected data elements in a view, click the Clear Selections icon at the top right of the slicer. This icon is pointed out in Figure 14-1.

Any filters applied by the slicer to the view are now removed. You will see that each element in the slicer list now has a small empty rectangle to its left, indicating that this element is not selected. No data is now filtered out of the report.

Tip   Another technique used to completely clear a slicer is to click (or Ctrl-click) the last remaining active element in a slicer. This leaves all elements inactive. Additionally, you can Ctrl-click to select every item. So, in effect, removing all slicer elements is the same as activating them all.

Deleting a Slicer

To delete a slicer and remove all filters that it applies for a view, select the slicer and press the Delete key. Alternatively, click the context menu button (the ellipses) that appears at the top right when you hover the mouse pointer over a slicer, and select Remove.

Any filters applied by the slicer to the view, as well as the slicer itself, are now removed.

You can even copy and paste slicers if you wish. This is very useful when you are copying slicers across different Power BI Desktop reports or between report pages.

Converting a Slicer to Another Visual Type

If you intend to use the field that was the basis for a slicer in a table or chart, you do not need to delete the slicer and re-create a table based on the same underlying field. You can merely

1.   Select the slicer.

2.   Click the Table icon in Visualizations pane.

The instant that a slicer becomes a table, it ceases to subset the data in the Power BI Desktop report.

Modifying a Slicer

If all you want to do is replace the field that is used in a slicer with another field, then it is probably simplest to do this:

1.   Select the slicer that you want to modify.

2.   Drag the new field over the existing field in the field area.

The current slicer field is replaced by the new field and the slicer updates to display the contents of the field that you added. Alternatively, you can delete the slicer and re-create it.

Note   You cannot add more than one data field to a slicer, nor can you drag a new field onto the slicer to replace the existing field.

When you start applying slicers to your Power BI Desktop reports, you rapidly notice one important aspect of the Power BI Desktop filter hierarchy. A slicer can only display data that is not specifically excluded by a report- or page-level filter. For instance, if you add a Color filter at page level and select only certain colors in this filter, you are only able to create a slicer that also displays this subset of colors. The slicer is dynamic and reflects the elements that can be displayed once any report and page filters have been applied—just like any other visual. Consequently, adding or removing elements in a filter causes these elements to appear (or disappear) in a slicer that is based on the filtered field.

If you wish, you can apply a filter specifically to a slicer. This allows you to restrict the elements that appear in a slicer.

Conversely, to remove a filter from a slicer, you need to switch it back to a table and remove the filter, and then switch back to a slicer.

Tip   When you save a Power BI Desktop file containing Power BI Desktop reports with active slicers, the slicer is reopened in the state in which it was saved.

Date Slicers

Selecting ranges of dates can extend the appearance and usefulness of slicers. As this is probably easier to appreciate if you see it in action, I suggest that you try out the following:

1. Open the sample file C:\PowerBiDesktopSamples\ PrestigeCarsDataForDashboards.pbix.

2. In the Visualizations pane, click the Slicer icon. An empty slicer will be added to the report canvas.

3. Expand the Date table and check the FullYear field.

4. Drag the left-hand (lower) threshold to the right until the left year field shows 2020. Any data in the page will be filtered to exclude dates outside this range of years. You can see this in Figure 14-3.

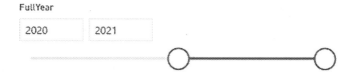

Figure 14-3. *Slicing on years*

You can, if you prefer, enter a year directly in one of the year fields in a slicer like this one. However, I feel that the usefulness of a slicer like this is precisely in its ability to alter the threshold values quickly and easily using the slider.

If you use a data field that is set as a *date type*, then the slicer can help you set dates quickly and easily, but in a slightly different way. Here's how:

1. In the Visualizations pane, click the Slicer icon. An empty slicer will be added to the report canvas.

2. Expand the Date table and check the DateKey field.

3. Click inside one of the date fields. The slicer will look like the one in Figure 14-4.

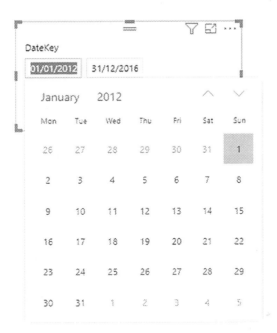

Figure 14-4. *A date slicer*

4. Select the date that you want to set for the date threshold.

To make the most of this calendar, you need to know a few tricks:

- Clicking the up and down chevrons displays the following or preceding month.

- Clicking the year in the calendar pop-up displays a list of years. From here you can select the required year.

- Clicking the month in the calendar pop-up displays a list of months. From here you can select the required month.

- You cannot select an upper date that is less than the lower date.

- The calendar *will* allow you to select dates that are not included in the underlying table of dates. This, however, can cause some unexpected results to appear in your reports.

Note   Certain fields in a date dimension (sometimes this can mean most of them) are considered as being simple selection elements. So, for instance, using the MonthFull field in a slicer will result in a list of months, without sliders. The best thing to do is to experiment with the various fields that are available in the Date table and use those that best suit your purposes.

Formatting Slicers

Slicers can be formatted just like any other Power BI Desktop visual. Indeed, many of the techniques that you use to format slicers are identical to those that you have already seen when formatting tables and matrices. Consequently, to avoid pointless repetition, this section concentrates on any formatting attributes that are slicer specific, and only refers in passing to formatting approaches that you have already covered in previous chapters.

Slicer Orientation

To help you to make the best possible use of report real estate, slicers can be configured to appear vertically (as in Figure 14-1) or horizontally. To switch a slicer's orientation:

1. Select the slicer that you want to modify. (I selected the colors slicer that you created previously.)

2. In the Visualizations pane, click the Format icon.

3. Make sure you are in the Visual tab and expand the Slicer settings card and then the Options tab.

4. In the Orientation pop-up, select Horizontal.

5. Resize the slicer to suit your dashboard. A horizontal slicer will look something like the one in Figure 14-5.

Figure 14-5. *A horizontal slicer*

As you can see in Figure 14-4, a horizontal slicer does not have the small check boxes that a vertical slicer does. Consequently, when a horizontal slicer element is selected, the entire element is in "reverse video."

You probably also noticed that Power BI Desktop alters the number of rows of text as well as the width of text elements when you resize the slicer. It follows that you are best advised to experiment when altering slicer height and width in order to get the effect that suits you best.

Note   When you resize a horizontal slicer, you will see that the slicer elements alter to take up the available space providing that they can all fit.

Adjusting Selection Controls

If you are not happy with the way that Power BI Desktop lets you select items in a slicer, then you can adjust the way that you interact with this particular visual. While the Power BI default mode of interaction is probably sufficient in most cases, it certainly does no harm to know that there are other ways of selecting elements in slicers.

Adding or Removing the Select All Box

You can add the Select All box to slicer as follows:

1. Select the slicer that you want to modify. (I used the original, vertical colors slicer that you created earlier.)

2. In the Visual tab of the Formatting pane, expand the Slicer settings card, and then also expand the Selection card.

3. Set the Show "Select all" option to On. This will add a Select All item to the top (or left) of the slicer.

Should you *not* want a Select All item in a slicer, all you have to do is ensure that the Show "Select all" option switch is set to Off in step 3.

Enabling Multiselect

A slicer's default mode is to select only a single item. This does not preclude you from selecting multiple items in a slicer, if you Ctrl-click on the slicer elements.

As this can get a little wearing for users, you can set a slicer to allow Multiselect. This allows users to select multiple items more easily. Should you need to activate—or disactivate—multiselect, follow these steps:

1. Select the slicer that you want to modify. (I used the original, vertical colors slicer that you created earlier.)

2. In the Visual tab of the Formatting pane, expand the Slicer settings card, and then also expand the Selection card.

3. Set the Multiselect with Ctrl switch to Off. This will allow multiple slicer elements to be selected without the Ctrl key.

Enabling Single Select

A slicer's default mode is to select only a single item, unless the user Ctrl-clicks several items. If you prefer to add items one at a time—and deactivate them individually too—you can enable Single Select to do just this. Simply follow these steps:

1. Select the slicer that you want to modify. (I used the original, vertical colors slicer that you created earlier.)

2. In the Visual tab of the Formatting pane, expand the Slicer settings card, and then also expand the Selection card.

3. Set the Single select switch to the On position. This will set the slicer interaction to single select. You can see the result of this operation in Figure 14-6, where the slicer check boxes have become radio buttons.

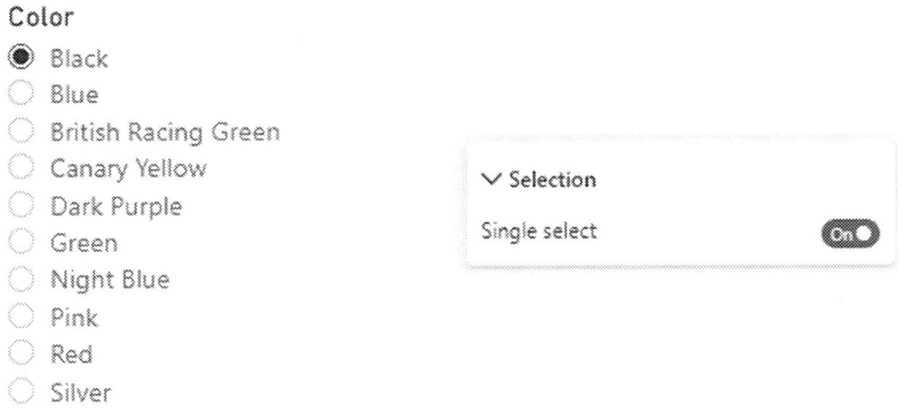

Color

◉ Black
○ Blue
○ British Racing Green
○ Canary Yellow
○ Dark Purple
○ Green
○ Night Blue
○ Pink
○ Red
○ Silver

∨ Selection

Single select   On

Figure 14-6. *Altering a slicer's selection controls*

Note   Setting single select to On makes the Multiselect with Ctrl and Show "Select all" option disappear from the Formatting pane. To make them reappear, you need to set Single select to Off.

Setting the Exact Size and X and Y Coordinates of a Slicer

If you want to place a slicer with total accuracy on a dashboard canvas, then you can set the X and Y (horizontal and vertical) coordinates for the slicer. You can also specify its exact height and width. The following explains how:

1. Select the slicer that you want to modify.

2. In the Formatting pane, activate the General tab.

3. Expand the Properties card and then the Position card.

4. Replace the X Position, Y Position, Width, and Height values with the pixel values that define the size and position of the slicer that you wish to apply. You can see an example of this in Figure 14-7.

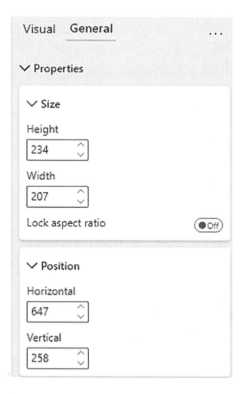

Figure 14-7. *Setting a slicer position on the dashboard canvas*

Formatting the Slicer Header

Should you want to add some visual flourish to a slicer, you can tweak the display of the slicer header. This can be a useful visual cue to users to help them distinguish slicers from other visuals. Here is an example of how to do this:

1. Select the slicer that you want to modify. (I used the horizontal colors slicer that you created earlier.)

2. In the Visual tab of the Formatting pane, expand the Slicer Header card.

3. Ensure that the Header switch is set to On.

4. Expand the Text card and choose a color for the header text.

5. Enter a different header text. I suggest **Car Colors:**.

6. Adjust the Text size and attributes to tweak the appearance of the header text.

7. Expand the Background card and choose a color for the header background using the Background color pop-up. You can see the results in Figure 14-8 in the next section.

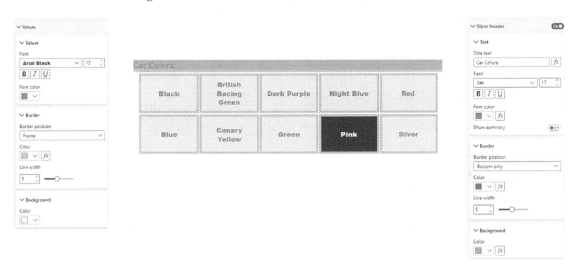

Figure 14-8. *A formatted slicer*

The available slicer header border options are explained in Table 14-1.

Table 14-1. *Slicer Header Options*

Option	Description
None	No border is visible
Bottom only	Adds a bottom border to the header
Top only	Adds a top border to the header
Left only	Adds a left border to the header
Right only	Adds a right border to the header
Top + bottom	Adds a top and bottom border to the header
Left + right	Adds a left and right border to the header
Frame	Adds a frame to the header

Formatting Slicer Items

Slicer items are the individual elements that make up the list of data that appear in a slicer, based on the underlying field. These, too, can be formatted to focus the attention of the reader. Here's an example:

1. Select the slicer that you want to modify (continuing with the colors slicer that you used in the previous section).

2. In the Formatting pane, expand the Values card.

3. Click the Font Color pop-up and choose a color for the item text.

4. Adjust the Text Size for the text of the items.

5. Expand the Background Color card and choose a color for the background of each item.

6. Expand the Border card and set the Border position to Frame from the options available in the Border position pop-up.

7. Choose a border color.

8. Set the border line width to **5**.

You can also format the following aspects of a slicer:

- Background

- Title

- Lock aspect ratio

However, since all of these are identical to formatting attributes that apply to tables and charts (and that you have seen in previous chapters), I will not repeat the description of them.

Finally, Figure 14-8 shows you a slicer with many of the formatting options that you just saw.

Sorting Slicer Elements

The elements in a slicer will be displayed in alphabetical order. If you wish, you can reverse this sort order, as follows:

1. Click the ellipses at the top right of the slicer.

2. Select Sort ascending or descending.

The slicer elements will now be ordered as you requested.

Tip   You can add a Sort By column to any data field that you wish to display in another sort order.

Switching to Dropdown Slicers

Slicers are amazingly useful, but they do have one drawback: they can take up a lot of valuable screen space. So the development team at Microsoft has come up with an elegant solution. This is to use dropdown slicers, where the slicer elements only appear when you click a pop-up menu.

To convert an existing slicer to a dropdown slicer:

1. Select an existing slicer (or hover the mouse pointer over it). I will use the colors slicer that you have used so far in this chapter.

2. Click the chevron on the top right next to the Clear Selections icon. A pop-up menu will appear, as you can see in Figure 14-9.

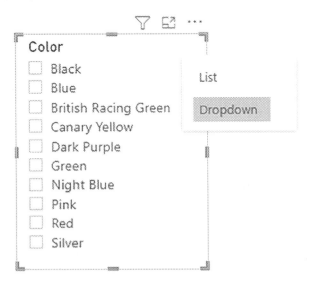

Figure 14-9. *Switching to dropdown slicer*

3. Select Dropdown. The slicer will convert to a dropdown slicer. You can see what this now looks like in Figure 14-10.

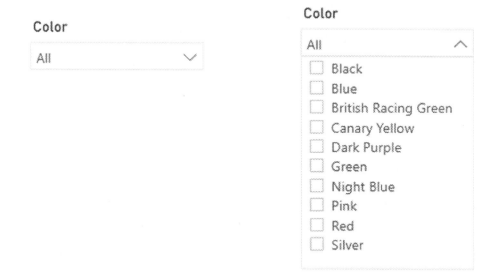

Figure 14-10. *A dropdown slicer*

4. Click the chevron for the slicer pop-up list and select the element that you want to slice the data on.

Tip   Dropdown slicers can be particularly useful when designing Power BI reports for mobile devices—as well as economizing on scarce screen real estate.

Exporting Slicer Data

Slicer data can be exported just like the data in any other visual:

1. Click the ellipses at the top right of the slicer.

2. Select Export Data.

3. Browse to the desired directory and enter a file name.

4. Click Save.

Using Charts As Slicers

You have seen how a table can become a slicer, which is a kind of filter. Well, charts can also be used as slicers. Knowing how charts can affect the data in a Power BI Desktop report can even influence the type of chart that you create, or your decision to use a chart to filter data rather than a standard slicer. Charts can be wonderful tools to grab and hold your audience's attention—as I am sure you will agree once you have seen the effects that they can produce.

Charts As Slicers

Charts can be used as a kind of slicer to filter data interactively for any or all of the visualizations in a Power BI Desktop report. This is also known as cross-filtering.

To see this in action, let's assume that we are aiming to produce a report using two objects:

- A Cost Plus Spares by Color table
- A Spare Parts by Make column chart

Let's create a Net Margin by Color table. It is principally used to show the effect that using a chart as a slicer in a Power BI Desktop report has on other objects. As an added extra, you will apply a filter to the page to demonstrate that filters and slicers work together, as described.

1. Open the C:\PowerBiDesktopSamples\
   PrestigeCarsDataForDashboards.pbix file and delete any existing
   visuals. You will need an entire uncluttered report for this
   example.

2. Add a table based on the following fields:

   a. Color (from the Vehicle table)

   b. SalePrice (from the Sales table)

3. Add a stacked bar chart based on the following fields:

   a. Make (from the Vehicle table)

   b. SpareParts (from the Sales table)

369

4.   Adjust the layout of the two visualizations so that it looks something like Figure 14-11. It is not important that only a subset of the makes is displayed.

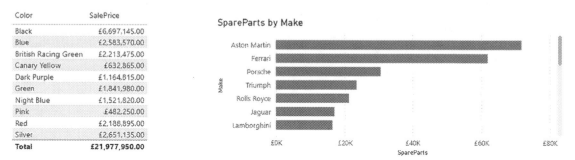

Color	SalePrice
Black	£6,697,145.00
Blue	£2,583,570.00
British Racing Green	£2,213,475.00
Canary Yellow	£632,865.00
Dark Purple	£1,164,815.00
Green	£1,841,980.00
Night Blue	£1,521,820.00
Pink	£482,250.00
Red	£2,188,895.00
Silver	£2,651,135.00
Total	**£21,977,950.00**

Figure 14-11. *Preparing a chart for use as a slicer*

To see how to use a chart as a slicer, click any column in the chart of parts costs by make. I will choose Jaguar in this example.

The Power BI Desktop report will look something like Figure 14-12.

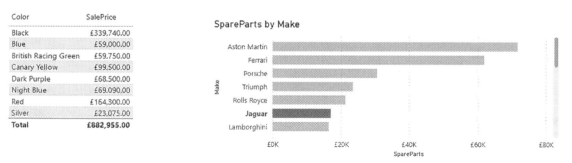

Color	SalePrice
Black	£339,740.00
Blue	£59,000.00
British Racing Green	£59,750.00
Canary Yellow	£99,500.00
Dark Purple	£68,500.00
Night Blue	£69,090.00
Red	£164,300.00
Silver	£23,075.00
Total	**£882,955.00**

Figure 14-12. *Slicing data using a chart*

You will see that not only is the make that you selected highlighted in the chart (the bars for other makes are dimmed), but that the *figures in the table also change*. They, too, only display the cost plus spares (for each color) for the selected make.

To slice on another make, merely click the corresponding column in the column chart. To cancel the effect of the chart acting as a slicer, all you have to do is click for a *second time* on the highlighted column.

Any bar chart, pie chart, or column chart can act like a slicer in this way, as can funnel charts, tree maps, scatter charts, bubble charts, and maps. The core factor is that for a simple slice effect, you need to use a chart that contains only one axis; that is, there will only be a single axis in the source data and no color or legend. What happens when you use more evolved charts to slice, filter, and highlight data is explained next.

Tip   It is perfectly possible to select multiple bars in a chart to highlight data in the same way that you can select multiple elements in a slicer. Simply Ctrl-click to select multiple items.

Cross-Filtering Chart Data

So far, we have seen how a chart can become a slicer for all the visualizations in a dashboard page. However, you can also use another aspect of Power BI Desktop interactivity to make data series in charts stand out from the crowd when you are presenting your findings. This particular aspect of data presentation is called *cross-filtering*.

Once again, cross-filtering is probably best appreciated with a practical example. First, we will create a stacked bar chart of parts and labor costs by CountryName; and then we will use it to highlight the various costs inside the chart.

1. In a blank Power BI Desktop report (so you do not get distracted), create a clustered column chart based on the following fields:

    a. CountryName (from the Geography table)

    b. SpareParts (from the Sales table)

    c. LaborCost (from the Sales table)

2. Click SpareParts in the *legend*. All the sales costs will be highlighted (i.e., remain the original color) in the column for each country, whereas the other cost will be grayed out.

After cross-filtering has been applied, the chart will look like Figure 14-13. This will also filter any other visuals on the page.

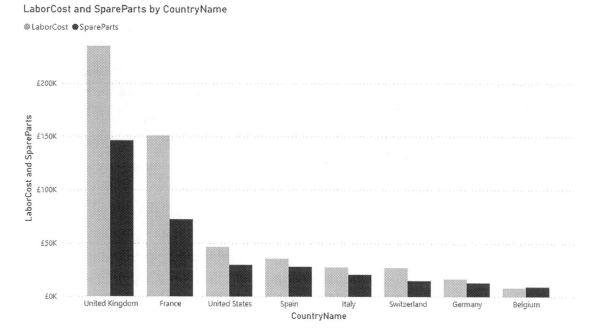

Figure 14-13. *Cross-filtering data inside a chart*

To remove the cross-filtering, all you have to do is click a second time on the same element in the legend. Or, if you prefer, you can click another legend element to highlight this aspect of the visualization instead. Yet another way to remove cross-filtering is to click inside the chart, but not on any data element.

Cross-filtering data in this way should suit any type of bar or column chart as well as line charts. It can also be useful in pie charts where you have added data to both the Axis and Legend boxes, which, after all, means you have multiple elements in the chart just as you can have with bar, column, and line charts. You might find it less useful with scatter charts.

Cross-Chart Cross-Filtering

Cross-chart cross-filtering adds an interesting extra aspect to chart cross-filtering and filtering. If you use one chart as a filter, the other chart is updated to reflect the effect of selecting this new filter not only by excluding any elements (slices, bars, or columns) that are filtered out but also by showing the proportion of data excluded by the filter.

As an example of this, create a pie chart of cost price by color and a column chart of direct costs by vehicle type. We will then cross-filter the two charts and see the results. The steps to follow are

1. Create a pie chart using the following fields:

   a. VehicleType (from the Vehicle table)

   b. CostPrice (from the Sales table)

2. Create a (clustered) column chart using the following fields:

   a. Make (from the Vehicle table)

   b. SalePrice (from the Sales table)

   For charts that are this simple, Power BI Desktop automatically attributes the fields to the correct boxes in the Fields list once the source tables are converted into charts. The result is shown in Figure 14-14.

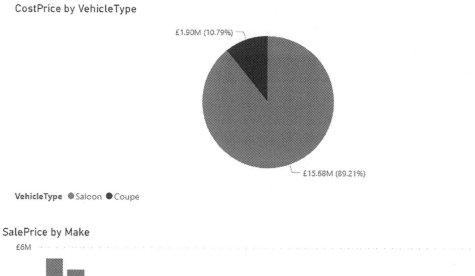

CostPrice by VehicleType

£1.90M (10.79%)

£15.68M (89.21%)

VehicleType ● Saloon ● Coupe

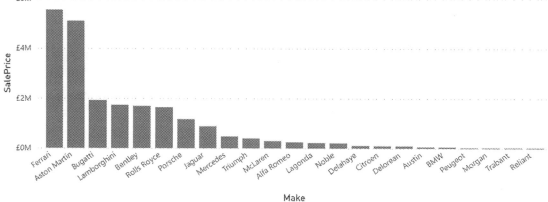

SalePrice by Make

Figure 14-14. *Preparing charts for cross-chart cross-filtering*

3. Now click a slice in the pie chart (I have selected the smallest slice which represents coupe). You should see the result given in Figure 14-15. Not only have all the other segments of the pie chart been dimmed, but the bars in the bar chart have been highlighted to show the proportion of the selected color of the total sales cost per vehicle cost.

CostPrice by VehicleType

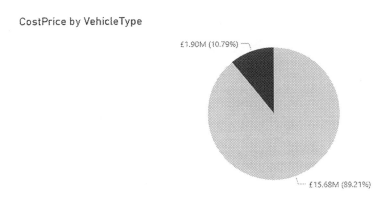

£1.90M (10.79%)

£15.68M (89.21%)

VehicleType ○ Saloon ● Coupe

SalePrice by Make

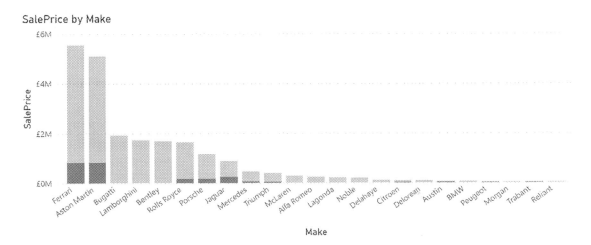

Figure 14-15. *Cross-chart cross-filtering*

4. Now click the bar in the bar chart representing Ferrari. You are now using the bar chart as a slicer. As you can see in Figure 14-16, the pie chart displays the proportion of Ferrari sales for each color.

CostPrice by VehicleType

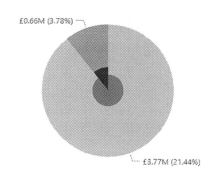

£0.66M (3.78%)

£3.77M (21.44%)

VehicleType ● Saloon ● Coupe

SalePrice by Make

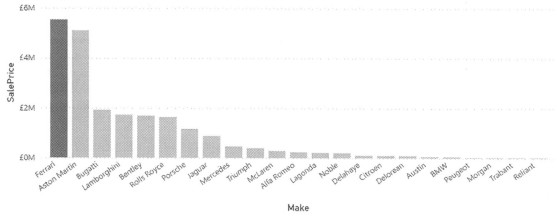

Figure 14-16. *Cross-chart cross-filtering applied to a pie chart*

Note   When you use a filter, you do not highlight a chart but actually filter the data that feeds into it; consequently, you remove elements from the chart. Cross-filtering leaves elements in a chart but accentuates certain aspects of the data relative to others.

Cross-Filtering Data in Bubble Charts

Often when developing a visualization whose main objective, after all, is to help you to see through the fog of data into the sunlit uplands of comprehension, profit, or indeed, whatever is the focus of your analysis, you may feel that you cannot see the forest for the trees. This is where Power BI Desktop's ability to highlight data in a chart visualization can be so effective.

Let's take a visualization that contains a lot of information; in this example, it is a bubble chart of vehicle types. Indeed, in this example, an audience might think that there is so much data that it is difficult to see the bubbles for specific makes of car, and so analyze the uniqueness for sales data by make. Power BI Desktop has a solution to isolate a data series in such a chart. To see this in action and to make the details clearer, you need to do as follows:

1. Create a bubble chart (remember that this is a scatter chart, really) using the following elements:

    a. *X Axis*: LaborCost

    b. *Y Axis*: SpareParts

    c. *Size*: CostPrice

    d. *Values*: SalePrice

    e. *Legend*: VehicleType

2. In the legend for the chart, click a vehicle type. I used saloon (the British word for sedan in the United States) in this example. The data for this vehicle type is highlighted in the chart, and the data for all the other vehicle types are dimmed, making one set of information stand out. This is shown in Figure 14-17.

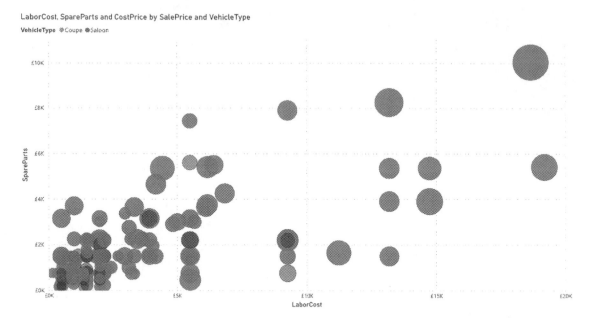

Figure 14-17. *Cross-filtering data in bubble charts*

This technique needs a few comments:

- To highlight another dataset, merely click another element in the legend.

- To revert to displaying all the data, click the selected element in the legend again.

- Cross-filtering data in this way also filters data in the entire page, as described previously.

Tip   You can add drill down to charts and still use chart cross-filtering in exactly the same way as you would use it normally, provided that you have disabled drill down using a chart element, as described in Chapter 10. In this case, you have to drill down (as well as up) using the Drill icons. The chart highlights an element at a drill down level or sublevel, as well as applying filtering to the Power BI Desktop report.

Charts As Complex Slicers

Now that you have seen how charts can be used as slicers, let's take things one step further and see them used as more complex slicer elements. To show this, I build on the principles shown in the previous example, but add a bubble chart that will slice data on two elements at once.

Follow these steps for the purposes of this example:

1. Build a Power BI Desktop report with the following:

    a. A matrix of SalePrice by CountryName (rows) and Color (columns)

    b. A clustered column chart using CostPrice and Make

2. Create a bubble chart using the following data (this is the one you created in the previous section):

    a. *X Axis*: LaborCost

    b. *Y Axis*: SpareParts

    c. *Size*: CostPrice

    d. *Values*: SalePrice

    e. *Legend*: VehicleType

3. Resize and tweak the bubble chart so that it is displayed under the existing column chart and table.

4. Click the top-right bubble in the bubble chart. The Power BI Desktop report should look like Figure 14-18. The tooltip indicates which bubble has been used to filter the other visuals.

CountryName	Black	Canary Yellow	Dark Purple	Green	Night Blue	Silver	Total
France		£2,000.00				£2,175.00	£4,175.00
Germany	£500.00			£2,175.00		£2,000.00	£4,675.00
Italy			£1,490.00				£1,490.00
Spain						£500.00	£500.00
United Kingdom	£2,175.00				£5,655.00		£7,830.00
Total	£2,675.00	£2,000.00	£1,490.00	£2,175.00	£5,655.00	£4,675.00	£18,670.00

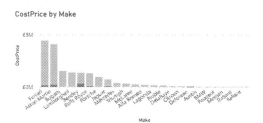

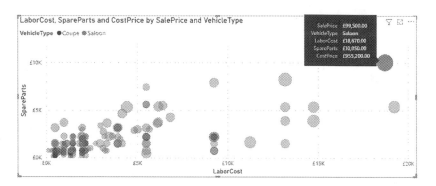

Figure 14-18. Cross-filtering and filtering using a chart

You can see that the other visualizations are filtered so that both the elements that make up the individual bubble (CountryName and Color) are used as filters (or double slicers if you prefer to think of them like that). This means that

- The table only shows colors where there are sales for this country and this color.

- The chart highlights data for this country and color only.

As was the case with simple chart slicers, you can cancel the filter effect merely by clicking for a second time on the selected bubble. Or you can switch filters by clicking another bubble in the bubble chart. You will also see the chart itself has data highlighted, but this is explained a little further on.

Clearly, you do not have to display the fields on which you are filtering and cross-filtering in all the visualizations in a report. I chose to do it in this example to make the outcome clearer. In the real world, all other visualizations in a report are filtered on the elements in the Details and Legend boxes of the bubble chart.

Bubble charts are not the only chart type that lets you apply two simultaneous filters, however. All chart types that display multiple fields allow this. However, I am of the opinion that some charts are better suited than others to this particular technique. Specifically, I am not convinced that line charts are always suited to being used as filters

380

for a Power BI Desktop report. Scatter charts may work—visually, that is—if you use cross-filtering, but it is just as likely that they will not. Stacked bar and stacked column charts can be ideal for cross-filtering, as you will see in the following sections.

Column and Bar Charts As Slicers

Column charts and bar charts can also be used to filter a Power BI Desktop report on two elements simultaneously. The only limitation is that you can only have one set of numeric data as the values for the chart. If the bar or column chart is a stacked bar, then you can click any of the sections in the stacked bar. In addition, if the chart is a clustered bar or column, you can click any of the columns in a group to slice by the elements represented in that section.

If this limitation is not a problem, then this is how you can use bar or column charts (whether they are clustered, stacked, or 100% stacked) to apply double filters to a report:

1. Create a Power BI Desktop dashboard using the C:\
   PowerBiDesktopSamples\PrestigeCarsDataForDashboards.pbix
   file with the following two elements:

   a. A matrix based on color and country name (as the rows), sales price, and cost price (as the values). Once the matrix is created, click the Expand all down one level icon in the hierarchy to see all the levels of data.

   b. A clustered bar chart of sales price by country name.

2. Then create a stacked column chart using the following data:

   a. *Values*: TotalDiscount

   b. *Axis*: Color

   c. *Legend*: Make

Once tweaked to clarify the appearance of the chart, the net result should look like Figure 14-19.

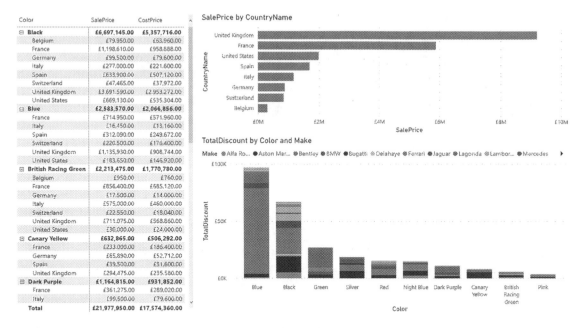

Figure 14-19. *A report ready for chart-based cross-filtering*

Clicking any segment of a column filters and highlights other visualizations on the same report for that country and color. An example of this is given in Figure 14-20, where the Ferrari has been selected for the black vehicle column.

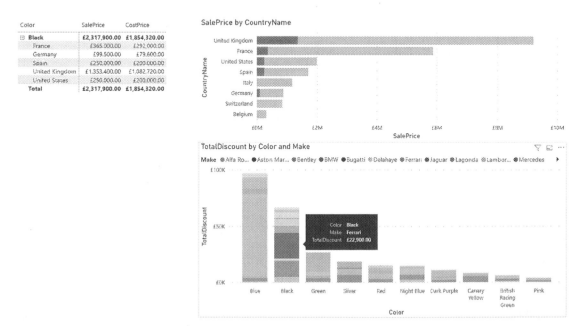

Figure 14-20. *Applying cross-filters*

Clicking any make in the legend will filter by make only. You see this in Figure 14-21, where the legend item for Bentley has been selected.

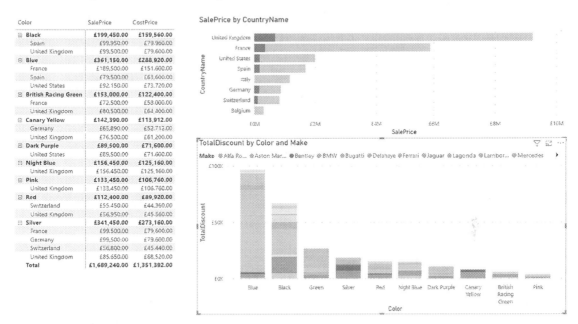

Figure 14-21. *Filtering using a legend element*

So in fact, you can choose to filter on a single element or multiple elements, depending on whether you use the chart or the legend as the filter source.

Note   A line chart will not produce the same effect when you click only a data point. If you click a series in a line chart, you are cross-filtering that series, which is numeric data, and so it cannot be used as a slicer. Similarly, if you click an element in the legend of a column or bar chart, you are selecting a data series, and this, too, cannot serve as a slicer (even though it highlights the series in the chart).

Specifying Visual Interactions

In the previous few sections, you saw that the effects of selecting one or more items in a slicer are applied automatically to every visual on a page, as will the effects of using a chart as a slicer. This is indeed true and is the default behavior of Power BI Desktop unless you specifically configure a visual *not* to react when a chart or slicer on the page has items selected.

In effect, this means that you can attain a tremendous degree of subtlety in your dashboards, because you can define which visuals are to remain interactive—and which must not change when a slicer, chart, or multiple slicers and charts are used.

The following explains how to alter the default setting and remove interactivity from a visual. You need to be aware that you need at least two visuals in a report to carry out this modification.

1.   Select the visual (this can be a text visual, a chart visual, or a slicer, for instance) that you want to prevent having a cross-filtering effect on other visuals.

2.   In the Format ribbon, click the Edit Interactions button. All the other visuals on the page will display the interaction icons that you can see in Figure 14-22.

Figure 14-22. *The visual interaction icons for visuals*

3.   Click the Stop Interaction icon (the "no entry" sign) in another visualization. I used the table of sales by country that you created previously. This icon will appear filled in, as shown in Figure 14-23.

Figure 14-23. *The visual interaction icons set to prevent interaction*

4. Repeat steps 2 through 5 for all visuals that you want to "disconnect" from the selected visual.

5. In the Home ribbon, click the Edit Interactions button to stop configuration of visual interaction. This will *keep* the existing interaction *settings*, but *prevent* the *display* of the interaction icons.

You can then iterate through all the charts and slicers on a page to set their dependency on another element.

Note   A slicer can also be linked to or dependent on another slicer on the page. Consequently, you can set the interaction for a slicer just as you can for any other visual.

What-If Slicers

A really interesting feature in Power BI Desktop is the ability to interact with data using what-if slicers. These allow you to define variable values that are then applied to the data in the data model for any fields that you choose. You can then adjust the what-if value in a slider on screen and watch the calculated values change in real time.

This feature is best appreciated if you experiment with it. So here is one example of a what-if slicer. Let's suppose that you want to see what happens to gross margin if suppliers increase the cost of spare parts.

1. In the Modeling ribbon, click the New parameter button.

2. Enter **SparePartsVariation** in the Name box.

3. Select Decimal Number as the data type from the Data Type pop-up list.

4. Leave the Minimum value as 0, and enter **0.5** (50 percent) as the Maximum value.

5. Set the increment to **0.02** (two percent). The dialog will look like the one in Figure 14-24.

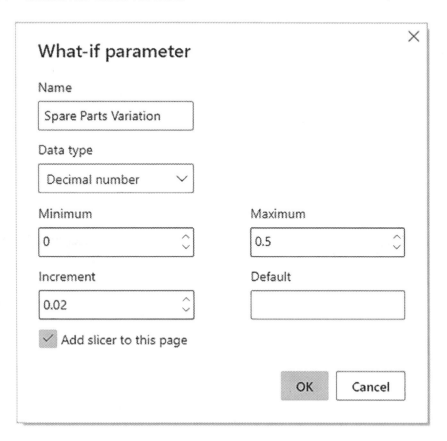

Figure 14-24. *The What-If Parameter dialog*

6. Click OK. Power BI Desktop will add a new table to the data model named SparePartsVariation as well as a slicer to the desktop canvas. After resizing the slicer, you can see these, as well as the data in the new table (from the Data View), in Figure 14-25.

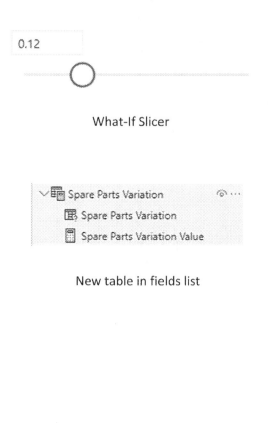

0.12

What-If Slicer

New table in fields list

Spare Parts Variation ▾
0
0.02
0.04
0.06
0.08
0.1
0.12
0.14
0.16
0.18
0.2
0.22
0.24
0.26
0.28
0.3
0.32
0.34
0.36
0.38
0.4
0.42
0.44
0.46
0.48

Table values

Figure 14-25. *A what-if slicer*

7. Click the SalesInfo table in the Fields list and then click New Measure in the Home or Modeling ribbons.

8. Enter the following formula in the Formula bar (this will calculate a new spare parts cost using the multiplier from the what-if slicer):

```
SparePartsNew = SUM(Sales[SpareParts]) +
(SUM(Sales[SpareParts]) * 'Spare Parts Variation'[Spare
Parts Variation Value])
```

9. Click the check box on the formula bar to confirm the creation of the new column. You can see this column in the Data View if you select the Spare Parts Variation table.

10. Create a clustered column chart using the following fields:

    a. Make (from the Vehicle table)

    b. SpareParts (from the Sales table)

    c. SparePartsNew (from the Sales table)

11. Adjust the slider to apply a new percentage increase in the cost of spare parts. The resulting chart and slicer will look like those in Figure 14-26 (I have formatted SparePartsNew to appear as a percentage).

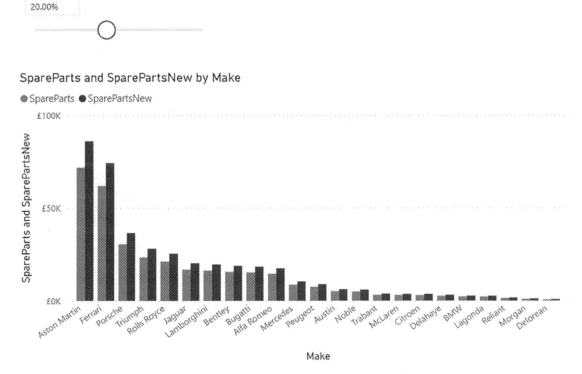

Figure 14-26. *A what-if slicer applied to a chart*

The values that you add in the table that underlies the what-if slicer can be fixed values, percentages—anything you like. Moreover, you can create as many new measures based on the what-if value as you want to.

Custom Visuals As Slicers

There are many excellent third-party visuals available that are designed to be slicers. This section provides a few pointers to some of the currently available third-party slicers. These are only a few of the slicers that you can find. Once again, I have limited the selection to third-party visuals developed by Microsoft.

All the third-party slicers that are explained in the following sections can be added to a Power BI Desktop file using the techniques that you saw in Chapter 11.

Timeline Slicer

The timeline slicer lets you drag the upper and lower limits of a date range. You can also define the date element (year, quarter, month, week, or day) to use interactively. You can see this in Figure 14-27, where the timeline slicer is using the DateKey field from the DataDimension table.

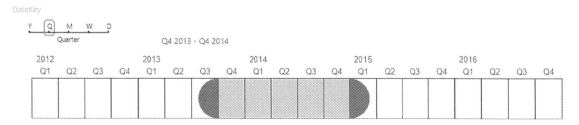

Figure 14-27. *The timeline slicer*

The timeline slicer allows you to specify

- The depth of detail that you wish to display from a hierarchy of time (year level, quarter level, month level, week level, or day level)

- A visual data range that you specify by dragging the ends of the data range left and right

Timebrush Slicer

A timebrush slicer allows you to highlight a section of a time-ordered dataset. You can see this in Figure 14-28, where you can see that selecting a time range has filtered the table. This approach allows you to "home in" on potentially interesting data expressed in the slicer and see the detail displayed in other visuals.

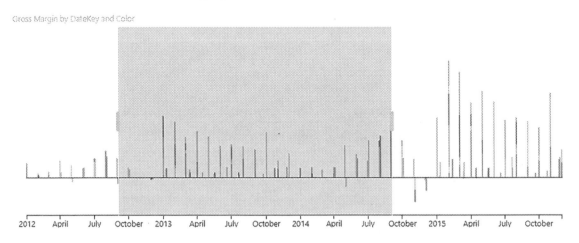

Color	SalePrice	LaborCost	CostPrice	Gross Margin
Black	£935,250	£11,179	£605,490	£329,760
Blue	£1,900,250	£16,162	£1,135,100	£765,150
British Racing Green	£1,380,000	£11,093	£919,490	£460,510
Canary Yellow	£1,878,940	£21,410	£1,272,315	£606,625
Dark Purple	£944,500	£8,221	£564,180	£380,320
Green	£1,055,490	£13,943	£690,715	£364,775
Night Blue	£779,600	£8,545	£594,290	£185,310
Red	£2,623,990	£23,276	£1,492,295	£1,131,695
Silver	£1,233,690	£11,783	£613,770	£419,920
Total	£12,731,710	£125,632	£8,087,645	£4,644,065

Figure 14-28. *The timebrush slicer*

Chiclet Slicer

A chiclet slicer is a slicer that you can arrange and format in a multitude of ways. You can see a simple example in Figure 14-29.

Figure 14-29. *The chiclet slicer*

This particular slicer really does add a multitude of options. I strongly recommend that you take a look at all that it can do. To whet your appetite, it is worth noting that you can

- Specify colors of selected and unselected elements

- Define the standard height and width of elements

- Add images to elements

Text Filter

The text filter is a kind of slicer in that it lets you enter a text—which need not be a complete word or even match any complete word in a field—to filter on the text interactively. You can see a text filter as well as the results of applying it (through clicking the magnifying glass icon) in Figure 14-30.

Figure 14-30. *A text filter in operation*

Choosing the Correct Approach to Interactive Data Selection

Now that you have taken a tour of the interactive options that Power BI Desktop offers, it is worth remembering that there is a fundamental difference between slicers and chart filters:

- Slicers and chart filters apply to all visuals on the Power BI Desktop page unless you have tweaked the visual interactions.

- Cross-filtering only applies to the selected chart, although it filters data in other tables and highlights the percentage of this element in other charts.

Conclusion

In this chapter, you have seen how to use the interactive potential of Power BI Desktop to enhance the delivery of information to your audience. You saw how to add slicers to a report and then how to use them to filter out data from the visualizations it contains. Then, you learned how to highlight data in charts. Next, you saw how to use charts as interactive slicers to isolate specific elements in a presentation.

You then extended your knowledge by learning how to apply what-if slicers and took a peek at some of the third-party slicers that are available. Finally, you took a quick tour of some of the third-party slicers that are available.

These techniques are powerful tools that can dramatically enhance the way that you present data to an audience. Used carefully, they will help your dashboards become more powerful and even more memorable. So all that remains is for you to start applying these techniques using your own data. Then you can see how you can impress your audiences using all the interactive possibilities of Power BI Desktop.

CHAPTER 15

Enhancing Dashboards

After spending a little time working with Power BI Desktop, I can assume that you have analyzed your data. In fact, I imagine that you have been able to tease out a few extremely interesting trends and telling facts from your deep dive into the figures—and you have created the tables, charts, maps, and gauges to prove your point. To finish the job, you now want to add the final tweaks to the look and feel of your work so that it will come across to your audience as polished and professional.

Fortunately, Power BI Desktop is on hand to help with all of these final touches, too. It can propel your effort onto a higher level of presentation—without you needing to be a graphic artist—so that your audience is captivated. With a few clicks, you can

- Align and distribute objects on the report canvas.

- Add free-form text.

- Add images to a report.

- Apply a report background.

- Add basic shapes to enhance your visuals.

- Superpose objects and define how they are placed one on top of another.

- Prepare reports ready for display on mobile devices.

- Apply predefined themes (or style sheets) to standardize the presentation of your reports.

So, while not attempting to rival expensive drawing applications, Power BI Desktop can certainly add the necessary design flourishes that will help you to seize your audience's attention and convince them of the value of your analysis.

This chapter takes you through these various techniques and explains how to use them to add the final touches to your analysis. We will use the C:\ PowerBiDesktopSamples\PrestigeCarsDataForDashboards.pbix file as the source data

© Adam Aspin 2022
A. Aspin, *Pro Power BI Dashboard Creation*, https://doi.org/10.1007/978-1-4842-8227-4_15

and as an example of all the dashboards in this chapter. You will also have to download the image files that are part of the source files to the C:\PowerBiDesktopSamples\Images folder from the Apress website, as described in Appendix A.

Formatting Ribbons

When enhancing dashboards, you will need to use three further ribbons:

- The View ribbon

- The Insert ribbon

- The Format ribbon

These three ribbons are described in the following sections.

The View Ribbon

The View ribbon options are illustrated in Figure 15-1 and explained in Table 15-1.

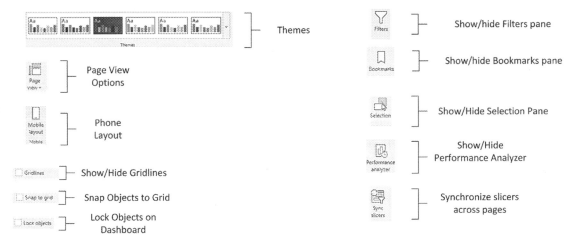

Figure 15-1. *The View ribbon*

Table 15-1. *View Ribbon Options*

Option	Description
Themes	Lets you choose a theme to apply to your entire dashboard.
Mobile Layout	Switches from desktop layout to phone layout and back.
Page View: Fit to Page	Scales the display to fit the available screen dimensions.
Page View: Fit to Width	Scales the display to fit the width of the screen.
Page View: Actual Size	Displays the page at its actual size.
Show or Hide Gridlines	Displays or hides the underlying grid.
Snap Objects to Grid	Forces visuals to align to the grid (hidden or visible) or leaves them free-floating.
Lock Objects	Fixes all objects in place and prevents them being resized or moved.
Filters Pane	Shows or hides the Filters pane.
Bookmarks Pane	Shows or hides the Bookmarks pane. You will learn about this in the upcoming chapters.
Selection Pane	Shows or hides the Selection pane. You will learn about this in the next chapter.
Performance Analyzer	Shows or hides the Power BI Desktop Performance Analyzer. This tool can help you monitor the time taken by each visual in a report to query the data and render the result.
Synch Slicers	Shows or hides the Synch Slicers pane. This allows you to enable slicers to filter data on the pages that you select.

The Insert Ribbon

The Insert ribbon options are illustrated in Figure 15-2 and explained in Table 15-2.

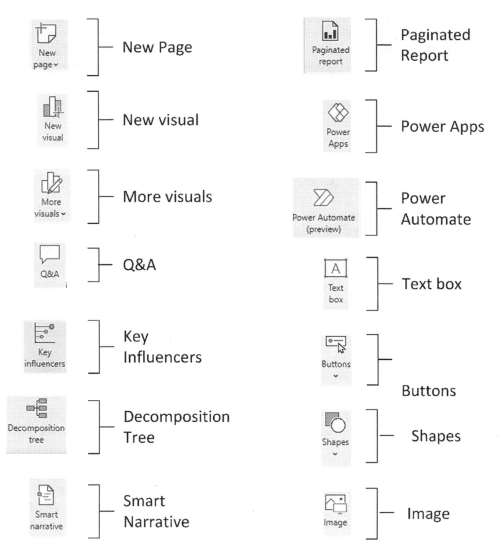

Figure 15-2. *The Insert ribbon*

Table 15-2. *Insert Ribbon Options*

Option	Description
New page	Lets you copy the current page or insert a blank page after the existing page
New visual	Inserts a new blank visual onto the current page
More visuals	Lets you add third-party visuals from disk or the App Store
Q&A	Lets you ask questions of the data using natural language
Key Influencers	Inserts a new blank Key Influencers visual onto the current page
Decomposition Tree	Inserts a new blank Decomposition Tree visual onto the current page
Smart Narrative	Inserts a new blank Smart Narrative visual onto the current page
Paginated Report	Inserts a new blank Paginated Report visual onto the current page
Power Apps	Inserts a new blank Power Apps visual onto the current page
Power Automate	Inserts a new blank Power Automate visual onto the current page
Text box	Inserts an empty text box onto the current page
Buttons	Adds a button to the current page
Shapes	Adds a shape to the current page
Image	Adds an image to the current page

The Format Ribbon

The Format ribbon options are illustrated in Figure 15-3 and explained in Table 15-3.

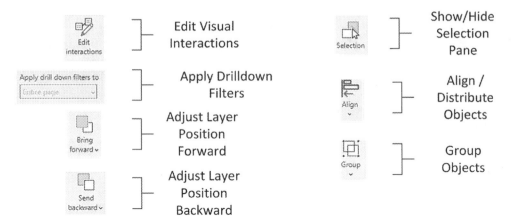

Figure 15-3. *The Format ribbon*

Table 15-3. *Format Ribbon Options*

Option	Description
Edit Interactions	Changes how visuals react when data points in other visuals are selected
Apply drill down filters to	Allows drill down to filter data in other visuals
Bring Forward	Brings a visual toward the top of a layer of objects
Send Backward	Sends a visual toward the bottom of a layer of objects
Selection	Displays the Selection pane which allows you to show and hide (and set the tab order for) all the visuals on the page
Align Objects	Aligns and distributes selected visuals
Group	Groups selected visuals

Formatting the Page

Before you spend a certain amount of time and effort finalizing a presentation, it is vital to define one fundamental aspect of the output—the page format. Power BI Desktop lets you select from among the following output device formats:

- 16:9

- 4:3

- Letter

- Tooltip

- Custom

To change the page size, follow these steps:

1. Click anywhere on the report canvas (and *not* on a visual).

2. In the Visualizations pane, click the Format icon.

3. Expand the Canvas settings card.

4. Select one of the page size presets from the Type pop-up list.

Should you wish to specify your own page size, simply select Custom from the Type pop-up list and then enter the required page height or width in pixels. You can use the scroll arrows to set the required figure if you prefer. You can see the results of this in Figure 15-4.

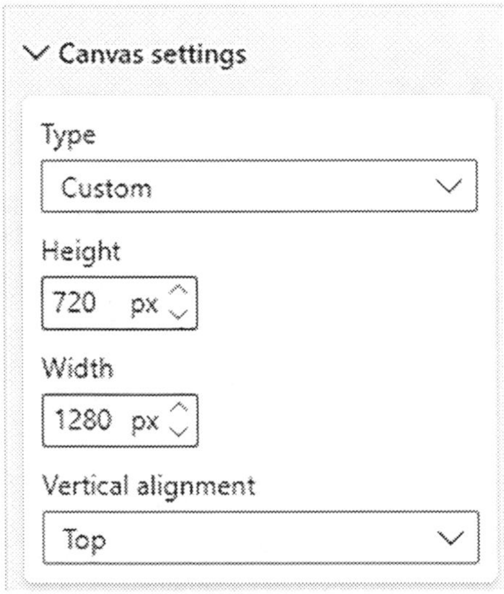

Figure 15-4. *Custom page size settings*

Note   Currently, the only available unit of measure is pixels.

Aligning and Distributing Visuals

There is one quick and easy tweak that is capable of adding a polished look to any dashboard. This is the simple decision to align visuals flawlessly so that you avoid giving an impression of ragged positioning. Like it or not, well-aligned visuals will help convince your audience that your analysis is valid.

To be clear, when I say *align visuals*, I include distributing visuals on the dashboard canvas. So here is how you can apply both techniques to give a patina of professionalism to your dashboards.

Aligning Visuals

A set of neatly aligned elements on a page will always please an audience. What is more, it literally only takes a couple of seconds to take a set of existing visuals and to present them harmoniously. The following explains what you do:

1. Select the visuals that you want to align (Ctrl-click each one).

2. In the Format ribbon, click the Align button to display the pop-up menu. It will look like Figure 15-5.

Figure 15-5. Alignment options

3. Select the required option.

The selected elements will be aligned along their tops, bottoms, left or right sides, or centered, depending on the choice that you made. The available alignment options are outlined in Table 15-4.

Table 15-4. *Alignment Options*

Option	Description
Align Left	Aligns all the selected visuals along their left sides
Align Center	Centers all the selected visuals
Align Right	Aligns all the selected visuals along their right sides
Align Top	Aligns all the selected visuals along their top edges
Align Middle	Aligns all the selected visuals in the middle of the elements
Align Bottom	Aligns all the selected visuals along their bottom edges

Note   You have to select more than one visual for this option to be available.

Distributing Visuals

One way to add a final touch that implies "attention to detail" to a dashboard is to make sure that all visuals are neatly distributed horizontally and/or vertically. This will simply guarantee that there is always the same amount of space between each element.

1. Select the visuals that you want to distribute (Ctrl-click each one).

2. In the Format ribbon, click the Align button to display the pop-up menu.

3. Select the required option.

4. The selected elements will be distributed horizontally or vertically, depending on the choice that you made. The available distribution options are outlined in Table 15-5.

Table 15-5. *Distribution Options*

Option	Description
Distribute Horizontally	Distributes a selected series of visuals along a horizontal plane
Distribute Vertically	Distributes a selected series of visuals along a vertical axis

Note   You may need to distribute a collection of visuals both horizontally and vertically to get the best effect. You will need to carry out the two alignment operations successively to obtain this result. Also, you must select at least three visuals.

Aligning to the Grid

The Power BI Desktop canvas includes a grid (like a sheet of squared paper) that you can use to align visuals and other objects. This can help you create more polished-looking presentations. To align to the grid, simply

1. Activate the View menu.

2. Select Snap Objects to Grid.

Now, whenever you move or resize an object, it will align to the grid or increase/decrease in size by one grid point (or pixel).

Displaying the Grid

If you prefer, you can also display the grid to help you align objects:

1. Activate the View menu.

2. Select Show Gridlines.

You will now see a pattern of dots (one every 10 pixels) representing the hidden grid.

Note   The number of pixels in the Power BI Desktop report canvas will depend on the selected page size.

Specifying the Exact Position of a Visual

A final option that you can apply when placing visuals is to specify their exact position, height, and width. This feature is particularly useful when you want to make a series of visuals the same size. Follow these steps:

1. Select the visual that you want to resize and/or reposition.

2. In the Visualizations pane, click the Format icon.

3. Expand the General section.

4. Expand the Properties card and then expand the Position card.

5. Set the X (horizontal starting) position, Y (vertical starting) position, height, and width.

Power BI Desktop uses pixels as the unit of placement as it does for the underlying grid.

Adding Text Boxes to Annotate a Report

Let's begin at the start. You have spent quite a while digging into data and have found effective ways of drawing your audience's attention to the valuable information that it contains. However, you need the one, final, cherry on the cake—a title for the report. As a title is nothing other than a text box, this is your introduction to adding, formatting, and modifying text boxes.

A text box is a floating text entity that you can place anywhere on the Power BI Desktop report canvas. They are especially useful for annotating specific parts of a dashboard.

Adding a Text Box

Adding a text box is so easy that it takes longer to describe than to do, but nonetheless, this is how you do it:

1. In the Insert ribbon, click the Text Box button. An empty text box will appear on the dashboard canvas.

2. Type in the text that you want to add; it will be a title. I entered **Sales for 2022**.

3. Place the mouse pointer over either the corner or lateral central indicators of the title box and drag the mouse to resize the title box.

4. Click the text box header bar (the gray area at the top of the text box) and drag the text box to the top center of the page.

5. Click outside the title anywhere in the blank report canvas.

Figure 15-6 shows you a text box added to a report. Moreover, should you want to modify a text, it is as easy as clicking inside the text box and altering the existing text just as you would in, say, PowerPoint.

Figure 15-6. *Adding a text box to a report*

Note   If a text box is too small to hold the entire text, vertical scrollbars are added to the text box when you select it. To make these disappear, you will need to resize the text box to ensure that all the text is visible.

Moving Text Boxes

Text boxes are a Power BI Desktop visualization like any other, and consequently, they can be moved and resized just as if they were a table or a chart. So all you have to do to move a title is to

1. Hover the mouse pointer over the text box. A container will appear indicating the text box shape.

2. Click the top bar of the text box and drag the text box elsewhere on the dashboard canvas.

Alternatively, you can select the text box and then place the mouse pointer over the edges of the text box (but not on the corner or side handles) and drag the text box to a new position.

Formatting a Text Box

A text box can be formatted specifically so that you can give it the weight and power that you want. Even though this is completely intuitive, for the sake of completeness, here is a short example of what you can do:

1. Select the text box that you created previously. The Format palette will be displayed under or above the text box.

2. Select the text that you wish to modify.

3. Click the Font pop-up and select the font that you want to apply to the selected text.

4. Click the Font Size pop-up and select the size (in points) that you want to apply.

5. Apply any font attributes that you require (bold, underline, italic) by clicking the relevant icons.

6. Align the text by clicking one of the three alignment icons. This will apply to all the text in the box.

Tip   Remember that you must highlight the text to format it. If you select the text box itself, then you can only alter the alignment of the text in the text box.

The formatting options for text boxes are explained in Table 15-6.

Table 15-6.   *Formatting Options for Text Boxes*

Element	Icon	Description
Font	Segoe UI ⌄	Lets you choose a font from those installed on the computer
Font Size	10 ⌄	Lets you choose a font size
Font Colors	A ⌄	Lets you choose a font color
Bold	B	Makes the text appear in boldface
Italic	I	Makes the text appear in italics
Underline	U	Underlines the text
Left	≡	Places the text on the left of the text box
Center	≡	Centers the text in the text box
Right	≡	Places the text on the right of the text box
Hyperlink	⊘	Adds a hyperlink for the selected text
Superscript	x^2	Makes the text appear as superscript
Subscript	x_2	Makes the text appear as subscript
Bulleted list	≣	Makes the text appear as a bullet list

Adding a Hyperlink

Power BI Desktop dashboards certainly do not exist in isolation. It follows that you can use them as a starting point to link to other documents or web pages. Remember, however, that a hyperlink will *only* work once a Power BI Desktop file has been deployed to the Power BI Service in the cloud.

To add a hyperlink:

1. Select the text box that you created previously.

2. Select the text that will be the hyperlink.

3. Click the Hyperlink icon. The Format palette will expand to display the hyperlink box.

4. Enter or paste in a URL.

5. Click the Done button in the Format palette.

Removing a Hyperlink

To remove a hyperlink that you have already added:

1. Select the text box containing a hyperlink that you created previously.

2. Click inside the hyperlink. The Format palette will expand.

3. Click the Remove button.

If you prefer, you can always simply remove the text that is the link.

Deleting Text Boxes

If you want to delete a text box, then be sure to

1. Select the text box.

2. Click the pop-up menu for the text box (the ellipses at the top right of the text box).

3. Select Remove. The text box will be deleted.

An alternative way to delete a text box is to select the text box and press the Delete key.

Note   Merely selecting and deleting the text inside the text box will not remove the text box itself; so to be sure that you do not leave any unnecessary clutter in a report, delete any unwanted and empty text boxes.

Text Box General Attributes

A text box can have a background, borders, and a title just like any visual. These are set as for any visual. This is explained in the first two chapters.

Modifying the Page Background Color

Power BI Desktop does not condemn you to presenting every report with a white background. To avoid monotony, you can add a different color background to each page in a report individually with a couple of clicks.

To apply a background to a report, all you have to do is

1.   Click inside the dashboard canvas, but not on any existing visuals.

2.   In the Visualizations pane, click the Format icon.

3.   Expand the Canvas background pane. The available options will look like they do in Figure 15-7.

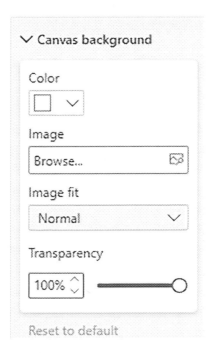

Figure 15-7. *Page background options*

4. Select a color from the palette of available colors.

5. Slide the Transparency button left or right to select a level of intensity for the chosen color.

Note   You have to format every page in a report individually. You cannot Ctrl-click to select multiple pages simultaneously.

Images

We all know what a picture is worth. Well, so does Power BI Desktop. Consequently, you can add pictures, or images, as they are generically known, to a Power BI Desktop report to replace words and enhance your presentation. The images that you insert into a Power BI Desktop report can come from the Web or from a file on a disk—either local or on an available network share. Once an image has been inserted, it is *not* linked to the source file. So if the source image changes, you will have to reinsert it to keep it up to date.

The following are some of the uses for images in Power BI Desktop:

- As a background image for a report.

- Images in tables instead of text. An example could be to use product images.

- Images in slicers. These could be flags of countries, for instance.

- Independent images—a logo, for instance, or a complement to draw the viewer's attention to a specific point.

- Images as a chart plot area background.

Once we have looked at the types of image formats available, we will see how images can be used in all these contexts.

Image Sources

There are multitudes of image formats. Power BI Desktop accepts all of the following industry-standard image types:

- *JPEG*: This is a venerable standard image file format.

- *PNG*: This is a standard file format for Internet images.

- *BMP*: This is a standard image type produced by MS Paint, for instance.

- *GIF*: This is a venerable image format frequently used in web pages.

- *TIFF*: This is a standard format for scanned images.

- *RLE*: Run length encoding format.

- *JPE*: The 24-bit compressed JPEG graphic format.

- *JFIF*: A Bitmap graphic that uses JPEG compression.

All of these formats (and their various descendant formats that Power BI Desktop can handle) can deliver reasonable quality images that should certainly suffice for Power BI Desktop reports. However, if you attempt to insert an image that is not in a format that Power BI Desktop can handle, you will get an alert and the image will *not* be inserted.

Note   When you attempt to insert an image from a file, the Open dialog filters the files so that only files with one of the acceptable extensions are visible. You can force the dialog to display other file formats, but Power BI Desktop may not be able to load them.

Adding an Image

You may still want to add completely free-form floating images to a report. However, before getting carried away with all that can be done with images, remember that Power BI Desktop is not designed as a high-end presentation package. If anything, it is there to help you analyze and present information quickly and cleanly. Inevitably, you will find that there are things that you cannot do in Power BI Desktop that you are used to doing in, say, PowerPoint. Consequently, there are many presentation tricks and techniques that you may be tempted to achieve in Power BI Desktop using images to get similar results. Indeed, you can achieve many things in a Power BI Desktop report by adding images. Yet the question that you must ask yourself is "Am I adding value to my report?" I am a firm believer that less is more in a good presentation. Consequently, although I will show you a few tricks using images, many of them go against the grain of fast and efficient Power BI Desktop report creation and can involve considerable adjustment whenever the data in a visualization changes. So I advise you not to go overboard using images to enhance your presentations unless it is really necessary.

Despite these caveats, let's add a floating, independent image to a Power BI Desktop report. In this example, it is a company logo—that of Brilliant British Cars, the company whose metrics we are analyzing throughout the course of this book.

Adding an image is really simple. All you have to do is

1. In the Power BI Desktop Insert ribbon, click the Image button. A classic Windows dialog will appear; it lets you choose the source image, as shown in Figure 15-8.

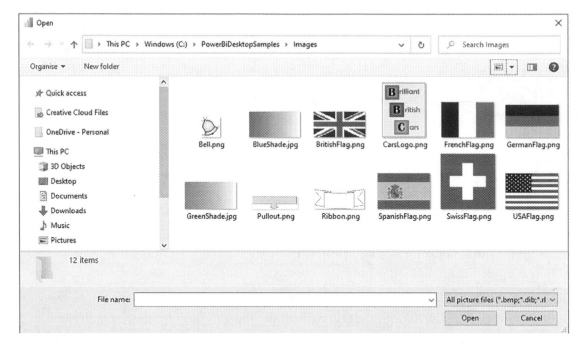

Figure 15-8. *Navigating to an image file*

2. Navigate to the directory containing the image that you wish to insert. There are several sample images in the C:\ PowerBiDesktopSamples\Images folder, which you can install as described in Appendix A.

3. Click the image file. I use the example image CarsLogo.png in this example.

4. Click Open. The selected image will be loaded into the page.

5. Drag the image to the top left of the page and resize it. The dashboard will look like it does in Figure 15-9.

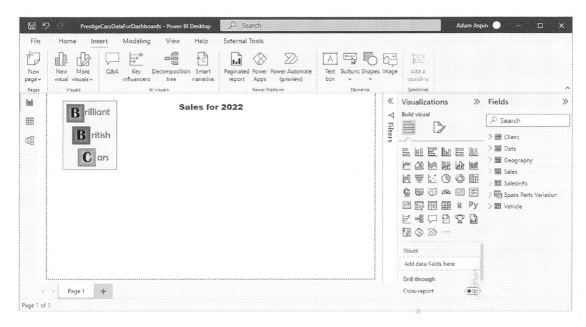

Figure 15-9. *An image added to a dashboard*

Removing an Image

To remove an image, all you have to do is

1. Select the image.

2. Click the pop-up menu for the image (the ellipses at the top right of the text box).

3. Select Remove. The image will be removed from the report. The original image file, of course, will not be affected in any way.

An alternative way to delete an image is to select the image and press the Delete key. The selected image will disappear from the report.

Resizing Images

An image is just like any other visual in a Power BI Desktop dashboard in that any of these elements can be moved and resized in exactly the same way. Simply do the following:

1. Select the image that you want to resize.

2. Place the mouse pointer over either the corner or lateral central indicators of the image and drag the mouse to resize the image.

Note   If you want an image—or any visual for that matter—to retain the same aspect ratio (the height-to-width ratio) when you resize it, simply hold down the Alt and Shift keys as you drag a corner handle.

Formatting Images

Once you have added an image, it can be tweaked to some extent in Power BI Desktop. The following are the parameters that you can modify:

- Image scaling

- Image title

- Image background

- Image border

- Aspect ratio

- Exact position and size

All of these modifications except for the first are common to most of the visualizations in Power BI Desktop. Indeed, you have come across some of them several times already. Consequently, I will not waste your time repeating things that you already know, or can find elsewhere in this book.

Image *scaling* is completely new, however. Here is how you can alter the way that an image is altered if you resize it:

1. Select the image whose scaling you want to modify.

2. In the Visualizations pane (which has switched automatically to show only formatting options), expand the Style card followed by the Scaling card.

3. In the Scaling pop-up, select Fill.

The image will adjust to take up all the available space in the image placeholder. The three available image scaling options are explained in Table 15-7.

Table 15-7. *Image Scaling Options*

Option	Description
Normal	The image maintains its height-to-width ratio (whatever the Lock Aspect setting) and resizes to fill the image placeholder as well as it can.
Fill	The image fills the image placeholder but it gets distorted.
Fit	The image fills the image placeholder but parts of the image are cut off rather than the image getting distorted.

Background Images

One major, and frequently very striking, use of images is as a background to a report—and possibly even to a whole series of reports. So let's take a look at how to use images for report backgrounds.

Adding a Background Image

Before anything else, you need to add a background image. This is, once again, extremely simple:

1. Click the dashboard canvas for the page where you want to add a background image. Make sure that no visuals are selected.

2. In the Visualizations pane, click the Format icon.

3. Expand the Canvas Background card.

4. Click Add Image. A classic Windows dialog will appear; it lets you choose the source image.

5. Navigate to the directory containing the image that you wish to insert. In this example, it will be C:\ PowerBiDesktopSamples\Images.

6. Click the image file. I will use the example image GreenShade.jpg in this example.

7. Click Open. The selected image will be loaded into the page.

8. In the Image Fit pop-up list, select Fit.

9. With the Page Background card of the Format panel expanded, slide the Transparency slider left or right so that the image is visible.

The selected image will cover the entire page behind any visuals.

There are three possible ways of adjusting the size of an image. These are given in Table 15-8.

Table 15-8. *Background Image Sizing Options*

Option	Description
Normal	The image stays the size it was created.
Fit	The image expands (and may be deformed) to cover the entire dashboard area.
Fill	The image is expanded proportionally to cover as much of the dashboard area as possible.

Note   There is nothing that you can do to resize an image manually in Power BI Desktop. If you need an image to be a certain size, you have to create it at the exact required size in an image editing application.

Some Uses for Independent Images

The limits of what images can do to a report are only those of your imagination, so it is impossible to give a comprehensive list of suggestions. Nonetheless, the following are a few uses that I have found for free-form images:

• *Company logos*, as we have just seen.

- *Images added for a purely decorative effect.* I would hesitate before doing this at all, however, as it can distract from the analysis rather than enhance it. Nonetheless, at times, this may be precisely what you want to do (to turn attention away from some catastrophic sales figures, for instance). So add decoration if you must, but please use sparingly!

- *To enhance the text in a text box* by providing shading that is in clear relief to the underlying image or background.

- *As a background* to a specific column in a table. Be warned, however, that the image cannot be made to move with a column if it is resized.

Adding Shapes

Sometimes your figures may need just a little help to stand out from the crowd. Maybe a small set of visuals (gauges or cards perhaps) are best grouped together. Whatever the need, Power BI Desktop can add a few final touches to your dashboards by adding one or more shapes to a page.

There is a whole range of shapes that you can add. You can see the available shapes in the Shapes pop-up that is shown in Figure 15-10.

Let's suppose that you want to add a decorative arrow to a dashboard to draw the reader's attention to a specific figure. The following explains how you can do this:

1. In the Insert ribbon, click the Shapes button to see a pop-up list of available shapes. You can see this in Figure 15-10.

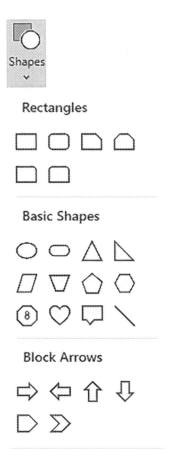

Figure 15-10. *Available shapes*

2. Select Rectangle. A square will be added to the dashboard canvas.

3. Resize the square in the same way that you would resize a chart or an image. If you use the top, bottom, or side handles, then the square will become a rectangle.

As the other available shapes can be inserted in exactly the same way, I will not explain them individually, but will let you have some fun by adding different shapes to a page to see how they can enhance a dashboard.

Formatting Shapes

You can tweak the following aspects of shapes:

- Border (which means the line enclosing the shape)

- Fill

- Rotation

- Title

- Background

- Aspect ratio

- Exact position and size (X and Y coordinates)

As it is only the first three that are new as far as formatting visuals is concerned, let's see them in action.

Lines and Fill Color in Shapes

When we say "lines" in shapes, we are really talking about the exterior boundary of the shape. Power BI Desktop lets you alter its

- Color

- Thickness (or weight, as it is known)

- Transparency

As well as you can set the fill color of the shape. Here is how you can alter basic characteristics for any of the available shapes:

1. Select the shape to format.

2. In the Visualizations pane (that now displays only the Format Shape options), expand the Style card and then expand the Border card.

3. Select a color for the line (border) from the pop-up palette of available colors. The exterior line of the shape will change color.

4. Adjust the Width to set the line thickness. The exterior line of the shape will grow thicker.

5. Move the Transparency slider to the left to adjust the intensity of the color.

6. Expand the Fill card.

7. Select a color for the fill from the pop-up palette of available colors. The interior of the shape will change color.

8. Move the Transparency slider to the right to adjust the intensity of the color.

9. In the Fill card, choose a fill color.

10. The Visualizations pane and the shape will look like they do in Figure 15-11.

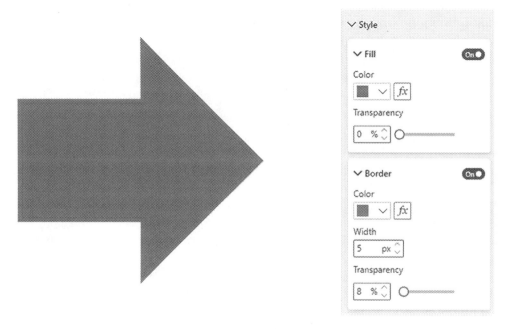

Figure 15-11. *Formatting a shape*

Note   If you want to change the color of a line, you need to change its fill color.

Adding Text to a Shape

You can add a text inside a shape if you wish like this:

1. Select the shape you want to add text to.

2. In the Visualizations pane (that now displays only the Format Shape options), expand the Style card and then expand the Text card.

3. Set the Text button to On and add a text. I suggest **Increased Sales!**

4. Select the appropriate font and adjust the font attributes to your taste.

5. Set the left, right, top, and bottom padding to **1**. The shape and Visualizations pane will look like they do in Figure 15-12.

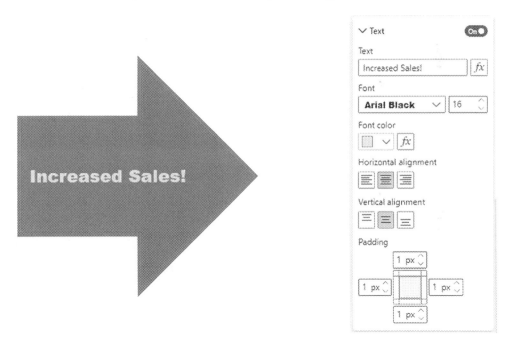

Figure 15-12. *Formatting a shape*

Shape Rotation

Some shapes need to be rotated to point in the right direction for the effect that you are trying to produce. The shapes that generally need adjusting in this way are arrows and triangles—though this technique can be applied to any shape. To rotate a shape:

1. Select the shape to rotate.

2. In the Visualizations pane (that now displays only the Format
    Shape options), expand the Rotation card.

3. Set Shape to **70** and Text to **15**. The shape and Visualizations pane
    will look like they do in Figure 15-13.

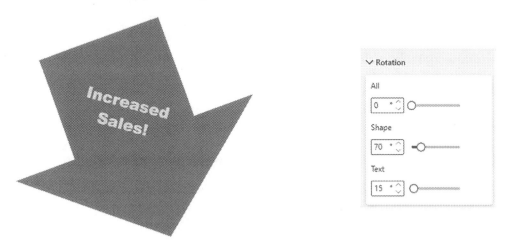

Figure 15-13. *Rotating a shape*

It is worth noting that you can enter a precise rotation value in the Rotation box if
you prefer. This is particularly useful when swiveling a shape through multiples of 45 or
90 degrees.

Note   If you want to rotate the shape and the text at the same time, simply
modify the All value only.

Adding Glow and Shadow to a Shape

You can enhance shapes by adding a glow and/or a shadow.

1. Select the shape to make glow.

2. In the Visualizations pane, expand the Style card and then the
    Glow card.

3. Set Glow to On.

4. Choose a glow color and increase the transparency and blur.

5. Expand the Shadow card and set Shadow to On.

6. Set the shadow attributes as you learned how to do in Chapter 2.
    The shape and Visualizations pane will look like they do in
    Figure 15-14.

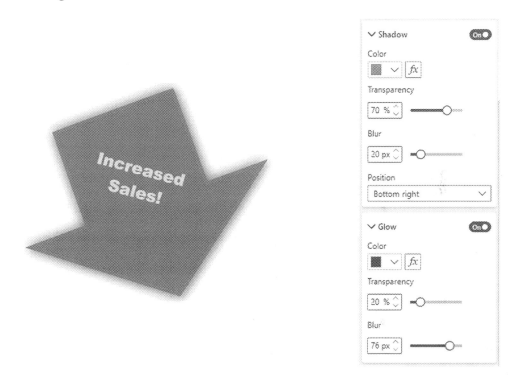

Figure 15-14. *Glow and shadow added to a shape*

Removing Shapes

To remove a shape, all you have to do is

1. Select the shape to remove.

2. Click the pop-up menu for the shape (the ellipses at the top right
    of the text box).

3. Select Remove. The shape will be deleted.

An alternative way to delete a shape is to select the shape and press the Delete key.
The selected shape will disappear from the report.

Switching Shape Types

You can also switch between shape types for existing shapes.

1. Select the shape to alter.

2. In the Formatting pane, expand the Shape card.

3. Choose a different shape type from the Shape pop-up.

Shape Effects

Some (but not all) shapes allow you to alter certain aspects of their layout. Any available options will be visible in the Shape card. These options are described in Table 15-9.

Table 15-9. *Shape Options*

Option	Applies To
Rounded corners	Rectangle, Rounded rectangle, Arrow, Chevron arrow, Pentagon arrow, Hexagon, Octagon, Parallelogram, Pentagon
Arrowhead size	Arrow, Pentagon arrow
Stem width	Arrow
Angle	Chevron arrow
Slant	Hexagon, Parallelogram
Cap Type	Line
Size of snips	Octagon

The best way to see the outcomes of applying these effects is to try them out!

Standardizing Shapes

If you are adding the final decorative (and hopefully also illustrative touches) to a dashboard, you might want to make a series of shapes all look identical. After all, you never want a dashboard to look like a patchwork quilt. A trusted tool from MS Office is available to help you rationalize dashboards in this way—the Format Painter.

1. Select the shape that will serve as the model for other shapes.

2. Click the Format Painter button in the Home ribbon.

3. Click the shape that you want to see formatted identically to the first shape.

Note   You cannot double-click the Format Painter to apply the same format several times to different shapes as you can when formatting in MS Word or Excel.

Organizing Visuals on the Page

A complex dashboard can consist of many elements (though hopefully not so many that you end up confusing your public). This is where some elementary polishing of the final appearance can help. Put simply...

- An audience gives more credence to a slickly organized dashboard.

- Clarity of layout is interpreted as clarity of thought—and so adds to the credibility of the facts and figures that you are presenting.

- Good aesthetics add to, rather than detract from, the points that you are making.

So to finish our tour of the ways that you can finalize and perfect your dashboards, you need to learn how to adjust the way that visuals (whether they are tables, charts, gauges, images, or shapes) relate to one another on the page; this essentially means layering visuals vertically.

Layering Visuals

As a report gets more complex, you will inevitably need to arrange the elements that it contains not only side by side but also one on top of the other. Power BI Desktop lets you do this simply and efficiently.

As an example of this, let's create a chart with another chart superposed on it:

1. Create a donut chart using the following two fields:

    a. LaborCost (from the Sales table)

    b. CountryName (from the Geography table)

2. Create a (clustered) column chart using the following two fields:

    a. Make (from the Vehicle table)

    b. SalePrice (from the Sales table)

3. In the donut chart, add a legend and set it to appear on the right. Also, set the Detail Labels option to Off. Set the Donut Background option to Off.

4. Place the donut chart in the top right-hand corner of the bar chart.

5. With the donut chart selected, choose Bring Forward ➤ Bring To Front from the Power BI Desktop Format ribbon.

6. Click outside all visuals on the dashboard canvas to deselect everything.

Your composite chart should look like Figure 15-15. Bringing the donut chart to the front means that the gridlines for the column chart are now under the donut chart.

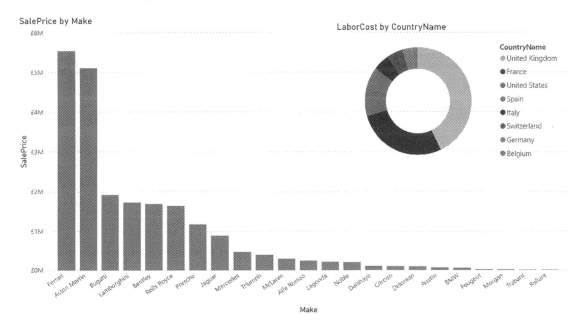

Figure 15-15. *Layering charts*

This technique is particularly useful when you are adding independent images as was described in the previous section. It is also handy when you are combining elements such as images and text boxes, as you will see in the next section.

Grouping Visuals

Power BI Desktop also lets you group multiple visuals into a single visual. This can be extremely practical when you want to copy, place, or resize multiple objects.

To do this:

1. Create the two charts described in the previous section.

2. Select both charts.

3. In the Format menu, click Group ➤ Group.

4. Resize the (single) visual that the two (previously separate) visuals have become. The two visuals will be resized together.

To ungroup a previously grouped visual:

1. Select the grouped visual.

2. In the Format menu, click Group ➤ Ungroup.

Mobile Layout

More and more information workers need their data on the move. This means consulting Power BI dashboards on their mobile phones. To make this easier, the Power BI team at Microsoft has added a valuable feature to Power BI Desktop—mobile layout.

This technique lets you take an existing report and define how each of the visuals that make up the dashboard is displayed on a smartphone or tablet. There are several advantages to this approach:

- You do not have to create duplicate reports, one for a computer screen and another for a phone or tablet, and then update them both.

- You do not have to include all the visuals in a dashboard on the phone or tablet version.

- Any changes in a visual for the dashboard are reflected in the corresponding phone or tablet layout.

As a simple example of this, here is how to create a report destined for a smartphone or tablet from the dashboard containing the superposed charts that you just created:

1. Open, or create, a Power BI Desktop dashboard.

2. In the View ribbon, click the Mobile Layout button. You will see a screen like the one shown in Figure 15-16.

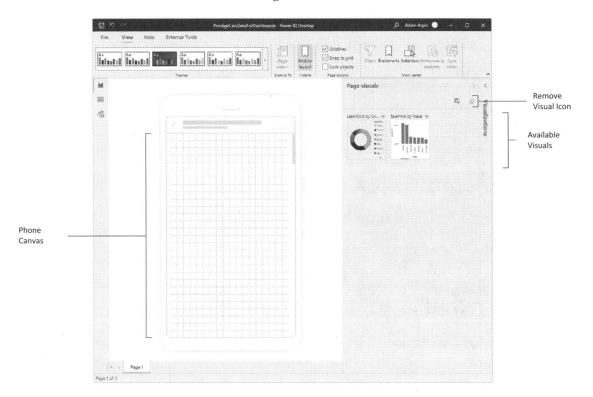

Figure 15-16. *Phone layout*

3. Drag the first visual that you want to use in a phone version of this report to the phone or tablet image.

4. Resize the visual so that it covers the required phone or tablet screen real estate.

5.   Add any other visuals that you wish to use and position them to
      suit your requirements. The phone or tablet layout screen could
      look like Figure 15-17.

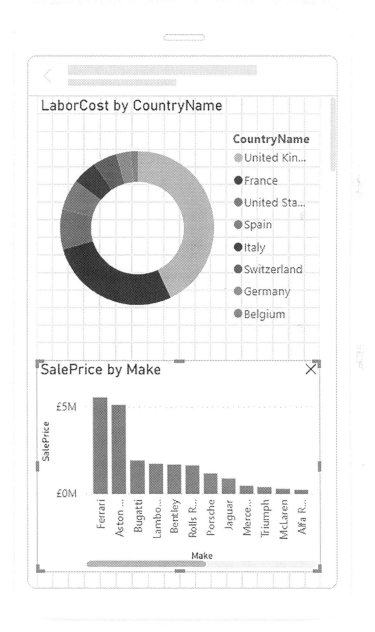

Figure 15-17. *A completed phone layout*

6. Switch back to desktop layout by clicking the Mobile Layout button once again.

Now, once this report is published to the Power BI Service (or an on-premises Power BI Report Server), any mobile users will see the phone layout on their smartphones.

Note   If a visual is not completely visible in phone layout, you will see ellipses and a small down-facing triangle in the visual to indicate that visibility may be an issue. You can see this in the donut visual in Figure 15-19.

Remove Visuals from the Mobile Layout

To remove visuals from the mobile layout, you need to

1. Select the visual in the mobile layout.

2. Click the remove icon at the top right of the visual on the mobile canvas.

3. Click Remove in the dialog that appears.

Note that this does not delete the underlying visual.

Exit Mobile Layout

To exit mobile layout and return to the standard dashboard canvas, simply click the Mobile Layout button in the View menu.

Report Themes

You can define your own set of colors that will be applied automatically to tables, matrices, and data in charts if you so wish. This involves creating a simple file in a specific format that you then load into Power BI Desktop. This file must contain the following elements:

- A name for the theme

- A set of data colors enclosed in square brackets and comma separated

- A background element

- A foreground element

- An accent element for tables

You can see a sample file in step 1 of the following example:

1. Open the file PrestigeCarsDataForDashboards.pbix from the sample data.

2. In the Format ribbon, click the Themes pop-up and select Browse for theme and browse to the theme file PrestigeCars.json.

3. Click Open. You will see the dialog shown in Figure 15-18.

Figure 15-18.   *The Import Theme dialog*

4. Click OK. The theme file will open and apply the theme to all the pages in the current file.

The background, foreground, and table accent colors will now apply to every table and matrix in the report. Moreover, the data colors will, by default, be those specified in the themes file. You can see this in Figure 15-19.

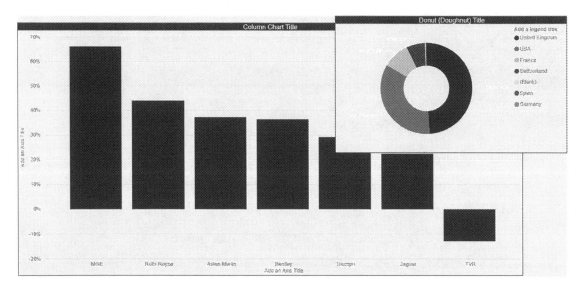

Figure 15-19. *Applying a theme to a report*

This theme file is also available in the folder C:\PowerBiDesktopSamples\ (assuming that you have downloaded the sample files from the Apress website).

Note   To remove the theme that you have just loaded and revert to the default theme, click Switch Theme ➤ Default Theme in the Home ribbon.

Report themes are very much a work in progress in Power BI Desktop and are currently in a constant state of flux. I imagine that the structure of the JSON file will have evolved considerably by the time that this book is published. It is such a complex subject that I can only refer you to the multitude of available resources available on this subject that can be found on the Web. So I cannot, with any certainty, delve any deeper into the question of report branding and creating the underlying JSON files in this edition of this book. What I can do is suggest that you look at the file BrilliantBritishCars.json from the sample data to get an idea of what is required. Indeed, you should be able to use this file as the basis for your own style templates.

If you want to learn about Power BI themes in detail, I recommend my book *Pro Power BI Theme Creation*—also by Apress.

Conclusion

In this chapter, you saw how to push the envelope when using Power BI Desktop to deliver particularly compelling presentations. You saw how adding images can turbocharge the impression that your analysis gives when you add graphic elements to tables and slicers. And, used sparingly, images, shapes, and free-form text elements can draw your audience's attention to the most salient features of your presentation. So now it is up to you to use these powerful Power BI Desktop features to deliver some really compelling interactive analyses to your audience.

In this chapter, you also saw how to take existing reports and prepare them for display on a mobile device. With very little extra effort, you were able to ensure that a complex report becomes perfectly adapted for a smartphone or tablet.

Finally, you learned how to create your own "branding" for Power BI Desktop reports using theme files. This lets you create a standardized look and feel across a range of reports automatically.

It is now time to learn how to assemble structured interactive reports that allow users to drill-through the data across multipage reports and delve deep into the levels of detail that the data contains. You will learn these approaches in the next two chapters.

CHAPTER 16

Multipage Dashboards

In the final two chapters of this book, I want to finish by introducing a series of techniques that you can use to add real power and depth to your dashboards. The approaches that you will discover in this chapter and the next are specifically designed to add structure to your reports. This means that you will be able to

- Guide your users in a path of data discovery from the highest to the lowest level of detail

- Provide navigation through multipage reports

- Use your data to tell a story

Taken individually, the techniques that you can use to achieve these objectives are all extremely useful and can drive insight and understanding. Used together, however, they can turbocharge your dashboard and wake up even the most jaded audience using the power and depth of the real meaning the data contains.

In this chapter, then, you will learn how to

- Add, remove, and rename dashboard pages

- Control how slicers act across dashboard pages

- Drill-through from one dashboard page to another

- Add page navigation buttons

- Create pop-up tooltips

- Create dashboard templates

The techniques that you will learn in this chapter use Power BI Desktop files from the sample data. They are available on the Apress website as part of the downloadable material that accompanies this book.

© Adam Aspin 2022
A. Aspin, *Pro Power BI Dashboard Creation*, https://doi.org/10.1007/978-1-4842-8227-4_16

Multipage Dashboards

In a previous chapter, I briefly touched on the subject of adding pages to Power BI Desktop reports. Although this is extremely simple, it is nonetheless worth exploring all the techniques that you can use when creating multipage dashboards.

Adding and Removing Pages

Adding pages is as easy as clicking the yellow plus icon at the right of the page tabs at the bottom of the Power BI Desktop window. When new pages are added, they are automatically given consecutive numbers.

Removing pages is equally simple. All you have to do is to click the small cross at the top right of the tab for the page you wish to delete. A dialog will confirm that this step is irreversible.

If a page contains structures that you wish to reuse in another page, you can duplicate pages too—like this:

1. Right-click the tab for the page you wish to duplicate. The page tab context menu will be displayed as shown in Figure 16-1.

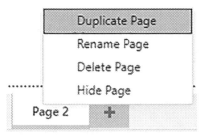

Figure 16-1. *The page tab pop-up menu*

2. Select Duplicate Page.

A copy of the page will be added at the right of any existing pages. You might have to scroll through the page tabs to see it. It will be named "Duplicate of (the name of the current page)."

Renaming and Moving Pages

You do not have to stay with the page names that Power BI Desktop provides. To rename a page:

1. Right-click the tab for the page you wish to duplicate. The page tab context menu will be displayed.

2. Select Rename Page. The current page name will be highlighted. Alternatively, double-click on the page name.

3. Enter the new page name.

4. Press Enter or click anywhere on the page canvas.

Moving pages is as simple as clicking a page tab at the bottom of the screen and dragging left or right.

Note   You cannot select multiple pages at once.

Page Visibility

When you deploy a Power BI Desktop file to the Power BI Service, all the pages in the Power BI Desktop file will be visible to the user. Unless, that is, you decide to make them invisible. To do this:

1. Right-click the tab for the page you wish to make invisible once published. The page tab context menu will be displayed.

2. Click Hide page. A small icon like the one shown in Figure 16-2 will appear to the left of the page name.

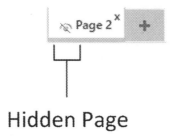

Hidden Page

Figure 16-2. *Hiding a page*

The page will remain visible in Power BI Desktop, but will not be visible once deployed. To make the page visible again, repeat the process.

Note   At least one page must remain visible or the file will not deploy to the Power BI Service.

Applying Slicers Across Multiple Pages

Chapter 14 introduced you to the concept and application of slicers to Power BI dashboards. Yet slicers still have more secrets to reveal. Specifically, you can fine-tune the application of slicers across multipage reports and specify which slicers apply to which pages in a Power BI report. This means that you can, for instance, create a "home" page for a report that contains a series of slicers and then tweak Power BI Desktop to ensure that any or all of the slicers on this page will automatically apply to—or even appear on—other selected pages. This guarantees a predictable and reassuring user experience for readers—as well as avoiding the necessity of having to copy and paste a set of slicers across multiple pages. Another non-negligible factor is this approach frees up considerable screen real estate across the pages in a report.

Suppose that you have a report with a first page named "Cover Page" that contains a couple of slicers and then three other pages. This is how you can apply a slicer from the initial page to other pages:

1.   Click the tab for the page containing the slicers.

2.   Select the slicer whose effect you want to extend to other pages.

3.   In the View ribbon, click the Sync slicers button. The Sync slicers
     pane will appear to the right of the dashboard canvas displaying
     the list of all the pages in the report. The third column of the list
     of pages (which indicates if a slicer is visible on the report page) is
     checked for the current page. You can see the Sync slicers pane in
     Figure 16-3.

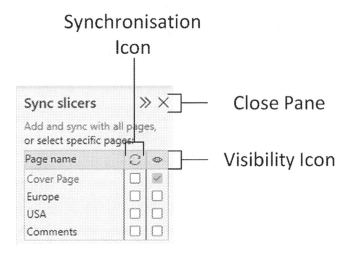

Figure 16-3.   *The Sync slicers pane*

4.   Check the second column (which specifies that the slicer is active
     on the page) for all the pages where you want the selected slicer to
     filter data *including the current page containing the slicer.*

5.   Uncheck the boxes in the third column for all columns *except the*
     current page containing the slicer. You can see this in Figure 16-4.

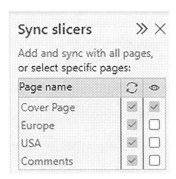

Figure 16-4.   *The Sync slicers pane with slicers synchronized across several pages*

6. Close the Sync slicers pane by clicking the cross icon in the top-right corner of the pane (or click the Sync slicers button in the View ribbon again).

Now, when you use the selected slicer to filter data interactively, the slicer's effect will extend beyond the current page to all the selected pages.

Note   It may seem counterintuitive, but you *have to check the sync box for the current page*—or the slicer will have no effect on the other pages.

Repeating Slicers on Multiple Pages

If you want slicers not only to produce an effect across several pages but also to appear on the pages where they will be actively filtering the data, then all you have to do is to check the box in the visibility column as well as the sync box. This avoids you having to copy and paste slicers across multiple pages. Another advantage is that formatting or repositioning the source slicer on the initial page will result in the slicers that have been made visible on other pages to automatically be updated to reflect any changes. Here is how to do this:

1. Click the tab for the page containing the slicers and select the slicer you want to copy to other pages.

2. In the View pane, click Sync slicers (unless the Sync slicers pane is already visible).

3. Check the second and third columns for all the pages where you want the selected slicer to appear and filter data. This must include the current page that contains the slicer. This is shown in Figure 16-5.

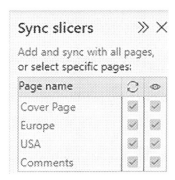

Figure 16-5. *The Sync slicers pane with slicers visible across several pages*

If you now switch to any of the pages where you synchronized slicers, you will see that the slicer appears on the other pages. What is more, selecting slicer options on any page will cause the same selections to appear on *all* the synchronized pages.

Note   It is not currently possible to select multiple slicers and define their application and visibility together by Ctrl-clicking the source slicers.

Synchronizing Separate Slicers

Sometimes you may want to set an existing slicer to be synchronized with another slicer. That is, you have two slicers that apply the same filter effect on separate pages, but you want each of them to reflect the changes made in the other. This, too, can be done through synchronizing slicers.

Suppose that you have a page named "Cover Page" that contains a slicer based on Color. Elsewhere in your report, you have a separate page named "Europe" that also contains a slicer based on Color. Here is how you can synchronize the two existing slicers. Of course, the slicers have to be based on identical fields.

1. Click the tab for the page containing the slicers and select the slicer you want to synchronize with slicers on other pages.

2. In the View pane, click Sync slicers (unless the Sync slicers pane is already visible).

3. Expand Advanced Options.

4. Enter a name to identify the two or more slicers that you want to synchronize. I will use ColorSlicer.

5. Ensure that the two check boxes under the group name are selected.

6. Switch to the page containing the slicer to synchronize and select the slicer.

7. Expand Advanced Options and enter exactly the same name that you entered in step 4. You can see what the Sync slicers pane for each of the synchronized slicers now looks like in Figure 16-6.

Figure 16-6.   *The slicer groups to sync slicers*

The two slicers are now synchronized. What is more, any changes that you make to the fields used in either slicer will also affect any other slicers in the group of slicers that you created.

This approach is not limited to a couple of slicers only. You can repeat steps 6 and 7 for as many existing slicers as you like.

Tip   As the name that you use to define the synchronized group of slicers has to be rigorously identical for every slicer in the group, it is a good idea to copy and paste the group name rather than entering it manually each time.

Drill-through

One of the key techniques that you can apply to shape your data narrative is the ability to drill down through the data and display progressively more detailed levels of information. In simple terms, Power BI Desktop lets you jump to another page based on an interactive selection criterion quickly and easily. This enables you—and your users— to delve into the detail about your data in a progressive and structured way.

Drill-through is a function that requires at least two pages in a report:

- The source page that contains data about many elements

- A destination (or detail) page that provides a different set of visuals that exist to provide a more detailed level of information on a single aspect of the data

Let's see this in action. To avoid pages of instructions, I will only ask that you create two very simple report pages. In practice, of course, your reports could be much more complicated than these.

The Source Page

The source page is the page that you will use for the high-level view of your data. For argument's sake, let's assume that this is the total sales for the company since it was founded, expressed as a chart:

1. Open the Power BI Desktop file `C:\PowerBiDesktopSamples\`
   `PrestigeCarsDataForDashboards.pbix`.

2. Rename the blank page **Sales**.

3. On this page, create a bar chart using the following fields:

   a. Make

   b. SalePrice

You can see this chart in Figure 16-9.

The Destination Page

This page must be designed to show more *detailed* data that is relevant to the single element that you used as the basis for the drill-through on the source page. In this example, that means information about a *make* of vehicle. This page will also have a couple of specific tweaks added that specify that it is the destination for a drill-through action.

1. Add a new page to the existing report.

2. Rename this page **Make Details**.

3. Add a card using the field Make. Don't worry about the actual make that is displayed at this stage.

4. In the Formatting pane for the card, set the Category label to Off.

5. Add a table using the following fields:

    a. FullYear

    b. CostPrice

    c. SalePrice

6. Add an area chart using the following fields:

    a. Color

    b. LaborCost

    c. SpareParts

You can see these two visuals in Figure 16-9.

7. Click the report canvas (outside any visual) and drag the Make field into the "Add drill-through fields here" area of the Visualizations pane. A back button appears automatically at the top left of the current page.

8. Place the Back button where you prefer it to appear on the dashboard.

9. Click the report canvas and take a look at the Drill-through section of the Visualizations pane. You can see the result in Figure 16-7.

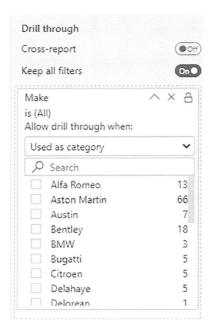

Figure 16-7. *The Drill-through Filters area*

The two pages—source and destination—are now linked and ready to drill down into the data.

Note   To disable drill-through, all you have to do is to delete the field from the Drill-through area by clicking the cross at the top right of the drill-through filter on the "destination" page.

Applying Drill-through

You can now use your drill-through report.

1. Go to the Sales page.

2. Right-click any bar in the chart. I am using *Rolls Royce* in this example. You will see the pop-up menu that is shown in Figure 16-8.

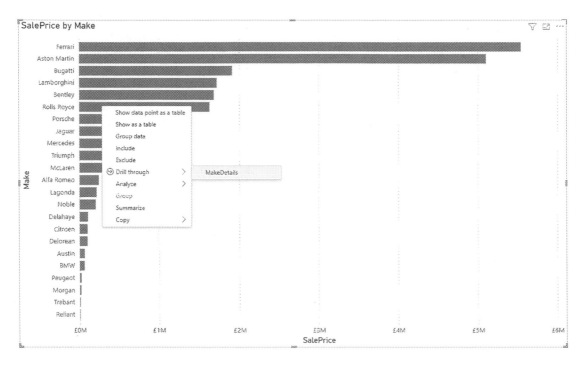

Figure 16-8. *The drill-through context menu*

3. Select Drill-through ➤ Make Details. Power BI Desktop will display
    the Sales Details page—where you can see the make that you clicked
    in the source page displayed in the card visual. In Figure 16-9, you
    can see the destination page after applying the drill-through.

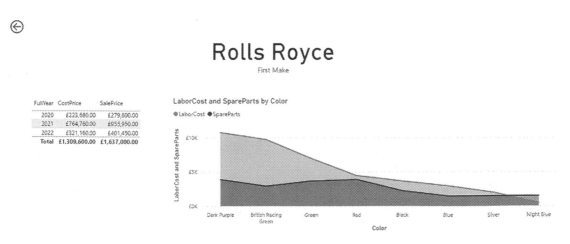

Figure 16-9. *The drill-through destination page*

4.   Ctrl-click the back button to return to the source report.

The Make Details report will be displayed and will filter the data to display the make of the row or data point that you right-clicked.

Power BI Desktop created a back button automatically on the drill-through report (the "destination" report page). However, you do not have to use this button if you do not want to. In fact, any shape or image can become a back button. If you consider it superfluous, you can delete it.

You need to be aware that you can set the same drill-through filter on more than one page. Doing this means that the drill-through menu that appears when you right-click on a data point and select Drill-through could contain several options that indicate multiple possible destination pages. You can see this in Figure 16-10.

Figure 16-10. *Multiple possible drill-through destination pages*

This allows you to define multiple possible data story paths through the data.

Tip   The list of destination pages will be in alphabetical order. Should you want to define the order of the pages in the drill-through pop-up, you will need to rename the destination pages so that each starts with a number.

Multiple Levels of Drill-through

Drill-through is not limited to a single level. Once you have drilled down into greater detail on a second page, there is nothing to prevent you drilling down yet again to an even deeper level of detail on a third page. All you have to do is to repeat the process that you learned in the previous section, only this time you use the "destination" page as the starting point—and create a third page as the new destination.

When drilling down to deeper and deeper levels of analysis, it is worth noting that you can choose to apply any existing filters that are in place when drilling down (which is a fairly standard approach)—or you can override any slicers and filters when drilling down except for the drill-through filter itself (i.e., the element that you clicked in step 3 of the previous example).

If you wish to inhibit filter propagation when drilling down between pages, simply set the Keep all filters option in the Values pane to Off. You can see this in Figure 16-11.

Figure 16-11. *Inhibiting filter propagation during drill-through*

Drill-through Across Power BI Files

Drill-through is not limited to a single report. You can also drill down across reports. However, this will only happen with reports that you have deployed to the Power BI Service.

To enable drill-through across reports, simply set the Cross-report button to On in the Values pane. You saw this button in Figure 16-5.

If you wish to see drill-through working, you can load the file PrestigeCarsDataForDrillthrough.pbix (from the samples folder) where you can find the example explained previously set up and ready for you to test.

Page Navigator

While moving from page to page is as simple as clicking the tab for the page that you want to view, this is not the most user-friendly technique that is available.

One alternative for page navigation is to create—automatically—a set of buttons in the dashboard itself that users can take advantage of to jump from page to page. Here is how you can set up this kind of interface. This example will use the sample file PrestigeCarsDataForButtons.pbix that you can find in the sample files. This file contains only four pages, but that is enough to show how this technique works.

1. Open the file PrestigeCarsDataForButtons.pbix and click the UK page tab.

2. In the Insert menu, click Buttons ➤ Navigator ➤ Page Navigator. You can see this in Figure 16-12.

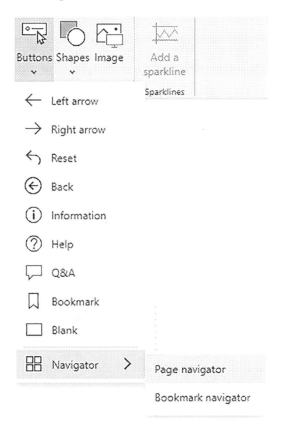

Figure 16-12. *Inserting page navigation buttons*

3. A set of buttons corresponding to the visible pages in the Power BI file will appear on the dashboard. For the sample file (which only contains four pages each containing the detailed sales for a separate country), it will look like Figure 16-13.

Figure 16-13. *Page navigation buttons*

4. Resize the button bar to make it smaller (while leaving the text readable).

5. Select the navigation buttons bar and copy it.

6. Paste the navigation buttons on all the other pages in the file.

You can now Ctrl-click to jump to any of the pages in the dashboard file. Of course, once the file is deployed to the Power BI Service, a simple click will suffice.

There are, inevitably, a few aspects of navigation buttons that you need to be aware of:

- The page navigation bar is a collection of buttons that are automatically grouped when the page navigation buttons are created.

- Buttons can be formatted—but this will be explained in the next chapter where buttons are dealt with in detail.

- The page navigation bar will only display visible pages. So if you don't want a dashboard page to appear in the button bar, simply hide the page before inserting the navigation buttons.

- The page navigation bar and the page tabs are synchronized. So if you ever change a page name, the new name will be updated in the page navigation bar.

- Any pages that are added, removed, or hidden will also appear in (or disappear from) the page navigation bar.

Pop-up Tooltips

Pop-up tooltips are among the most impressive capabilities that Power BI Desktop has to offer—at least in the opinion of most of the users that I have spoken to. Pop-up tooltips allow you to hover the cursor over, for example, a pie chart segment or a bar chart element (or indeed just about any metric in a dashboard) and immediately display a selected chart, table, or a combination of both that hovers over the existing dashboard visual. This allows you to add an immediate level of detail to a dashboard page without having to leave the page.

In essence, pop-up tooltips are a *separate page that has been configured in a specific way* to host a small number of visuals (anything above two or three generally defeats the object of the exercise). The main steps that are explained in the following are

- Add a new page

- Specify that the page is a tooltip

- Reduce the page size

- Add a tooltip filter

Before actually creating a tooltip page, it is important to know what metric you will be filtering on. This is because a tooltip filter is designed to provide a more granular level of detail for a specific element. Consequently, you need to know what the filter element will be when you are building the pop-up tooltip.

In the following example, you will be using the file `C:\PowerBIDesktopSamples\`
`PrestigeCarsDataForDashboards.pbix`. Here, you will add a pie chart with sales by make. The aim is to add a tooltip filter that provides further details about each make. So the field *Make* is the tooltip filter field that we will use.

1. Open the file `PrestigeCarsDataForDashboards`.pbix.

2. On any page, create a pie chart using the fields Make and SalePrice.

3. Add a new page and name it **CostsTooltip**.

4. Click the Format icon for the page in the Visualizations pane.

5. Expand the Page information card and set Allow to use as a tooltip to On.

6. Expand the Canvas settings card and select Tooltip from the pop-up list of available sizes. The page canvas will shrink to show the actual size of the tooltip.

7. Expand the Canvas background card and select a color and a transparency for the tooltip page background (this will make the pop-up tooltip stand out more clearly from the underlying dashboard). The format options are shown in Figure 16-14.

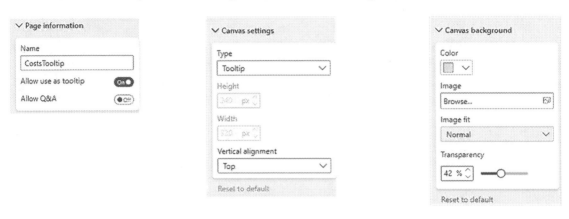

Figure 16-14. *Tooltip formatting options*

8. Click the Build icon in the Visualizations pane to switch back to the Fields information.

9. Drag the Make field into the "Drag tooltip fields here" well as shown in Figure 16-15.

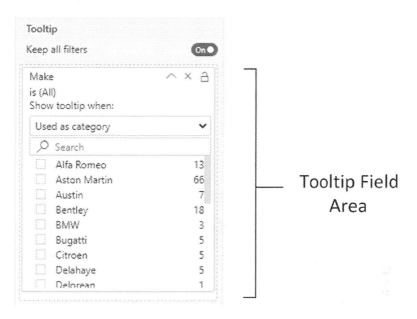

Tooltip

Keep all filters   On

Make   ∧ × 🔒
is (All)
Show tooltip when:

Used as category   ∨

🔍 Search

☐ Alfa Romeo   13
☐ Aston Martin   66
☐ Austin   7
☐ Bentley   18
☐ BMW   3
☐ Bugatti   5
☐ Citroen   5
☐ Delahaye   5
☐ Delorean   1

Tooltip Field
Area

Figure 16-15. *Specifying a tooltip filter*

10. Create a clustered column chart of LaborCost and SpareParts by
     Model in the new tooltip page.

11. Resize the chart to take up all the available space in the
     tooltip page.

12. Format the chart to your liking.

Now, when you hover over any segment of the pie chart on the *initial* page, the pop-
up tooltip appears, as shown in Figure 16-16.

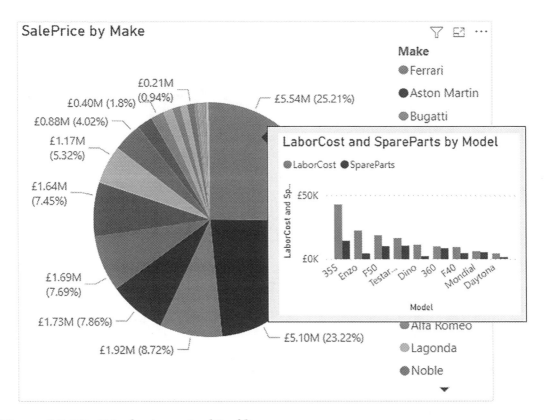

Figure 16-16. *Displaying a tooltip filter*

There are several important points to note when creating tooltip visuals:

- You may prefer to specify the exact size of the page used for a pop-up tooltip in pixels, rather than using the preset value "tooltip." To do this, first select Custom in the Type pop-up of the Page size section of the Page formatting options, and then enter a height and width for the pop-up tooltip in pixels.

- You might also want to hide the tooltip page once created to prevent users from clicking it and displaying it as a page, rather than a tooltip. To do this, all you have to do is to right-click the page tab and select Hide page from the available options in the context menu.

- The tooltip pop-up will appear any time the filter metric is used. In other words, any visual that contains (in this example) the Make field will display the pop-up tooltip, whichever page the visual is on.

- You can format the tooltip visual(s) and the page that becomes a tooltip just as you would any standard visual or page.

- Tooltip visuals can contain several different visuals on the tooltip page if you wish.

- Tooltip visuals cannot, themselves, invoke other tooltip visuals.

Defining the Tooltip Page

It is perfectly possible to specify several tooltip pages that all use the same tooltip field. You can then specify, for any visual that contains this field, which tooltip page will be invoked.

1. Select the pie chart that you created in step 2 earlier.

2. In the Formatting pane, activate the General tab and expand the Tooltips card.

3. Select Report Page as the Type.

4. Select the relevant tooltip page from the Page pop-up list. You can see this in Figure 16-17.

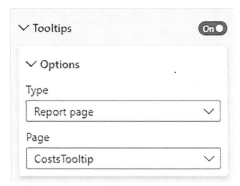

Figure 16-17. *Choosing a tooltip page*

Note   If you want to prevent a tooltip page from displaying, then select Default as the tooltip type in the Tooltips card.

Templates

To conclude this chapter, I want to draw your attention to one Power BI technique that can save you a considerable amount of time when mass-producing dashboards. This is the use of templates that contain

- Standard layouts (such as logos and graphic elements).

- Predefined styles (in a JSON style sheet that you have attached to the template file). You saw this in Chapter 15.

- Selected third-party visuals.

A Power BI template is nothing more than a standard Power BI Desktop file that contains some or all of the preceding elements ready for you to use as a basis for a dashboard that will deliver a standardized corporate look and feel that will also save you time as you do not have to add the same graphic elements every time to a new dashboard.

To save a file as a dashboard:

1. Create a standard Power BI Desktop file that contains all the elements (logos, styles, decorative graphics, repeating elements such as the date of the last data update, etc.).

2. In the File menu, click Save As....

3. Select Power BI Template files (*.pbit) as the Save As type in the pop-up list of file types.

4. Give the file a name and click Save.

5. The Export a template dialog will appear, where you can enter a description for the template. You can see this dialog in Figure 16-18.

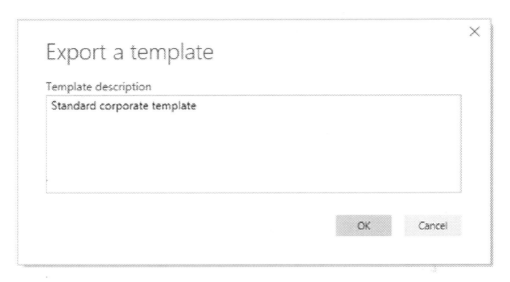

Figure 16-18. *The Export a template dialog*

6.   Click OK.

Now, when you want to create a new dashboard based on the template:

1.   Click File ➤ Open and click the Browse button. The Windows Open dialog will appear.

2.   On the bottom right of the dialog, select Power BI Template files (*.pbit).

3.   Navigate to the template file that you created, select it, and click Open.

The template will open as a new file. This means that when you save the file, Power BI Desktop will prompt you for a file name—which prevents you from opening an existing file (to use as a model) and accidentally overwriting the original.

Conclusion

In this penultimate chapter, you learned how to enhance dashboards and develop them into structured reports that guide the user to a progressively deeper understanding of the data that they are analyzing with Power BI.

First, you learned the basics of adding and removing pages. Then you saw how to create a data story by adding drill-through paths into the data both inside a report and across separate reports.

You also discovered how to synchronize slicers across multiple pages and how to insert page navigation buttons to add a seamless user experience to your multipage dashboard. To add pizzazz to your dashboards, you learned how to implement pop-up tooltips. Finally, you saw how to save complex dashboards as templates for reuse.

The time has come to move on to the final chapter of this book. Here, you will learn to add further interactivity to your dashboards and deliver an exciting user experience that will entrance even the most jaded end user.

CHAPTER 17

Bookmarks and Buttons

This chapter is all about using Power BI to tell a data story. It is where you will learn to shape the dashboard interface to guide the user by controlling the visibility and appearance of visuals on the dashboard page.

This control extends to

- Hiding and displaying visuals

- Switching between different filters at visual, page, and all pages levels

- Adding buttons that you can use to allow users to interact with the dashboard—and activate bookmarks

In this chapter, you will be using the sample file PrestigeCarsDataForBookmarks. pbix. It is available in the downloadable data on the Apress website.

Bookmarks

Bookmarks are one of the most powerful and useful features of Power BI. They help you to take analytics from the merely interactive to the totally meaningful by helping your data to tell its own story. Bookmarks are a method of memorizing selected aspects of a dashboard so that you can reset them quickly and easily. In practice, this means that you can remember the state of

- The current page.

- Any active filters.

- Slicers—this includes both the slicer type (dropdown or list) and the slicer state (the selected elements).

- Visual selection state (such as any cross-filtering applied).

- Any sort order that has been applied to some or all visuals.

A. Aspin, *Pro Power BI Dashboard Creation*, https://doi.org/10.1007/978-1-4842-8227-4_17

- Drill state.

- Object visibility (using the Selection pane—as you will learn in a few pages time).

- The focus or Spotlight modes of any visible object.

- And much else...

As with most Power BI Desktop features, bookmarks are best understood through seeing them in action. So here is an example of how to create two bookmarks and then apply them in turn. The two bookmarks will be

- A "revert" bookmark that captures the initial "plain vanilla" state of the dashboard page. The idea behind this is that it will let you clear any slicers and filters to revert to the initial state of the page.

- A "filtered" bookmark that will remember slicer and filter settings so that these can be reapplied quickly and easily.

Here is how you can do this:

1. Open the sample file PrestigeCarsDataForBookmarks.pbix. This contains a table and a bar chart—as well as a couple of slicers (all of which are extremely simple). You can see the initial dashboard page in Figure 17-1.

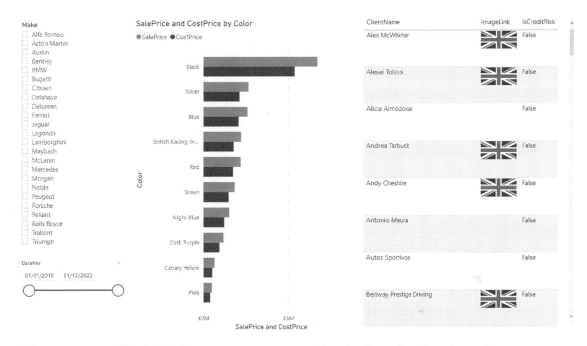

Figure 17-1. *The initial page state captured by the Baseline bookmark*

2. In the View ribbon, click the Bookmarks icon. The Bookmarks pane will appear.

3. Click Add. A new bookmark (called Bookmark 1, probably) will appear in the list of bookmarks. This bookmark will remember the filters and slicers exactly as they were when you created the bookmark.

4. Click the ellipses to the right of the new bookmark to display the context menu (alternatively, you can right-click the bookmark name) and select Rename. Indeed, if you prefer, you can double-click inside the bookmark name instead.

5. Enter the new name and press Enter. I suggest **Baseline** in this example. The Bookmarks pane will look like the one in Figure 17-2. What you have done is to "memorize" the state of the page and all the visuals it contains before any slicers or filters are applied.

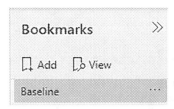

Figure 17-2. *The Bookmarks pane*

6. Apply one or two slicer choices.

7. Click one of the bar chart sections to cross-filter the data.

8. Expand the Filters pane and drag the CountryName filter into the Filters on this page area and select United Kingdom.

9. Collapse the Filters pane. These modifications will alter the data displayed on this page. You can see an example in Figure 17-3.

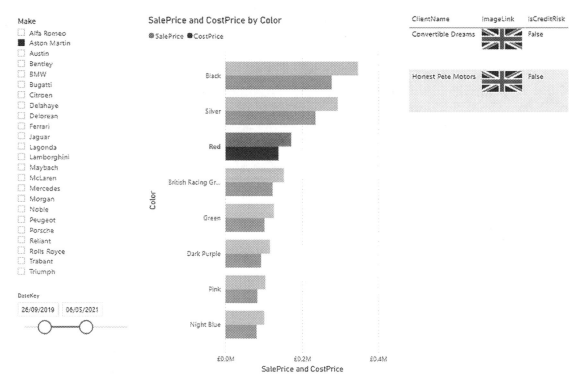

Figure 17-3. *The filtered page state captured by the SlicedData bookmark*

10. Create a second bookmark (as described in steps 3–5) named **SlicedData**. You have now "memorized" the new, altered state of the page after the slicers and spotlight were applied.

Clicking either of the bookmarks in the Bookmarks pane will reapply the state of the slicers, filters, and cross-filters that were active when you created the bookmark. This means that you can switch between different filter, slicer, and cross-filter states in a single click.

Note   This example does not contain any drill down that has been applied. However, drill down is "memorized" by a bookmark just like as filter or slicer is. The same is true for the visibility of any object.

Updating a Bookmark

A bookmark, once created, is never set in stone. You can update an existing bookmark at any time as your analytics requirements evolve.

1. Click the bookmark that you want to update to activate the bookmark settings.

2. Add or remove slicer elements, filters, and cross-filter selections to adjust the dashboard display.

3. Click the ellipses to the right of the new bookmark to display the context menu (alternatively, you can right-click the bookmark name). You can see the context menu in Figure 17-4.

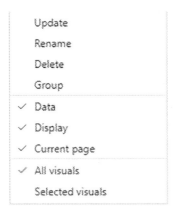

Figure 17-4. *The bookmark context menu*

4. Select update.

The bookmark is updated (even if nothing is immediately visible to indicate this), and the new state of the page is now memorized.

Note   You will have to remember to update the appropriate bookmark(s) *every time* that you alter a previously bookmarked page.

Defining the Extent of a Bookmark's Application

As I mentioned earlier, bookmarks can be applied to several aspects of a dashboard. However, you do not have to apply a bookmark to *every* aspect of a dashboard. You can choose to have a bookmark apply to the range of options that are described in Table 17-1.

Table 17-1. *Bookmark Application*

Extent	Description
Data	This means that any filters, slicers, cross-filtering, or sorting that have been applied are memorized with the bookmark.
Display	This means essentially that any visuals that have had the spotlight option applied will have this attribute "remembered" with the bookmark. Equally, the Filters visual state (expanded or collapsed) will be remembered.
Current page	The current page is included in the definition of the bookmark—and applying the bookmark will make display the page where the bookmark was applied.
All visuals	All visuals on the page will be "remembered" by the bookmark.
Selected visuals	You can select one or more visuals to restrict the number of visuals that will be affected when the bookmark is used.

Essentially, this means that a bookmark has a variable scope and effect—and you decide how far-reaching this should be. As the various interactions can appear a little confusing at first, it is probably best to see these functions applied to a dashboard in order to understand their ramifications.

Note   At least one of the bookmark options (data, display, or current page) must be selected—or the bookmark becomes inactive.

Display and Data in Bookmarks

To begin with, let's see how using a bookmark to memorize a page's display settings works. Here, you will be extending the PrestigeCarsDataForBookmarks.pbix file that you modified previously. The objective is not to apply filters and slicers when activating the bookmark, but to keep any slicers, filters, or cross-filtering as it is and only affect the display of the dashboard page.

1.   Click the Baseline bookmark to revert to an unfiltered page.

2. Click the ellipses at the top right of the bar chart and select Spotlight from the context menu. This will dim all other visuals on the page.

3. Click Add to add a new bookmark.

4. Click the ellipses to the right of the new bookmark to display the context menu (alternatively, you can right-click the bookmark name) and uncheck Data and Current page, leaving Display checked.

5. Rename the new bookmark **HighlightChart**.

To see this in action, you need to apply either of the other bookmarks. Then apply the HighlightChart bookmark. This will apply the highlighting only—as it is a display attribute—and will have no effect on the filters or slicers as these are set by the Data bookmark context menu option, and this is not applied to this bookmark. Figure 17-5 shows this.

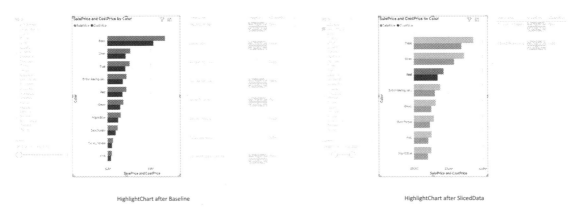

HighlightChart after Baseline   HighlightChart after SlicedData

Figure 17-5. *Using bookmarks to highlight a visual*

If the Filters pane was expanded when this bookmark was created, then it would also appear, expanded, when you activate this bookmark.

Note   As the HighlightChart bookmark applies highlighting only, you can cancel the highlighting simply by clicking anywhere on the blank report canvas.

It is important to note that this bookmark affected two aspects of the page:

- Display elements (specifically the state of the Filters pane and any highlighting) *were* remembered.

- Data elements (specifically any filters, slicers, cross-filtering, or drill down) were *not* remembered.

Applying Bookmarks to Selected Visuals

The bookmarks that you have created until now in this chapter have been fairly expansive in their application. That is, they have been applied to every visual on the dashboard page. This does not have to be the case, and you can apply a bookmark to a selected group of visuals only should you need to. Let's see this in action.

1. Still in the PrestigeCarsDataForBookmarks.pbix file, click the Baseline bookmark to revert to an unfiltered page.

2. Select the table.

3. Expand the Filters pane and drag the SalesRegion field into the empty Filters on the visual area.

4. Check the North America check box in the SalesRegion filter area. This will display only customers in the United States in the table.

5. Collapse the Filters pane.

6. Add a new bookmark, and in the bookmark context menu, check Selected visuals.

7. Rename the new bookmark to **USAList**.

To see this in action, apply the bookmark "SlicedData." This will display only two UK-based customers. Then apply the bookmark Sliced data followed by USAList. This will remove all customers from the table—but leave the chart as it is—because this bookmark only applies to a specific visual.

Note   You can preselect more than one visual (by Ctrl-clicking the required visuals) when choosing to apply a bookmark to selected visuals.

Bookmark Page Settings

Bookmarks also have the option of remembering the page to which the bookmark applies. While this is required for most bookmarks, there will certainly be times when you will want to apply bookmark settings globally—that is, to all pages.

Suppose, for instance, that you want a bookmark that applies a filter to all pages. Here is how to do this:

1. In the Power BI Desktop file that you have been modifying through this chapter (PrestigeCarsDataForBookmarks.pbix), click the Baseline bookmark to return to an initial, unfiltered dashboard.

2. Expand the Filters pane and drag the Model field into the Filters on all pages area.

3. Select a dozen or so models in the newly added filter.

4. Collapse the Filters pane.

5. Add a new bookmark and name it **SelectedModels**.

6. Display the context menu for this new bookmark and unselect Display and Current page.

Now, when you apply this filter, it will apply the list of selected models to every page in the report.

Arranging Bookmarks

Once you have learned to appreciate just how useful bookmarks can be, you may find yourself creating quite a collection of them. So it is worth noting that there are a few techniques on offer to make managing bookmarks easier. They are

- Changing the order in which bookmarks appear in the Bookmarks pane

- Deleting bookmarks

For example, to change the order in which bookmarks appear in the Bookmarks pane:

- In the Bookmarks pane, drag a bookmark vertically to a new position in the list of bookmarks.

Deleting bookmarks is as simple as right-clicking a bookmark and selecting Delete from the pop-up menu.

Note   It is not possible to delete more than one bookmark at a time.

Grouping Bookmarks

You can easily end up with dozens and dozens of bookmarks in a complex dashboard. Because this scenario could easily become unmanageable, Power BI Desktop has a solution to help you to control things. This involves grouping bookmarks. As with most aspects of Power BI Desktop, this is best seen using an example:

1. In the Bookmarks pane, Ctrl-click to select a set of bookmarks to group. In the sample file, I suggest selecting *Baseline* and *SlicedData*.

2. Click the ellipses for any of the selected bookmarks and choose Group in the context menu. A new group will appear.

3. Double-click the group name and enter a new name. In this example, I will apply **Main**. Press Enter to confirm the name.

4. Expand the new group (by clicking the down-facing chevron to the left of the group name). You can see this in Figure 17-6.

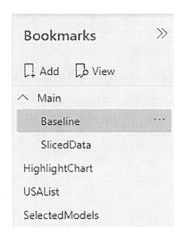

Figure 17-6. Using bookmarks to highlight a visual

It is worth stressing that a bookmark group is purely administrative in that all it does is allow you to collect bookmarks into sets for easier management. There is no limit to the number of bookmarks that you can add to a group.

To extract the bookmarks from a group and remove the group (while keeping the bookmarks that it contains), simply select Ungroup from the group's context menu. This, in effect, removes the group and leaves the bookmarks it contained intact.

To add a bookmark to an existing group:

1. In the Bookmarks pane, expand the bookmark where you want to add another bookmark.

2. Drag the required bookmark into the expanded group.

The Selection Pane

As dashboards grow more complex, they can contain literally hundreds of visuals—from tables and charts to images, drawing elements, and buttons. Keeping track of all these elements and even selecting them on a dense (not to say cluttered) page can become difficult.

Power BI Desktop's solution to this challenge is called the Selection pane. This allows you to

- List all the objects on a page

- Give meaningful names to each object

- Make elements visible or invisible

- Change the layering order for multiple objects (to stack them one on top of another)

Here, I am using the word *object* to describe any element added to a dashboard page, be it a chart, table, filter, or decorative element such as a text box or image.

Renaming Objects

Let's take a look at this in action. To begin with, let's give more meaningful names to objects on the page to help us find them again later. For this section, I suggest that you close the file PrestigeCarsDataForBookmarks.pbix (assuming that you have been using it) *without saving* and reopen it in a pristine state.

1. In the View menu, click the Selection button. The Selection pane will appear. It should look like Figure 17-7.

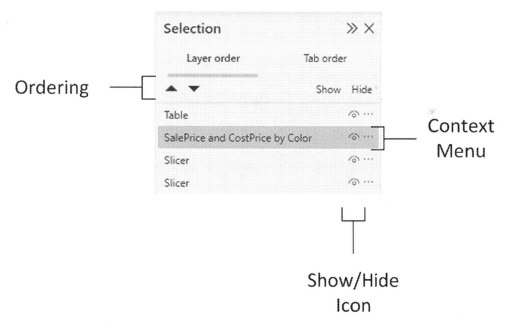

Figure 17-7. *The Selection pane*

2. Click on the Table element in the Selection pane. The table will appear selected in the dashboard canvas.

3. Double-click the table name and replace with something more meaningful. I suggest **ListOfMakes** in this example.

4. Press Enter to confirm the name.

After adding meaningful names to all the objects on the page, the Selection pane could look like the one shown in Figure 17-8.

Figure 17-8. *The Selection pane with objects renamed*

Admittedly, in a page that only contains a handful of objects like this one, the Selection pane is probably not a fundamental tool. However, if you have

- Dozens of objects on the page

- Objects superposed on one another (and consequently difficult to select)

- The need to select multiple objects at once (to be used in a bookmark or formatted together, for instance)

- A requirement to place an object at the bottom of a superposed set of objects above other objects

then the Selection pane can be fundamental in allowing you to work more easily.

Using the Selection Pane

Now that you have seen what the Selection pane is, it is time to see how to use it:

1. In the Selection pane, click on the element named ListOfMakes. This will select the table with this name.

2. Click the Show Hide icon for this element in the Selection pane. This will hide (but not delete) the table. The Show Hide icon will look like the one shown in Figure 17-9.

Hidden Icon

Figure 17-9. *The Selection pane icon for a hidden object*

There are a few final points about the Selection pane that you ought to be aware of:

- To make a hidden object reappear, simply re-click the Show Hide icon for the required element in the Selection pane.

- The Selection pane merely reflects the current objects in a dashboard. So, to remove an item from the Selection pane, you must delete the object in the dashboard itself.

- You can select objects directly inside the Selection pane.

- You can move an object up or down (the same thing as using Bring forward/Send backward in the Format ribbon) by either

  - Selecting an item in the list of objects in the Selection pane and clicking the up and down Layer order triangles

  - Dragging the item up or down in the list

Note   You can collapse the Selection pane (to maximize available screen real estate) by clicking the Collapse icon (the double chevron) at the top right of the Selection pane. To remove the Selection pane, click the Selection button in the View menu.

Grouping Items in the Selection Pane

As was the case for bookmarks, you can also create groups of items in the Selection pane to make managing multiple objects easier.

1. In the Selection pane, Ctrl-click to select a set of bookmarks to group. In the sample file, I suggest selecting *MakeSlicer* and *DateSlicer*.

2. Click the ellipses for any of the selected items and choose Group ➤ Group in the context menu. A new group will appear.

3. Double-click the group name and enter a new name. In this example, I will apply **Slicers**. Press Enter to confirm the name.

4. Expand the new group (by clicking the down-facing chevron to the left of the group name). You can see this in Figure 17-10.

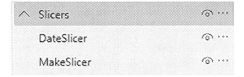

Figure 17-10. *Grouping items in the Selection pane*

As was the case for bookmarks, you need to be aware that this is just a management technique to apply rationality to large numbers of elements in the Selection pane list. You can ungroup a group of items by

- Clicking the ellipses for any of the groups and choosing Group ➤ Ungroup in the context menu. The group will disappear and the items that it contained will reappear in the main list.

Note   You cannot always see the last selected element when using Ctrl-click to select multiple elements. This does not mean that the final element is not selected.

Selection and Bookmarks

The Selection pane really comes into its own when used in conjunction with bookmarks. This is essentially because bookmarks often involve hiding objects on the page. However, if something is hidden, it is impossible to select it. However, hidden or not, you can select any object in the Selection pane.

So it can be fundamental to have the Selection pane open (and also to give meaningful names to objects in the dashboard) when you are updating bookmarks so that you can more easily identify bookmarks. And remember—you can select objects directly inside the Selection pane. This can avoid having to select multiple objects inside a crowded report canvas.

Slideshows Using Bookmarks

Power BI Desktop is not only a superb analytical tool. It can also help you in presenting data to tell a meaningful story—and bookmarks can be a valuable assistant when it comes to making the data speak for itself. This is because a series of bookmarks can be played back as a slideshow.

1. In the Bookmarks pane, organize the bookmarks from top to bottom in a meaningful sequence that represents the order of your data-driven narrative.

2. In the Bookmarks pane, click View. The first bookmark in the list will be activated. A new bar appears at the bottom of the report. You can see this in Figure 17-11.

Figure 17-11. *The SlideShow bar*

3. Click the right-facing chevron to activate the next bookmark in the list.

4. Once the slideshow is finished, click the Exit button at the top right of the Bookmarks pane.

It is probably self-evident, but clicking the left-facing chevron activates the previous bookmark in the list.

Note   The sample data folder contains the file PrestigeCarsDataWithSample Bookmarks.pbix. You can open this to see all the bookmark techniques that I have described here applied to a simple dashboard.

Buttons

Power BI is, above all, a reporting tool. However, this does not mean that it has to be static in any way. To allow you to develop more interactive reports, you can add buttons to any dashboard page. Once set up, buttons let users

- Jump to a specific page

- Return to the previously used page

- Open the Power BI Q&A dialog

- Open a web or intranet page

In this example, you will see how to add a button that will display a selected page. This will mean creating a new "destination" page that you will jump to by clicking a button in a different page.

1. Open the Power BI Desktop file `C:\PowerBIDesktopSamples\ PrestigeCarsDataForDashboards.pbix`.

2. Insert a new page and rename it **DetailedAnalysis**.

3. Add a bar chart of SalePrice and CountryName.

4. Add a bookmark (as described previously) named **Destination**.

5. Return to Page 1.

6. In the Insert menu, click the pop-up chevron in the Buttons icon. You will see the selection of available buttons in the pop-up menu as shown in Figure 17-12.

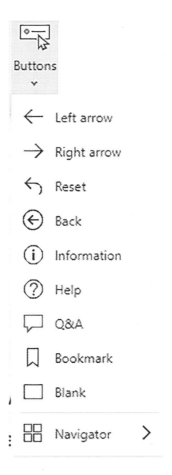

Figure 17-12. *The Buttons pop-up menu*

7. Select Bookmark as the button type. A bookmark-style button will be added to the dashboard.

8. Place the button in a suitable location in the dashboard, and leave the button selected.

9. In the Visualizations pane (which now is entitled Format button), expand the Style card and set Text to On.

10. Enter **Click to Jump** as the button text.

11. Center the text and alter any font attributes that you feel enhance the presentation of the bookmark.

12. Expand the Icon card (inside the Style card) and set Icon to Off.

13. Expand the Fill card (inside the Style card) and set Fill to On. Select a fill color from the color palette.

14. Expand the Border card (inside the Style card) and set Border to On. Choose a border color and set its width.

15. Expand the Shadow card (inside the Style card) and set Shadow to On. Choose the type of shadow that you want to apply.

16. Ensure the Action card is set to On and expand it.

17. Ensure that the action type is set to Bookmark.

18. Select Destination (the name of the bookmark that you created in step 4) as the bookmark to link to this button. The bookmark settings will look like Figure 17-13.

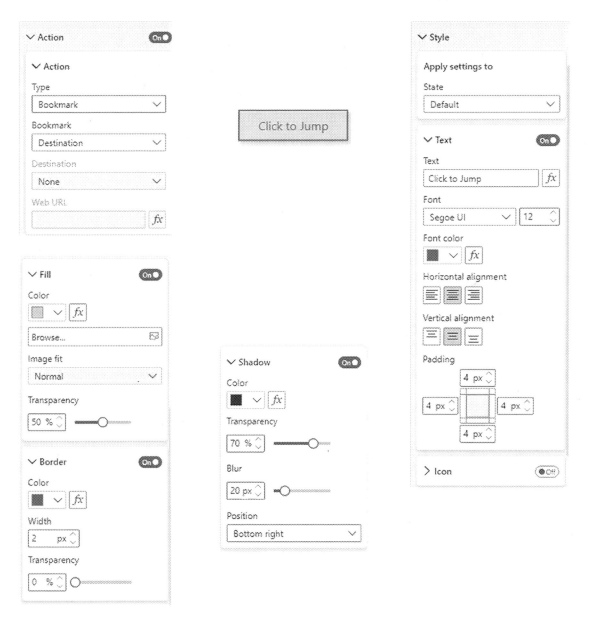

Figure 17-13. *Setting a button action to Bookmark*

If you now Ctrl-click the button, this will make the new page appear.

Note   It is only in Power BI Desktop that you have to use Ctrl-click to activate a button action. Once deployed to the Power BI Service in Azure, a simple click will suffice.

Warning   If you leave a button selected and insert another button, the existing button will be converted to the new button type.

Button Options

Power BI Desktop gives you a series of button types that you can choose from. Choosing a button type that is appropriate to the interaction that you want to define will help you create interactive dashboards quickly and painlessly. It is worth noting, however, that you can change any button type once it has been created and that selecting the button type merely applies presets that you can override later if necessary.

Table 17-2 lists the built-in button types that you can choose from.

Table 17-2. *Button Types*

Option	Description
Left arrow	Inserts a button with a left-facing arrow. No action is specified by default.
Right arrow	Inserts a button with a right-facing arrow. No action is specified by default.
Reset	Inserts a button with a left-facing arrow. No action is specified by default.
Back	Inserts a button with a left-facing arrow in a circle. The action is set automatically to return to the previous page used.
Information	Inserts a button with an information symbol. No action is specified by default.
Help	Inserts a button with a help symbol. No action is specified by default.
Q&A	Inserts a button with a callout box. The action is specified as active Q&A.
Bookmark	Inserts a button with a bookmark symbol. The action is set automatically to invoke a bookmark—you only have to specify which one to use.
Blank	Inserts a button without an icon. No action is specified by default.

Changing the Button Type

Fortunately, the button type that you originally choose is not set forever. You can switch between button types quickly and easily.

1. Select the button you wish to modify.

2. In the Visualizations pane, expand the Action section.

3. Ensure the Action section is set to On and expand it.

4. Select a different action from the list of available actions.

Button Actions

There are currently six predefined actions that you can "attach" to a Power BI dashboard button to add interactivity to your reports. Table 17-3 shows the actions that you can associate to a button.

Table 17-3. *Button Actions*

Option	Description
Back	This adds a back button that is preset to return to the previously used page.
Bookmark	This type of button lets you select a bookmark to apply. This allows you either to modify page filters, slicers, and sort order or move to a different page—or a combination of both.
Drill-through	Drills through to a destination page and applies the drill-through filter.
Page navigation	Jumps to a selected destination page.
Q&A	Presents a Q&A Explorer window.
Web URL	Jumps to the URL that you enter in the Action section of the Visualizations pane once Web URL is selected.

Note   When you are using buttons merely to move between pages, it is often best to define the bookmark for the destination page that you will be using *without* the data and display options enabled for the bookmark (as described previously). This will ensure that you jump to the destination page without adding unexpected filters or slicers.

Each of the various actions that a button can trigger has its own subtleties and quirks. So we will look at some of these in the following sections.

Drill-Through Buttons

A button can also drill-through to a page containing detailed analysis. This is a fairly similar operation to the drill-through that you saw in Chapter 16. You will need two elements to be in place for a drill-through button to work correctly:

- A destination page with a drill-through filter set up

- A slicer or cross-filter active on the page containing the drill-through button

To see this in action, you will need the following in place:

- A page named DrillthroughDestination where you have set up a drill-through filter on the Make field. You can always refer back to Chapter 16 if you need to remind yourself how this is done.

- A slicer using the Make field on the page containing the drill-through button.

The process is as follows:

1. Add a new page to the dashboard file named **DrillthroughDestination**. Drag the Make field into the Drill-through area of the Visualizations pane.

2. Add a new page to the dashboard file.

3. Add a slicer using the Make field.

4. Insert a new button.

5. Set Action to On and expand the Action card.

6. Set the Type as Drill-through.

7. Select the destination page (DrillthroughDestination) from the Destination pop-up list. You can see this in Figure 17-14.

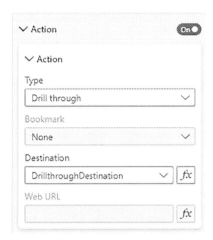

Figure 17-14. *Setting a button action to Drill-through*

8. Select a single make from the slicer.

9. Ctrl-click the button. The DrillthroughDestination page will be activated.

You need to be aware that the button will not work unless a single make is selected on the page containing the button. This can be in a slicer or a cross-filter. It cannot be set using a filter, however.

Page Navigation Buttons

Page navigation buttons are mercifully simple. As their name suggests, they simply allow the user to click and jump to another page.

1. Insert a new button.

2. Set Action to On and expand the Action card.

3. Set the Type as Page navigation.

4. Select a destination page from the Destination pop-up list. You can see this in Figure 17-15.

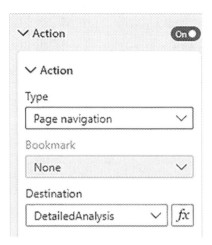

Figure 17-15. *Setting a button action to Page navigation*

Web URL Buttons

A button can also be used as a classic hyperlink to a web page, like this:

1. Insert a new button.

2. Set Action to On and expand the Action card.

3. Set the Type as Web URL.

4. Insert a valid URL in the Web URL. You can see this in Figure 17-16.

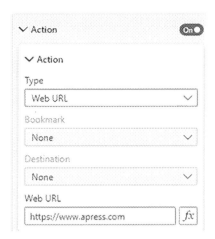

Figure 17-16. *Setting a button action to Web URL*

Ctrl-clicking the button in Power BI Desktop (or simply clicking in the Power BI Service) will open your browser and display the Apress website.

Back Button

The back button is probably the simplest action button of them all. It reverts to displaying the page that you used before the current page.

Q&A Button

The Q&A button displays the Questions and Answers screen. This is where you can ask Power BI questions of your data in natural language. Here is an example of this in action:

1. Insert a new button and set the Action to On and expand the Action card.

2. Set the Type as Q&A. You can see this in Figure 17-17.

Figure 17-17. *Setting a button action to Q&A*

3. Ctrl-click the button. The Q&A dialog will appear.

4. Enter **What are sales by make** as the question. You can see the output in Figure 17-18.

Figure 17-18. *The Q&A dialog*

5. Close the Q&A dialog.

Actions Using Images and Shapes

Actions can also be set for images and shapes. This is virtually identical to setting actions for buttons, so I will not repeat everything here. The only difference is that for images and shapes, there are only five actions available. This is because drill-through is not an available action for images and shapes.

Formatting Buttons

As you might expect, Power BI allows you to format buttons much as you can format any visual in a dashboard.

The essential elements that you can format are

- Text

- Icon

- Outline

- Fill

- Background

- Shape

- Rotation

You can also, technically, add a title and a border to a button, but in my opinion these are largely superfluous given the other available options.

You have already seen how to format many of these attributes before when learning about shapes (and in many ways buttons are a kind of shape object). However, there is a level of subtlety that applies to buttons alone. This is the *state* of a button.

A button can have any of four different states. These are

- *Default state*: The standard appearance of the button text

- *Hover state*: The text that is displayed when the cursor is placed over a button

- *Pressed state*: The state of a button once pressed (assuming that any button action does not immediately display a new page)

- *Disabled state*: The state if a button is disabled

You can set completely different formatting for the button state as far as the actual shape and the style (text, icon, fill, border, and glow) of a button are concerned.

Let's see some of these options applied to a button.

1. In the Insert menu, click Button and then Information to add a new button with the information (i) icon.

2. Leaving the button selected, in the Visualizations pane (which is now entitled the Format Button pane), expand the Style card.

3. Select On Hover from the pop-up list of possible button states.

4. With the Text card expanded, set Text to On.

5. Add a text for the hover state. I will simply add **Hovering**. You will not see any text yet as this will only appear when the pointer is hovering over the button.

6. Modify the font, font color, alignment, and text size.

7. Expand the Icon card and select a different icon from the list of those available.

8. Modify the line color and line weight.

9. Expand the Fill card, ensure that Fill is set to On, and choose a different fill color.

10. Select Default from the pop-up list of possible button states.

11. Modify the outline color and outline weight (this will be for the default state this time—so you will see the formatting changes as you apply them).

12. With the Text card expanded, set Text to On.

13. Add a text for the default state. I will simply add **Click Here**.

14. Modify the font, font color, alignment, and text size.

15. Set Icon to Off.

16. Expand the Fill card, ensure that Fill is set to On, and choose a different fill color. You can see the results of altering the formatting for two button states in Figure 17-19.

Click Here

Hovering

Default State   On Hover State

Figure 17-19. *Button formatting*

This example does not exhaust the limits of all that you can do to format buttons. So, now that you have seen the basics, I want to extend the formatting of the button you created with a couple of other options.

1. Select the button you created previously.

2. Expand the Shape card and ensure that Default is the selected state.

3. Select Chevron arrow from the pop-up list of available shapes.

4. Expand the Rotation card and set All to **45**.

5. In the Shape card, select On Hover as the state.

6. Select Heart from the pop-up list of available shapes.

7. Expand the Rotation card and set All to **-45**. You can see the (slightly wacky) results of altering the formatting for two button states in Figure 17-20.

Default State   On Hover State

Figure 17-20. *Further button formatting*

Note   Certain formatting effects—such as the button shape and rotation—need you to define a fill or border for the button.

Images in Buttons

You can add your own images to buttons instead of (or as well as) the standard Power BI button icons.

1. Click Buttons in the Insert ribbon and select the Blank button type.

2. Leaving the button selected (and in the Button tab of the Formatting pane), expand the Style card and then the Fill card (and set Fill to On).

3. Click the Browse area and select an image (I have selected the bell image from the images folder of the sample files).

4. Set the Image fit to Normal. You can see the result in Figure 17-21.

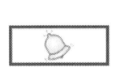

Figure 17-21. *Adding images to buttons*

Note   The image fill options are the same as those that you saw in Chapter 15.

Using Images and Shapes As Buttons

Power BI Desktop also allows you to use images and shapes as buttons. This is mercifully easy—as it simply parallels the method that you just saw for setting actions for buttons.

As an example, here is how to jump to a page using the bookmark that you created previously:

1. Ensure that you have added a bookmark to the page that you wish to move to (the "destination" page).

2. On a different page, add—or select—the image you wish to use as the clickable element to jump to the destination page.

3. With the image selected, expand the Action section in the Visualizations pane.

4. Ensure the Action section is set to On and expand it.

5. Select a bookmark from the list of available actions.

6. Select the bookmark name from the list of available bookmarks.

Note   You can apply exactly the same technique to any of the shapes added from the Insert ribbon.

Bookmark Navigator

Power BI Desktop also allows you to add a bookmark navigator to provide you with an instant set of buttons that are linked to the bookmarks in the report.

1. In the Insert ribbon, click Buttons ➤ Navigator ➤ Bookmark navigator. A group of buttons will appear as a button bar. You can see a (very simplistic) example of this in Figure 17-22.

Figure 17-22.   *The bookmark navigator*

There are a few points you need to be aware of concerning the Bookmark pane:

- The order of the buttons will reflect the order of the bookmarks in the Bookmark pane.

- Any new bookmarks will automatically appear in the Bookmark pane.

- Any bookmarks that you delete will be removed from the Bookmark pane.

Otherwise, a Bookmark navigator is identical to a Page navigator. So you can format it and copy and paste it across pages exactly as described in Chapter 16 for the Page navigator.

Conclusion

In this final chapter, you learned how to further enhance dashboards using buttons and bookmarks. While these techniques may seem mercifully simple (because they are), they nonetheless open the door to wide-ranging possibilities when it comes to creating powerful yet intuitive interfaces with Power BI. With a little practice, you can use these possibilities to create compelling data stories for your users to follow.

You have now reached the end of your journey through dashboard creation with Power BI Desktop. I sincerely hope that you have enjoyed this experience and will have amazing fun delivering analytics with this truly awesome tool.

APPENDIX A

Sample Data

Sample Data

If you wish to follow the examples used in this book—and I hope you will—you will need some sample data to work with. All the files referenced in this book are available for download and can easily be installed on your local PC. This appendix explains where to obtain the sample files, how to install them, and what they are used for.

Downloading the Sample Data

The sample files used in this book are currently available on the Apress site. You can access them as follows:

1. In your web browser, navigate to the following URL: github.com/apress/pro-power-bi-dashboard-creation.

2. Click the button Download Source Code. This will take you to the GitHub page for the source code for this book.

3. Click Clone or Download ➤ Download Zip and download the file PowerBIDesktopSamples.zip.

You will then need to extract the files and directories from the zip file. How you do this will depend on which software you are using to handle zipped files. If you are not using any third-party software, then one way to do this is as follows:

1. Create a directory named `C:\PowerBIDesktopSamples`.

2. In the Windows Explorer navigation pane, click the file PowerBIDesktopSamples.zip.

A. Aspin, *Pro Power BI Dashboard Creation*, https://doi.org/10.1007/978-1-4842-8227-4

3. Select all the files and folders that it contains.

4. Copy them to the folder that you created in step 1.

Images

The images used in various chapters can be found in the directory
`C:\PowerBIDesktopSamples\Images.`

APPENDIX B

Visualization Icons

A Power BI dashboard is built up of visuals placed on the dashboard canvas and connected to data. The currently available visuals are displayed in the Visualizations pane. The icons for these visuals are explained in Table B-1.

Table B-1. *Visualization Icons*

Visualization	Icon	Description
Stacked bar chart		Uses cumulative horizontal bars displaying one or more series of data
Stacked column chart		Uses cumulative vertical bars displaying one or more series of data
Clustered bar chart		Uses side-by-side horizontal bars displaying one or more series of data
Clustered column chart		Uses side-by-side vertical bars displaying one or more series of data
100% stacked bar chart		Uses cumulative horizontal bars displaying one or more series of data presented as percentages of the total
100% stacked column chart		Uses cumulative vertical bars displaying one or more series of data presented as percentages of the total
Line chart		Displays series of data as lines
Area chart		Displays series of data as lines with filled areas between the line and the axis

(*continued*)

© Adam Aspin 2022
A. Aspin, *Pro Power BI Dashboard Creation*, https://doi.org/10.1007/978-1-4842-8227-4

Table B-1. (*continued*)

Visualization	Icon	Description
Stacked area chart	⬔	Displays series of data as cumulative lines with filled areas between the line and the axis
Line and stacked column chart	⬔	Combines a line chart (for one or more data series) with a stacked column chart for one or more data points using two axes
Line and clustered column chart	⬔	Combines a line chart (for one or more data series) with a clustered column chart for one or more data series using two axes
Ribbon chart	⬔	Uses cumulative vertical bars display one or more series of data and links the data points
Waterfall chart	⬔	Displays the cumulative result of positive and negative data points
Funnel chart	⬔	Shows a series of values in descending order
Scatter chart	⬔	Plots data points between two numerical axes
Pie chart	⬔	A circular chart using slices to indicate data points proportionally
Donut chart	⬔	A circular chart with a blank center using slices to indicate data points proportionally
Tree map	⬔	Displays hierarchical data as proportional rectangles
Map	⬔	A geographical representation of data points
Filled map	⬔	A geographical representation of data using shading
Shape map	⬔	Compares regional data on a map
Gauge	⬔	Shows progress toward a target as a gauge
Card	⬔	Displays a single value
Multirow card	⬔	Displays a selected set of key figures for a chosen category of data
KPI	⬔	Displays a key performance indicator visual
Slicer	⬔	An interactive filter visual on the dashboard canvas

(*continued*)

Table B-1. (*continued*)

Visualization	Icon	Description
Table		A list of data
Matrix		A crosstab or pivoted table of data
R script visual	R	The visual output of a script using the R language
Python visual	Py	The visual output of a script using the Python language
Key influencers visual		A visual that helps you to understand the drivers behind a metric
Decomposition tree		Breaks down data across multiple dimensions in a lateral hierarchy
Q&A		Uses artificial intelligence to ask natural language questions of the data
Smart Narrative		Uses artificial intelligence to return analyses of the data
Scorecard		Monitors performance
Paginated report		Displays a SQL Server Reporting Services "pixel-perfect" report
ArcGIS map		A detailed map visual from ArcGIS
Power Apps		Integrates with Power Apps
Power Automate		Integrates with Power Automate
Get more visuals		Allows you to access third-party visuals to add to a dashboard

Note   As Power BI Desktop is continually evolving, the set of available icons may have changed since this book went into print.

APPENDIX C

Blank Visual Representations

Whenever you create a blank visual on the report canvas, Power BI Desktop displays a different type of visual representation depending on the type of visual that you selected. The representations for these visuals are explained in Table C-1.

Table C-1. *Visualization Icons*

Visualization	Representation
Stacked bar chart	
Stacked column chart	
Clustered bar chart	
Clustered column chart	
100% stacked bar chart	

(continued)

© Adam Aspin 2022
A. Aspin, *Pro Power BI Dashboard Creation*, https://doi.org/10.1007/978-1-4842-8227-4

Table C-1. (*continued*)

Visualization	Representation
100% stacked column chart	
Line chart	
Area chart	
Stacked area chart	
Line and stacked column chart	
Line and clustered column chart	
Ribbon chart	
Waterfall chart	
Funnel chart	
Scatter chart	

(*continued*)

Table C-1. (*continued*)

Visualization	Representation
Pie chart	
Donut chart	
Tree map	
Map	
Filled map	
Shape map	
Gauge	
Card	
Multirow card	
KPI	

(*continued*)

Table C-1. (*continued*)

Visualization	Representation
Slicer	
Table	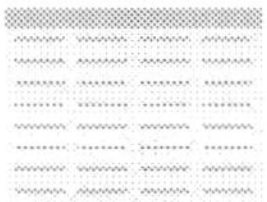
Matrix	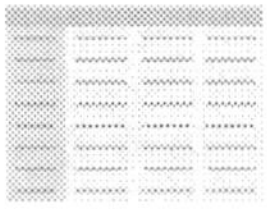
R script visual	
Python visual	
Key influencers visual	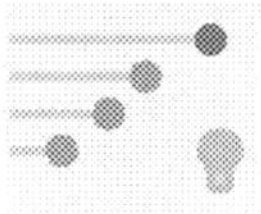
Decomposition tree	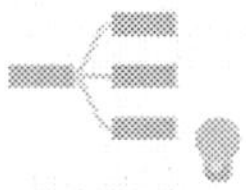
Q&A	
Scorecard	
Paginated report	

(*continued*)

Table C-1. (*continued*)

Visualization	Representation
ArcGIS map	
Power Apps	
Power Automate	
Custom visual	

Index

A

ArcGIS mapping
    basemap type, 299, 300
    dashboards, 297–299
    geospatial representation, 297
    infographics, 303, 304
    placeholder, 298
    reference layer, 301–303

B

Bing Maps, 276
Bookmarks
    analytics requirements, 463, 464
    application, 465
    arranging techniques, 468
    baseline, 461
    button action, 479
    context menu, 464
    dashboard page, 467
    display/data, 465–467
    features, 459
    filtered page, 462
    grouping options, 469, 470
    initial pane, 462
    page navigation, 491, 492
    page setting, 468
    Power BI Desktop, 460
    selection pane, 470
        grouping items, 474
        hidden object, 473, 474
        renaming objects, 471, 472

    selection pane, 475
    slideshow (*see* Slideshows)
Bubble charts
    initial process, 142
    net margin ratio, 143
    printed page, 143, 144
    types, 141
    visualizations pane, 142, 143
Buttons
    actions, 481, 482, 486
    back button, 485
    bookmark, 479
    built-in types, 480
    dashboard page, 476
    different page, 476
    drill-through, 483, 484
    formatting pane, 487–489
    images, 490
    page navigation, 483, 484
    pop-up menu, 477
    questions and answers screen,
        485, 486
    shapes, 491
    types, 481
    URL page, 485
    web page, 484, 485

C

Cards
    description, 103
    display units, 107, 108
    formatting card, 107–110

© Adam Aspin 2022
A. Aspin, *Pro Power BI Dashboard Creation*, https://doi.org/10.1007/978-1-4842-8227-4

G, H

I, J

K, L

M, N, O

Printed in the United States
by Baker & Taylor Publisher Services